NAVAL ADMINISTRATIONS

1827 TO 1892

NAVAL

ADMINISTRATIONS

1827 to 1892

THE EXPERIENCE OF 65 YEARS

BY THE LATE
SIR JOHN HENRY BRIGGS
READER TO THE LORDS AND CHIEF CLERK OF THE ADMIRALTY

EDITED BY LADY BRIGGS

ILLUSTRATED WITH EIGHT PHOTOGRAVURE PORTRAITS AND
FACSIMILE AUTOGRAPHS

My Dear Wife,

It was only at your earnest entreaty that I, at my great age and with my failing sight, was prevailed upon to undertake this work, and had you not kindly performed the duty of amanuensis, and volunteered to correct the proof sheets and verify the accuracy of the dates, it never could have been brought to completion; and as it is a joint production (every line having been written by you at my dictation) it is my express desire that your portrait shall appear on the TITLE-PAGE as a lasting recognition of my grateful appreciation of the services you have rendered me.

To you I dedicate it in the sincerest hope that it may be productive of some good to my country, and confer some benefit upon your dear self.

Your affectionate husband,

JOHN HENRY BRIGGS.

M170171

EDITOR'S PREFACE.

THIS work, which my late husband has entrusted to me, is not of that character that is usually confided to ladies, and I could not have taken upon myself the responsibilities of editing a book which deals with such professional subjects as this one does had not the Author, to a certain extent, prepared me for it; and, under all circumstances, it must have been beyond the capabilities of a woman had he not possessed a thorough grasp of the subject, which rendered it, comparatively speaking, a matter of easy accomplishment. In submitting this volume to the criticisms of the naval profession and general public, I do so in the hope that they will be to "its faults a little blind and to its merits very kind." I would likewise request the readers to bear in remembrance the great object the Author had in undertaking the work, namely, the necessity of an adequate navy, thoroughly organised and prepared for war, to protect the best interests of this great Empire; and also the development and general improvement of that grand profession which obtained its first glories in the reign of a Woman, and which has been revived and restored to its former strength and vigour in the reign of Another—and that not in response to the note of war and danger, but during a prolonged peace— by the splendid, although tardy, appreciation of those whose lives and destinies it is the guardian.   An event which is likely to rank in importance second to none in the memorable reign of Her Most Gracious Majesty Queen Victoria.

ELIZABETH CHARLOTTE BRIGGS.

24th May, 1897.

CONTENTS.

CHAPTER VII.

CHAPTER VIII.

CHAPTER IX.

CHAPTER X.

CHAPTER XI.

CHAPTER XII.

CHAPTER XIII.

LIST OF PHOTOGRAVURE PORTRAITS.

——◦◦◦——

INTRODUCTION.

It has been my earnest endeavour, throughout the pages of this volume, to set before the public the extent to which the defences of the Empire and the requirements of the navy have been neglected by successive administrations. The real perils to which this country has been exposed, and from which she has happily escaped, are known to few, and probably would not be acknowledged by those who held office at the time, though subsequent events have proved it only too truly. They have been indifferent to the condition of the navy and the means of providing adequate protection for our colonies, immense commerce, coaling-stations, and the safety of our own shores.

When war broke out in the United States they were unprepared for it; the consequence was a wasteful expenditure of £500,000,000 and a protracted conflict of four years Prussia, on the other hand, was prepared for war, having been made to feel, in the days of Napoleon, the bitterness of subjugation; and had, during a period of profound peace, calmly and dispassionately considered all those arrangements that would be required upon the first outbreak of hostilities In 1866, in a short and brilliant campaign lasting but a few weeks, she defeated the Austrians, added ten millions to her war-like population, and became the first military power in Europe. This was followed by the Franco-German War in 1870, when the contrast between the state of her preparations, as compared with those of France, resulted in a glorious victory for the former, and a disastrous defeat of unparalleled magnitude for the latter.   But this grand success could never have been achieved had it not been for the deep thought bestowed upon it, and the elaborate calculations made by Count von Moltke, and the offices of the Prussian Intelligence Department during many years of peace.   It was a grand achievement and deserves all the honour and glory so justly accorded to the War Department of Germany.   Twenty years have elapsed since that eventful period, but to what extent have we, as a nation, profited by this example ?   To concentrate a large army so successfully upon the frontier of France in so brief a period was no doubt a wonderful feat, splendidly executed, but it is dwarfed into insignificance when we consider what will devolve upon the English Board of Admiralty and the Naval Intelligence Department—the latter only in its infancy—at the first outbreak of a naval war.

In spite of all that has been done by the Government of the Marquess of Salisbury there are serious grounds for apprehension that adequate preparations have not, as yet, been made, and that the forces available would not be equal to meet the numerous duties devolving upon the Admiralty. In confirmation of these views I have only to refer to the evidence adduced before the Royal Commission, of which the Marquess of Hartington was president in the year 1890   It is far from encouraging to read the strongly expressed opinion of Lord Randolph Churchill, a rigid economist, a statesman selected by Lord Salisbury to fill the reponsible offices of Chancellor of the Exchequer and leader of the House of Commons, and a prominent member of the Royal Commission.   At the close of his separate memorandum on the report of the Commission he begs the Commissioners to " bear in mind that the evidence before us discloses, in many particulars, a state of things more seriously unsatisfactory, and possibly more pregnant with danger than Parliament or the public imagine"; but it is still more depressing to discover that it appears "in evidence before us that no conceived plan of operations for the defence of the Empire, in any given contingency, has ever been worked out or decided upon by the two departments." Such is the present state of affairs as represented by a Commission composed of the first statesmen of the day, belonging to the two great political parties in the country.

The great object which induced me, at my advanced age, to undertake this work was to place before and, if possible, to bring home to, the public the want of method and system which has for so many years prevailed in the naval and military establishments of the country, and the utter want of union and preparation for meeting those contingencies which must arise at the first outbreak of war, as success will mainly depend upon being able to take the initiative with promptness and decision.

The great question of coast defence has commanded far more attention in France, Germany, and Italy than in England; and, unless public opinion is very strongly expressed in Parliament and by the Press, the Government of the day will plead, as an excuse for still more delay, the differences of opinion which must necessarily prevail between naval officers, the Engineers, and the Artillery—the first very properly demanding freedom of action, the second considering that submarine mining will secure safety, whilst the Artillery maintain, rationally enough, that these mines must be defended by heavy and quick-firing guns, as it is as easy to pull submarine mines up as it is to lay them down, and, in the opinion of many experts, they are likely to prove more dangerous to our own shipping than to the cruisers of the enemy. Therefore the probability is that there will be

b

more commissions, more committees, more perplexity, and nothing done; the object of each government being to throw upon their successors the responsibility and unpopularity incidental to increased expenditure, and to escape from the recognition of the inevitable.

I cannot adduce a better instance in proof of the inadequacy of the navy to meet the requirements of the Empire than, when put to. the practical test, during the administration of the Earl of Northbrook between the years of 1880–1885. The noble lord (an experienced Admiralty official, having filled for many years responsible offices in that department) stated in July, 1884, in his place in the House of Lords, that so satisfactory did he consider the condition of the navy that, if three millions of money were thrust into his hand, he would really be at a loss to know how to spend it. Nevertheless, upon the mere rumour of a war with Russia, a very speedy and different conclusion was arrived at. Before the expiration of that very year his lordship disposed of not only the three millions but actually exceeded it, and felt himself bound to propose a programme entailing an annual increase upon the navy estimates. This, naturally, excited considerable apprehension and alarm in the public mind, which was not by any means allayed by the strongly expressed opinions and outspoken language of the most distinguished admirals and experts in the naval profession, amongst whom may be mentioned Sir Thomas Symonds, Sir Phipps Hornby, Lord Alcester, Sir Edward Fanshawe, Admiral de Horsey, Lord Charles Beresford, and others. The result was that, in 1888, Lord George Hamilton, as First Lord of the Admiralty, came down to the House of Commons and demanded a vote for £21,500,000 to augment the fleet, which was as readily granted as patriotically demanded.

It is most satisfactory to observe that Lord George Hamilton, instead of following the bad precedent of former

Boards in adding to the numerical rather than to the fighting efficiency of the fleet (though his lordship fully recognises the importance of numbers), has in his programme, under the Naval Defence Act, laid down vessels embodying the three great qualifications required in ships of war, namely, size, speed, and coal capacity. And what is still more to his credit is that shortcomings are no sooner discovered than measures are taken to avert them in all sister ships, as is especially the case in the second-class cruisers, which have been gradually increased in tonnage from 2900 to 4360.

I have placed before my readers the increase made to the navy by Lord Northbrook and the more important augmentations made by Lord George Hamilton   They will, therefore, be able to judge for themselves the crippled and impoverished condition of the fleet prior to 1884, and its utter inadequacy to meet the requirements of so great a commercial Empire as Great Britain and its numerous dependencies.

In order to avoid the errors of bygone days I have put prominently forward the too tardy recognition of the changes which have taken place in the numerous branches of the naval service and the serious perils to which the country has, on so many occasions, been subjected from the want of prudence and forethought on the part of successive governments, principally attributable to that ill-judged parsimony which has unhappily characterised the political procedure of the two great parties in the State.

I should not have presumed to have expressed my opinions so strongly and decidedly in this volume had I not had the practical experience of forty-four years in the Admiralty at Whitehall, and spent no less a period than thirty-five years in the Admiralty Board-room itself, having held the responsible office of deputy-reader and reader to my lords during the whole of that period, previous to my promotion to the office of chief clerk.   During my tenure of office I had the honour of serving with fifteen First Lords and upwards of fifty admirals. My position as reader afforded me unusual advantages. It placed me in daily personal communication with the members of the Board and secretaries; and, as all despatches passed through my hands, I was cognisant of all that was taking place throughout the department. It also afforded me ample opportunities of discussing the varied subjects of naval interest, submitted for the consideration of the Board, with the most distinguished flag-officers of the day, thereby becoming thoroughly acquainted with their real opinion as to what they considered should be done in the way of augmentation and organisation, the want of which they recognised and frequently deplored I joined the Admiralty before a single steam-vessel belonging to the Royal Navy was put into commission I quitted office in 1870, when there was a fleet of ironclad battleships and cruisers armed with guns throwing a shot the weight of which was equal to that of the whole broadside of the *Victory*, whereas, in my early days, it was with difficulty that the Admiralty could be prevailed upon to substitute 32-pounders for 24- and 18-pounders. Thus I have witnessed, during my official career, more important changes in the navy, both as regards construction and armaments, than are ever likely to occur during a similar period.

The interior economy and management of any large public department must always be a matter of general interest, more especially when it relates to a department so important to the country as that of the Admiralty. I have, therefore, endeavoured to give expression to the views and opinions I have entertained for a long series of years, consequent on the circumstances which have come under my personal observation, and that in the simplest language, with the object of really enlightening the general public as to the manner in which various duties of this great department of the State have been conducted for the last sixty-five years. This I have done in the earnest hope that it may induce the public to take in future years the same lively interest which, happily, was so apparent during the successful administration of Lord George Hamilton.

During my long tenure of office Sir James Graham was the only First Lord of the Admiralty who had any support in the Cabinet. In his first administration he was supported by Lord Palmerston, Lord Stanley, and Lord John Russell; and in his second administration, which was during the Crimean War, he had a *carte blanche* from the then Prime Minister, the Earl of Aberdeen

Many First Lords have used their best endeavours with the Cabinet, and more particularly with the Chancellor of the Exchequer, to obtain increased grants for the navy, with a view to augment it and to increase its general efficiency, but they, alas! failed in their laudable attempts. Political considerations and financial difficulties were invariably advanced as the grounds of refusal, and a favourite phrase with all Cabinets was, "The moment really is so inopportune" No moment ever was opportune to grant money for the navy previous to the administration of Lord George Hamilton. I have reason to believe that this was especially the case with the Duke of Somerset, who, during his seven years of naval administration, had had so many and urgent representations in regard to the inadequacy of the fleet from his naval advisers that he, in consequence, frequently brought this important subject before the notice of the Cabinet His Grace's pertinacity in requesting financial assistance practically led, upon a change of administration, to Mr Gladstone filling the office his Grace had held for that protracted period with the junior member of his own Board.* Not that this

* The Author alludes to Mr. Childers, who succeeded Mr. Stansfeld as Civil Lord in 1864, and became First Lord in 1868 —Ed.

observation is intended to cast the slightest reflection on his able successor.

Mr. Ward Hunt, as a member of a Conservative Cabinet, was not more fortunate than his Grace; for, after having stated in the House of Commons the inefficient condition in which he had found the fleet, and in consequence preferred a request for an increase to the navy estimates, he was obliged to retract what he had advanced to make an excuse for his hasty judgment, having thereby incurred the displeasure of the Cabinet of Lord Beaconsfield, pledged, like its predecessor, to economy and retrenchment.

Lord George Hamilton, like Sir James Graham, was so fortunate as to have substantial support within the Cabinet. His lordship not only had the generous and patriotic assistance of Mr. W. H. Smith, who held the high appointment of First Lord of the Treasury, but the not less valuable support of Mr. Goschen, who was Chancellor of the Exchequer Both these influential ministers had themselves held the office of First Lord of the Admiralty, and were consequently thoroughly cognisant of the requirements of the navy, and were ready and willing to do all in their power towards providing the necessary funds for placing Her Majesty's fleet upon an effective footing as soon as public opinion had been roused as to the inadequacy of the navy. The resignation of Lord Charles Beresford, and his subsequent forcible remarks as to the condition of the fleet and want of war organisation, started public thought on the matter, which was afterwards taken up by many other distinguished naval officers and civilians, besides those already mentioned, they being cordially supported by the entire press of the country Hence the Naval Defence Bill of 1889.

The people of England, that is to say, Her Majesty's subjects in all parts of the Empire, are only too ready to vote money to make efficient the naval and military establishments of the country, and to provide for Imperial Defence as soon as they are placed in possession of the facts, and know their real requirements. Preceding governments, both Liberal and Conservative, had allowed them to fall into a dangerous and discreditable condition from an unwise and mistaken policy of economy.

JOHN HENRY BRIGGS.

NAVAL ADMINISTRATIONS

1827 to 1892

———•◦•———

CHAPTER I.

THE ADMINISTRATION OF H R H THE DUKE OF CLARENCE, 4TH MAY, 1827, TO 12TH MARCH, 1828

Commanders appointed instead of first lieutenants to flagships and line-of-battleships—Sent the guardships to sea for the purposes of exercise and gunnery practice—Established half-yearly reports "On the state of preparation for battle from each ship in the Royal Navy"—Put a check upon corporal punishments—Established naval A.D.C. to the Sovereign—An admiral to be principal A.D.C.—Commissioned the first steam-vessel in the Royal Navy, etc.

ON the 4th of May, 1827, H R H. the Duke of Clarence took his seat as Lord High Admiral and President of the Council upon the accession of Mr. Canning to office. The members of his Council were—

> Vice-Admiral Sir William Johnstone Hope, G.C.B.;
> Vice-Admiral the Right Hon Sir George Cockburn, G.C.B.;
> The Hon. W. R. Keith Douglas;
> John Evelyn Denison, Esq ;
> First Secretary, John Wilson Croker, Esq.;
> Second Secretary, John Barrow, Esq.

All the members of the Council and the First Secretary were members of Parliament.

B

Little or no interest was taken in naval affairs at this period, but the appointment of His Royal Highness was favourably received both by the service and the country. The administration of His Royal Highness was decidedly one of progress; he was a sincere friend to the navy, and had its best interests at heart.

The benefits conferred upon the service by His Royal Highness were far more important and substantial than the public are wont to recognise, and scant praise has been awarded to him.

His Royal Highness was singularly successful in carrying into practical effect several very important measures, the permanent and beneficial results of which could not at that time have been anticipated. Foremost amongst these I may mention the appointment of "commanders" to flagships and line-of-battleships in the place of first lieutenants.

It has been the invariable custom of the service to allow captains and commanders to select their own first lieutenants. This secured the selection of first-rate officers, as captains were sufficiently alive to their own interests to obtain the services of officers of good reputation

In such estimation was the appointment of first lieutenant held throughout the service that the most distinguished admirals looked back with pride and satisfaction upon the days when they had filled that responsible post.

It unfortunately too often happened for these officers that when they attained, by their merits, to the rank of commander their professional career came to an untimely end, as they rarely had sufficient interest to secure the command of a sloop.

The new regulation of the Lord High Admiral opened to them an unlooked-for prospect of advancement, as flag-officers and captains of line-of-battleships were only too glad to get their old first lieutenants to fill the post of commander. Strange to say, in the first instance, several commanders were imprudent enough to decline the offer, but when the three commanders of the *Asia, Genoa,* and *Albion,* after the battle of Navarino, were, at the expiration of a year from the date of their appointments, promoted to the rank of captain, and were made Companions of the Bath, with three foreign orders, the appointment was regarded in a totally different light, and was anxiously sought after.

The benefits conferred by this regulation may be regarded as threefold. It secures the promotion of many meritorious officers, who without it would have but little chance of further advancement in their profession. It greatly assists the First Lord in his choice of officers for promotion to the rank of captain, as it is perfectly clear that officers who have filled the responsible duties of first lieutenant and commander are able and efficient; and, therefore, it only remains for the First Lord to select the best from amongst the most capable. Nor is this all, for it secures to the country the appointment of captains of undoubted and proved experience to the command of our ironclads. This admirable regulation of His Royal Highness, combined with the well-thought-out scheme of naval retirement devised by Mr. Childers, enables naval officers on the active list to rise to the highest point in their profession, which in days gone by they had not the slightest chance of attaining, except in the case of those possessing political or family interest.

The next measure of importance which His Royal Highness carried out calls for great commendation, namely, the sending to sea, for purposes of exercise and gunnery, the guard-ships at the several ports which had remained stationary in harbour for years.

To prove the necessity for such a measure, it is only necessary to mention that when a three-decker at Sheerness was ordered to proceed to sea, three of her lieutenants requested to be superseded, as they felt unequal to take charge of a watch in a vessel of that size. In addition to this it was well known that of late years gunnery had been greatly neglected, and it was reported to His Royal Highness shortly after his accession to office that, upon a sloop being paid off at Sheerness after a three years' commission, the ship's company had never been exercised at target practice upon any single occasion. So fully impressed was His Royal Highness with the neglect into which the fighting efficiency of our warships had been permitted to lapse, that to him is the merit due for establishing a half-yearly report "of the state of preparation for battle" from each ship in the Royal Navy from the commanders-in-chief upon all stations, as well as a quarterly return of the gunnery exercises and the expenditure of ammunition.

In order to secure a uniform system of gunnery throughout the service (it appearing that a diversity of practice prevailed), His Royal Highness appointed a committee to consider that important question; and this subsequently led to a most satisfactory result

There was another most important matter in which His Royal Highness took a very earnest and humane interest— I allude to the infliction of corporal punishment in the navy.

Upon a careful examination of the quarterly returns of punishment, His Royal Highness was painfully impressed with the conviction that, in some instances, both the number and the severity of the punishments were far in excess of what His Royal Highness regarded as necessary for the maintenance of good discipline. This led to the establishment of several salutary regulations calculated to check the use of the "cat" except in extreme cases, such as mutiny, insubordination, and such like, and suggested milder treatment for offences of a more venial character.

So very decided was the opinion of the profession at this date upon the subject of corporal punishment, that it would have been utterly impossible to bring naval officers to believe that a period would arrive when that punishment could be safely dispensed with. Nevertheless this important change has been gradually effected and, happily, brought about by improving the condition of the seamen, and by the tact, judgment, and temper of commanding officers, combined with the strongly expressed opinions of the public press. His Royal Highness showed the great interest he took in the navy by endeavouring to obtain for that service certain privileges enjoyed by the commissioned officers of the army, as well as certain marks of distinction conferred upon the non-commissioned officers of every branch of the military service.

Upon His Royal Highness's earnest recommendation the Sovereign was pleased to nominate six captains of the Royal Navy to be his aides-de-camp, and to appoint an admiral to fill the distinguished post of principal aide-de-camp. His Royal Highness, equally solicitous to promote the welfare and respectability of the working petty officers of the fleet, obtained for them badges of distinction corresponding with those of the sister service. The first-class petty officers were to be distinguished by an anchor and crown worked in gold upon their jacket, and the second-class by an anchor.

This regulation, it need scarcely be added, afforded great satisfaction to the service.

His Royal Highness had the proud gratification of putting into commission the first steam vessel upon the list of the Royal Navy. The officer selected as lieutenant and commander to the *Lightning* was Lieutenant George Evans, whose commission I myself made out. He subsequently attained to the rank of admiral and held a highly responsible appointment at Liverpool, and in after days often reminded me of the important step in his professional career.

The Duke of Clarence unfortunately held office for a very brief period—only ten months; but during that short time he certainly accomplished a very great deal. There is but little doubt that he intended, had he been a free agent, to have introduced many important improvements in the construction of our men-of-war, and to have advocated the employment of steam-vessels, with the necessity for which he was fully impressed. But Sir George Cockburn was First Sea Lord, and Mr. John Wilson Croker was Secretary, the latter exercising a departmental and political influence on account of his superior abilities, to which no secretary had hitherto attained He was an orator, a poet, and a distinguished man of letters, and during the passage of the Reform Bill through Parliament exhibited talents of the highest order.

Two individuals whose opinions were more in unison than those of Sir George Cockburn and Mr. Croker it would have been impossible to find The former was as professionally prejudiced as the other was politically biassed Both were opposed to everything in the shape of reform and improvement, and I verily believe conscientiously convinced that their views were right.

The disasters of the American War of 1813 had been brought about by the mismanagement of Lord Melville's former naval administration, and was mainly attributable to an obstinate determination to adhere to a system which, it was maintained, had swept the fleets of the world from the face of the ocean and to effect a change in which it was held would be fatal to British naval supremacy. The consequence was that small vessels, inferior in tonnage, armament, and complement, were sent to sea to contend with men-of-war superior in these three important elements, the result being that our ships were overmatched and subjected to unmerited discomfiture.

The elements of naval power in those days were threefold: tonnage, broadside weight of metal, and complement, and where these elements were equal the British superiority was fully maintained, as in the glorious combat between the *Shannon* (Captain Brooke) and the United States frigate *Chesapeake.* But when an English frigate of 1200 tons, with 18-pounder guns and 275 men and boys, was most injudiciously and improperly sent to contend with an American frigate of 1800 to 2000 tons, carrying 32-pounders and 500 men and boys, the result proved, as might have been anticipated, disastrous in the extreme. The unfortunate events connected with this war have been so ably set forth in 'James' Naval History,' that any of my readers desiring further information cannot do better than peruse its masterly and interesting pages.

The war having proved a failure, it was considered necessary to defend the policy of the Government, and every argument that naval prejudice, departmental cleverness, and administrative ingenuity could devise was had recourse to, to uphold what was known to be wrong and universally condemned throughout the country.

Such being the case, it can easily be understood that the difficulties His Royal Highness had to contend with were of no ordinary character; for almost every reform and improvement he was desirous of carrying into effect directly implied neglect or mismanagement on the part of those with whom he was officially associated. Therefore, the greater is the merit that ought to be accorded to an administration which, though brief, has left to the present day practical and valuable results.

CHAPTER II.

THE ADMINISTRATION OF RT. HON VISCOUNT MELVILLE, KT.,
19th SEPTEMBER, 1828, TO 25TH NOVEMBER, 1830.

Retrograde proclivities—The impossibility of obtaining a steam-vessel to convey mails from Malta to the Ionian Islands—The era of donkey-frigates, overmasted sloops, and coffin gun-brigs—Character sketch of Sir George Cockburn and Sir Thomas Masterman Hardy—Incidents of bravery—The necessity of employing young officers to important commands—The effect of habit and discipline.

IN 1828 Lord Melville (the office of Lord High Admiral being put in commission) became First Lord of the Admiralty, returning to the post he had filled previously for so many years The members of his Board were—

> Vice-Admiral Right Hon. Sir George Cockburn, G.C.B., M.P.;
> Vice-Admiral the Hon. Sir Henry Hotham, K.C.B.;
> Sir George Clerk, Bart., M.P.;
> The Viscount Castlereagh, M.P.;
> First Secretary, the Right Hon. John Wilson Croker, M P.;
> Second Secretary, John Barrow, Esq.

Lord Melville's retrograde proclivities were only too well known, and therefore nothing in the shape of reforms or improvement could reasonably be expected during his tenure of office ; expectation was not disappointed

No First Lord ever more completely represented in his own person the views entertained by the members of his board, which certainly were neither enlightened or progressive.

Mr Hay, then Under Secretary of State for the Colonies, preferred a request, on behalf of the Colonial Office, that a steamer might be employed for the conveyance of the mails between Malta and the Ionian Islands. This afforded a grand opportunity for the Board of Admiralty to give full expression to their opinion as to the value of steam navigation

Lord Melville, in an elaborate minute written by himself, regretted the inability of my lords commissioners to comply with the request of the Colonial Department, as they felt it their bounden duty, upon national and professional grounds, to discourage, to the utmost of their ability, the employment of steam-vessels, as they considered that the introduction of steam was calculated to strike a fatal blow to the naval supremacy of the Empire; and to concede to the request preferred would be simply to let in the thin edge of the wedge, and would unquestionably lead to similar demands being made upon the Admiralty from other departments.

Such is a brief summary of his lordship's minute.

The administration of Lord Melville was the era of donkey-frigates, overmasted sloops, and coffin gun-brigs, and was rendered memorable, in naval annals, by the substitution of carronades for long guns, whereby the numerical strength of a man-of-war was increased at the expense of her fighting efficiency except at close quarters.

Fortunately for the country a brighter period was about to dawn upon the navy. In 1830 Earl Grey became Prime Minister, and the high and responsible office of First Lord of the Admiralty was then filled by Sir James Graham, who was most happy in his selection of Sir Thomas Masterman Hardy as the First Sea Lord, one of the ablest, most distinguished and popular flag-officers who ever held a seat at the Board of Admiralty.

By a singular coincidence the out-going First Sea Lord

(Sir George Cockburn) was captain of the celebrated *Agamemnon*, bearing the broad pennant of Commodore Horatio Nelson, in which ship the incoming First Sea Lord (Sir Thomas Hardy) was first lieutenant, and subsequently captain of the *Victory* at the battle of Trafalgar Nothing could be in better taste than the manner in which Sir George Cockburn offered his congratulations to his old first lieutenant upon resigning into his hands the appointment he himself vacated.

These two distinguished admirals, with whom I was placed in personal communication for several years, and from both of whom I received great kindness, made a very deep impression upon my mind in the early days of my official career.

Previous to entering upon the important changes in the naval service carried into effect by the administration of Sir James Graham, it is necessary to institute a comparison between the professional opinions and respective characters of Sir George Cockburn and Sir Thomas Hardy.*

Nothing could be more marked than the differences of opinion entertained by these two conspicuous followers of Lord Nelson upon naval affairs.

Sir George Cockburn was a very highly educated gentleman, gifted by nature with a powerful intellect. He could pen a despatch like a Secretary of State, and dispute a point of law with almost the ability and acumen of his talented nephew, Sir Alexander Cockburn. He could make the most of a good case, and most unquestionably the very best of a bad one, and in debate in the House of Commons (where he was regarded as a great naval authority) could defend the navy estimates in a manner that proved his powers of debate

---

* Sir George Cockburn was First Sea Lord from March, 1828, till 25th November, 1830, when Sir Thomas Hardy came in with Sir James Graham.—ED.

Sampson Low, Marston & Co. Ltd.

F. Jenkins, Photo, Paris

Admiral Sir George Cockburn G.C.B.

were of no ordinary character He was a man of the world, a man of fashion, and a courtier, and, when he chose, could exhibit tact and persuasion.

Now for the other side of the picture He could assume a haughty and dictatorial bearing, totally at variance with his natural disposition. He also had very decided likes and dislikes, and possessed an indomitable will; considered he could carry everything by mere brute force, and imagined that when he gave an imperative order that which he had commanded must be done.

In his naval capacity he was the most uncompromising representative of things as they were He seemed to live in the past, and was impressed with the conviction that everything that had been done was right; that what was being done was questionable, and every step in advance was fraught with danger.

It often surprised me that a man of his powerful intellect could not be brought to see that this world did not stand still.

The result of the American War taught him no fresh lesson. The superiority of the American vessels in tonnage, broadside weight of metal, and complement made no adequate impression upon him. He considered it was only necessary for a captain to run his ship alongside of her enemy, pour in a broadside, board, and take her.

Upon my mentioning this to Sir Thomas Hardy, he quietly remarked: "I have no doubt this is Cockburn's opinion, but he would find himself most confoundedly mistaken, for his ship would be sent to the bottom long before he got alongside. What might have been accomplished in days gone by is now utterly impracticable"

In politics Sir George was an unyielding Tory of the old Tory school, and, in conjunction with Mr Croker, did his best to bolster up the calamitous policy of Lord Melville's administration. To make any change in the construction of our men-of-war would virtually be to admit the error of their ways.

Although France and the United States were building large and powerful vessels of every class, England persisted in constructing men-of-war of the obsolete type, totally inadequate to contend successfully with them. Thus political partisanship, combined with professional prejudice, impaired the efficiency of the navy then, as too often has been the case in later days.

I will here mention an incident related to me by a very experienced and talented predecessor of mine in office, being at that time head of the Military Branch and Intelligence Department. He, upon one occasion, felt it his duty to direct the attention of Sir George Cockburn to the superior size and armament of the frigates of the United States and France as compared with our 46-gun frigates Mr. Croker overheard the conversation, and, taking up a Navy List, said: "I have observed, Sir George, that we are very short of 46-gun frigates, and have consequently made the following minute 'Navy Board to prepare designs for six 46-gun frigates, to be armed with 18-pounders, and to carry a complement of two hundred and seventy-five men and boys'" And, turning round to Mr. Amedroz, said: "Execute this minute at once and bring it to me for signature." This will convey some idea of how, in days gone by, ships were ordered, money was spent, and experienced officials, anxious to do their duty, were subjected to rebuke.

Sir George was, both politically as well as professionally, greatly opposed (like Lord Melville) to the introduction of steam, and on one occasion went so far as to declare that since the introduction of steam-vessels he had never seen a clean deck or a captain who, when he waited upon him, did not look like a sweep.

Again, he could not be induced to look upon gunnery from

a scientific point of view, and when I one day ventured to suggest to him that sights should be affixed to every gun instead of to every other one, or to the guns on the starboard or larboard side, as was then the ridiculous regulation, he replied: "My young friend, it seems to me you have gone gunnery mad, for they are little more or less than d—— gimcracks"

Strange to say, Sir George Cockburn entertained the same opinion as to the small value to be assigned to concentrated fire, and all those modern inventions which render naval artillery so terrible and destructive. He further maintained that it would be impossible to give up impressment, as no other substitute could be found for manning the fleet in time of war, and that, in spite of the Reform Bill, the strong expression of public opinion, and the powerful influence of the *Times* and the press generally, it must be continued. Nevertheless he was disposed to check all undue severity in the use of the cat, but he held a very decided opinion that it would be extremely dangerous to discipline to entirely dispense with corporal punishment

He likewise entertained the antiquated belief, then so prevalent in the service, that seamen could only require leave to go on shore for one of two purposes, namely, to get tipsy or to desert. Such were the opinions entertained and openly expressed by one of the most talented, highly educated and respected admirals that ever sat at the Admiralty Board or in the House of Commons.

Barring these professional peculiarities Sir George Cockburn was very kind, humane, and the friend of all naval officers in trouble and difficulty; and at the Admiralty Board invariably took the lenient view of every case submitted for decision. He was a true friend to the widow and orphan and lavish in the distribution of his charities, but too often bestowed upon unworthy objects.

My representation would not be complete if I omitted to mention two incidents illustrative of his personal courage and presence of mind. Upon one occasion, when in command of a frigate, he was chased by a superior force which appeared at the moment to be gaining upon him, when a man fell overboard; he instantly ordered boats to be lowered and the frigate to lay to. The man's life was saved, and the effect of this act upon the ship's company can be better imagined than described, especially when all the circumstances of the case are duly considered.

The late Admiral Sir James Scott related to me the following anecdote:—At the taking of Washington he was standing beside Sir George Cockburn, who was on horseback. They were under a heavy fire, when a bullet, passing close by Sir James's whiskers, induced him involuntarily to bend his head, which Sir George observing, said: "Don't bob your head, Scott—it looks bad." He himself sitting as firm and immovable as a statue.

The contrast between the outgoing and the incoming First Sea Lord was most remarkable. Sir Thomas Hardy was no politician, had no seat in Parliament, and was selected solely on account of his high professional attainments, and his nomination under such circumstances established a precedent which has been fortunately followed with great benefit to the country and marked advantage to the naval service. A high naval reputation has been happily substituted for a seat in Parliament and a party allegiance. Sir Thomas did not possess the gift of eloquence and could not indite a despatch with the felicity of Sir George Cockburn, though no one knew better than he what ought to be written; for nothing could be more true than the remark of Lord Nelson respecting him, that "Providence had imbued him with an intuitive right judgment."

Sir Thomas Hardy was frequently heard to say "that he

Sampson Low Marston & C.º Ltd.   J. Jenkins, Heliog. Paris

Sir Thos. M. Hardy

could not argue against Cockburn, Croker, and Barrow, for they carried far too heavy a broadside for him. They would prove him wrong in two minutes, though he knew he was right for all that" This was unquestionably the case, for he was never known to be wrong on any professional point, thus confirming beyond all doubt, in the presence of all impartial hearers, the opinion of Lord Nelson.

The brilliant services of Sir Thomas Hardy as a naval officer are of wide-world fame, but his administrative abilities and as First Sea Lord of the Admiralty have never received a fair meed of honour by the country at large, though thoroughly appreciated in the service. He took a large and comprehensive view of all subjects, and clearly foresaw the many changes that must inevitably take place in the navy.

If Sir George Cockburn dreamt of the past, Sir Thomas Hardy lived for the future; he was not only a reformer, but a most prudent reformer, for he considered how far the leading members of the profession would be likely to go with him, so as not to provoke needless opposition.

He was unquestionably thirty years in advance of the opinions held by the admirals of that day; and seemed to behold, in prophetic vision, the mighty changes which science and steam are now effecting in the naval service.

No admiral had taken a more prominent part in the grand naval battles of the great war than Sir Thomas Hardy, and he may therefore be regarded as a very high authority as to the composition of a fleet.

He was strongly impressed with the conviction that our naval superiority could only be maintained by large and powerful line-of-battleships, carrying heavy armament, as in action nothing could resist their concentrated fire. He was no less an advocate for numerous and powerfully armed frigates as indispensable appendages to a fleet. He considered all large sums of money expended upon small craft as money wasted, as they must necessarily become a prey to vessels of a superior force.

In Sir Thomas's opinion, the fleet should consist of the most powerful vessels, as far as possible of the same class, and with equal sailing power, so as to prevent the movements of the fleet being impeded by dull sailers, the speed of the fleet being that of the slowest vessel.

He took an enlightened and far-seeing view in respect to the introduction of steam, and seemed thoroughly convinced in his own mind that it must play a most important part in any future naval war. Had he lived in the present day he would have been first to tender his support to those distinguished admirals, Sir Thomas Symonds and Sir G. Phipps Hornby, in advocating length, speed, and coal capacity in our ironclads, and the protection needed alike for the ship and fighting crew, as well as a revision of the armaments and guns appropriated to the naval service.

Sir Thomas Hardy served in the American War with Sir George Cockburn, and arrived at a conclusion, in reference to its management, diametrically at variance with that of the out-going First Sea Lord.

The policy of Sir Thomas Hardy was never to allow any foreign power to gain, even temporarily, an advantage over us, for it must be borne in mind, as he very justly remarked, that the naval system which had been successful with us had proved the reverse with our opponents, and it was but natural they should have recourse to other measures.

As soon as they commenced building larger vessels with more powerful armaments it became imperatively necessary that we should do the same, and he further added that, if foreign powers thought fit to have recourse to the introduction of steam, there was no alternative left to us but at once to introduce it likewise, and endeavour to maintain that superiority under the new system which we held under the old. He used to say: "Happen what will, England's duty is to take and keep the lead."

This surely is a policy of sound practical common sense, of which Sir Thomas Hardy may be regarded as the personal embodiment, and it will be for the good of the country, and the best interests of the commercial community, if this policy is far more consistently adhered to in the future than has unfortunately been the case, on too many occasions, during the last half century.

The interests of commerce are so completely identified with those of the Empire, that it becomes the bounden duty of the various chambers of commerce to render their utmost support to every government irrespective of party which exhibits a determination to uphold our naval supremacy, and prevent it from being subjected to any temporary unpopularity consequent upon any proposed addition to the navy estimates.

Upon one subject, however, there was no difference of opinion between Sir George Cockburn and Sir Thomas Hardy, namely, the necessity of employing officers in the prime of life to command our ships. Sir George was of opinion that thirty was a proper age for a captain to command a line-of-battleship, and if he was not fit then he never would be.

Sir Thomas Hardy was equally in favour of young officers being placed in command, provided they were thoroughly efficient.

When we consider the nerve required in the present day on the part of a captain in command of an ironclad, steaming from sixteen to twenty knots an hour, and keeping her place night and day in her proper station, and that the vessel entrusted to his charge has cost the country half a million of money or more, it is evident that youth and nerve are indispensable qualifications, and are not incompatible with professional experience.

It is greatly to be feared that many commanders of ability

C

and experience are not made captains until they have attained
to an age when they would be better qualified for flag-rank.

Sir Thomas Hardy's views upon discipline differed *in toto*
from those of Sir George Cockburn and those generally entertained by the service at that time. He exhibited a knowledge of human nature very rarely met with in any position
of life.

At a time when all leave was refused, and boats rowed
round the ships to prevent men deserting, he gave leave to
his men to go on shore, watch by watch, for forty-eight hours
at a time. The result was that, at the end of ten days or
a fortnight, only about one-half availed themselves of the
privilege, for they had spent their money, enjoyed their fun,
and experienced no particular amusement in strolling about
the streets.

On one occasion, when the fleet put to sea and the men
were weighing anchor, there were very strong expressions of
dissatisfaction heard from the whole ship's company. Upon
inquiry it turned out that two hands were missing, and that
the crew therefore considered their word and honour com-
promised. Suddenly loud cheers were heard, and the two
missing men were seen fast approaching in a bumboat.

When the ship's company was mustered not a single
hand was found to be missing—a striking proof of what
may be accomplished by tact, prudence, and kindness
judiciously administered.

Sir George Cockburn's aim always seemed to be to excite
admiration, inspire fear, and instil awe into the hearts
of all with whom he came in contact, whilst, on the other
hand, Sir Thomas Hardy inspired confidence and gained the
affections of all his followers.

In corroboration of what I have stated in reference to
Sir George Cockburn, I may mention the following incident
as a very curious fact:—The morning that Sir George Cock-

burn, appointed Commander-in-chief in the West Indies, was to wait upon Sir Thomas Hardy to receive his instructions, Sir Thomas assured me he always felt in his presence exactly as he did when serving as his old first lieutenant, notwithstanding their relative change of position, and asked me to remain in the room

Nothing could be better calculated to remove embarassment than the deportment of Sir George Cockburn, who, upon entering the room, said, "My dear Hardy, I have come to receive your instructions, as you know I am now under your orders."

Sir Thomas said, "Pray make any corrections in them you think fit, sir;" when Sir George with a smile replied, "It is not for me, Hardy, to make corrections, but merely to offer any suggestion that may occur to me for your better consideration."

I then proposed to Sir Thomas Hardy that it might perhaps be agreeable to Sir George Cockburn to take the instructions home with him, so as to peruse them at leisure. Sir George said, "This seems a good suggestion, Hardy. If you have no objection I will take them with me," which he accordingly did, and then left, to the great relief of Sir Thomas Hardy. As soon as Sir George had gone Sir Thomas said, " I really cannot believe I am First Sea Lord, the tables seem so entirely turned."

Is it not wonderfully strange that a man, the bravest of the brave, who, during the raging of the storm and the fury of the battle, would stand cool and collected and not lose his presence of mind for an instant, should be temporarily disconcerted upon finding himself in authority over one to whom he had for years paid professional obedience? Yet such is the effect of habit and discipline.

CHAPTER III.

THE FIRST ADMINISTRATION OF THE RIGHT HON. SIR JAMES R. G. GRAHAM, 25TH NOVEMBER, 1830, TO 11TH JUNE, 1834.

Reasons why an admiral is not placed at the head of the Admiralty instead of a civil first lord—Reorganisation of the navy and civil departments —Mistaken policy in ship-building—The *Excellent* commissioned as a school for teaching gunnery—Grievances in regard to promotions— An anecdote in reference to an officer preferring charges he could not substantiate—The division of the business of the Board—The want of inter-communication between the various departments of the State— A story to illustrate party feeling—"Master of the subject"—Sir John Pechell makes a speech in the House of Commons—The personal influence of Sir James Graham in the Cabinet.

THE question is often asked why an admiral is not placed at the head of the navy in the same manner as a military officer is placed at the head of the army. The cases are analogous. The Secretary of War holds precisely the same office in regard to the army as the First Lord of the Admiralty does in regard to the navy; both departments being presided over by civilians The First Sea Lord for the time being virtually exercising the functions of naval commander-in-chief.

The First Lord of the Admiralty must be a Cabinet minister. He must also be a statesman, a finance minister, a politician, and a ready debater; able to make the most of a good case and the best of a bad one. He ought also to be a patient listener and capable of weighing the arguments of both sides of a question calmly and dispassionately, and unbiassed by any professional prejudice; and, above all, he must be prepared to meet with contradiction, and to have the worst interpretation put upon everything that he does, and regard it as a mere matter of course.

Now several of the qualifications enumerated could scarcely be expected from a distinguished naval officer; although in these days there are many possessing great ability and high pretentions, so far as a knowledge of their profession is concerned, but wanting that parliamentary training which alone can be acquired after long experience in the House of Commons.

The remarks made in reference to the requirements of the First Lord of the Admiralty are equally applicable to the Secretary of State for War.

The staff of the Horse Guards is intended to give that professional assistance and experience to the Secretary of War which the naval members afford to the First Lord, with this difference, that at the Admiralty everything is concentrated in one department under one head, whilst the business of the War Office is conducted by numerous departments corresponding with one another, which leads to differences of opinion and considerable delay.

I have had many years' experience in the Admiralty Board-room, and I am very disinclined to admit the principal charges which are preferred by many against the Board at large, namely, that much unimportant business is brought before it, and valuable time wasted by irrelevant discussion. Such an admission would simply imply that the First Lord and secretaries were unequal to the discharge of their duties. First Lords have different modes of conducting their business, but an able minister has invariably a good system of his own.*

A general opinion prevails that the First Lord is bound to act under the advice of his Board, thereby ignoring the fact that they are only his advisers, and that he it is who is individually responsible to the Cabinet of which he is usually a leading member. First Lords have upon their own

* Formal Boards are now seldom assembled at the Admiralty.—ED.

responsibility acted in opposition to the strongly expressed opinions of the naval members of the Board upon certain occasions when it was evident that they were under a strong bias in reference to the administration of certain branches of the service, which perhaps it would be invidious for me to designate.

It has frequently been assumed that a naval officer of distinction must necessarily be able to form a sounder judgment upon naval subjects than a civil First Lord; but it unfortunately happens that the proposal of one distinguished admiral is totally at variance with that of another of equal ability; and it is in such cases that a calm and impartial opinion of a civil First Lord, who hears both sides of the question, is so indisputably necessary, more especially as professional subjects are often debated with as much warmth in the Admiralty Board-room as political questions in the House of Commons.

The naval administrations of Sir James Graham will be long remembered, the first as the one which reorganised the navy and effected all those important changes in the civil departments so much needed, such as the abolition of the navy and victualling boards, etc., and the second for the zeal and ability displayed in the preparations of the Baltic Fleets upon the outbreak of the Crimean War, and the brilliant success which characterised the management of the transport service in the conveyance of troops and stores during that most eventful period.

Sir James Graham's Board of 1830 was an unusually strong one. It comprised—

Rear-Admiral Sir Thomas Masterman Hardy, Bart., K.C.B., 1st Sea Lord,

Rear-Admiral Hon. George H. L. Dundas, C.B., 2nd Sea Lord;

Captain Sir Samuel John Pechell, Bart., C.B., R.N., M.P.,
  3rd Sea Lord;
Captain Hon. George Barrington, R.N., 4th Sea Lord;
Captain Hon. George Elliot, M.P., Secretary;
John Barrow, Esq., Permanent Secretary.

One of the first measures adopted by the new Board was
to reverse at once the naval policy of their predecessors, who
had persisted for years, in direct opposition to the strongly
expressed consensus of naval opinion, in spending hundreds
of thousands annually upon vessels inadequate in size and
deficient in armament to compete successfully with the new
classes of vessels in course of construction in the naval dockyards of France and the United States.

There is, perhaps, no subject more difficult to deal with
than the construction of vessels for the Royal Navy or one
upon which more mistakes have been made, more party spirit
enlisted, or public money wasted. However, upon the
present occasion nothing could be more sound or judicious
than the course pursued. In 1830 the fleet consisted, with
the exception of a few powerful 120 and 80-gun ships, of
nothing but line-of-battleships of 74 and 60 guns, together
with a very large number of 46-gun frigates, carrying
18-pounders and frigates of 26 guns (designated donkeys);
also of overmasted sloops of 16 and 18 guns, and coffin
10-gun brigs; of the last named, several foundered annually, and hence their name.

The first question for consideration was how to turn these
vessels to the best advantage, and, after calm and careful
reflection, it was decided to cut down the 74's and convert
them into 50-gun frigates, carrying 32-pounders, and to
adopt the same plan with the 46-gun frigates, and turn them
into powerful corvettes. To abolish at once the donkey
frigates, do away with the 10-gun brigs, and to reduce

the heavy masts of the sloops, which were almost as dangerous
as the coffin gunboats.

Sir Thomas Hardy, who had taken a distinguished part in
all the great naval battles of his day, was strongly impressed
with the conviction that what the navy stood most in need
of were line-of-battleships of 120 and 90 guns.

He attached as much importance to three-deckers and
90-gun ships as Voltaire did to strong battalions, who
is reported to have said, with more truth than reverence,
that he observed that the Almighty generally fought on
their side.

The amount of national wealth that has been wasted on the
construction of ships for the Royal Navy, many of which have
never hoisted the pennant or proceeded to sea, would amount to
millions. The system has been radically vicious, and utterly
opposed to practical common sense. The diversity of opinion
expressed in reference to the classes of vessels of which the
fleet should be composed has been influenced not only by
financial and political considerations, but by flag-officers,
members of the Board of Admiralty, professionally disinclined
to introduce those changes which scientific progress has
rendered imperatively necessary. The amount of capital
sunk in the several dockyards at various periods giving no
return has at times attained to an amount of five or six
millions. The stocks have been crowded with vessels, many
of which had been for years in course of construction, and
were regarded as obsolete before they were launched, whilst
in other cases ships were pulled to pieces to introduce modern
improvements, and almost entirely rebuilt, and very few
were completed according to their original design. The result
generally ending in disappointment and increased expense,
as is inevitable in such a course of proceeding.

It is much to be regretted that even in these days the
mistakes which I deplore are still only too apparent.

Another most important measure represented by Sir Thomas Hardy as necessary for the efficiency of the navy was carried into effect by Sir James Graham.

The ships placed in ordinary were absolute hulks, and considerable time elapsed before they could be got ready for sea; it was therefore deemed desirable that a given number of line-of-battleships and frigates at each of the several ports should be advanced to a certain stage of equipment, so as to expedite their completion, should any augmentation to the fleet be required to meet a sudden or unexpected emergency. This judicious arrangement proved subsequently on several occasions of great advantage to the public service, and may justly be regarded as the first step taken towards that system of reserve which has been gradually brought by successive Boards of Admiralty to that state of efficiency which is now visible in our several dockyards.

Perhaps one of the most important and successful innovation was the commissioning of paddle-wheel steam-vessels. Commander Austin of the *Medea*, an officer of great ability, obtained for himself considerable credit by steaming that vessel from the Thames into the basin at Woolwich Dockyard, and proving to the naval profession that a man-of-war steam-vessel skilfully handled was as completely under control as a penny steamboat.

The success of the *Medea* led to the construction of the *Gladiator*, a paddle-wheel steamer of a larger type; and so gratified was Sir James Graham with these vessels that, on quitting office in 1834, he left a minute on record expressing his opinion that in the event of war the service ought to be provided with at least six additional *Medeas* and four *Gladiators*.

Little did he then foresee what would be the requirements of the navy when, twenty years afterwards, he resumed his seat at the head of the Board of Admiralty, just previous to the breaking out of the Crimean War, or that he would derive so much benefit from the advanced views of Sir Thomas Hardy's naval policy in the construction of powerful line-of-battleships, and urging on the introduction of steam-vessels for purposes of war.

For many years the important subject of gunnery had been grievously neglected, as was apparent during the war with the United States in 1813, and it was only too evident that proper attention had not been paid to the drill and exercise of the officers and men in this essential part of their duty, and that both stood greatly in need of scientific instruction, they being as ignorant of the theory as they were deficient in practice in the art of war. There were a few creditable exceptions, however, to what was the general rule, amongst whom may be mentioned Sir Thomas Hardy, Sir Philip Brooke, Sir Samuel John Pechell, Captain the Hon. Henry Duncan, and others, who were keenly alive to the shortcomings of the service in this most important particular.

It was mainly owing to the great attention paid by Lord St. Vincent to the training of the men in gunnery that our brilliant successes during the great war were attributable Of such paramount importance did he regard it, that he gave orders that "every day, whether in harbour or at sea, a general or partial exercise should take place on board every ship in the squadron."

So fully impressed was Sir James Graham with the urgent necessity of establishing a permanent school for the scientific and practical teaching of gunnery to the naval officers and seamen of the fleet, that, upon the strong representations of the naval members of the Board, he decided to commission at once a ship for that particular purpose.

Captain Sir Thomas Hastings was the officer selected for the command of the *Excellent* at Portsmouth, which from that day to this has been regarded as the headquarters of that valuable school of naval artillerists which of late years has done so much to raise the scientific reputation of the navy.

Sir Thomas Hastings was peculiarly fitted to undertake the formation and organisation of so important an establishment, and to place it upon an efficient footing He possessed high scientific attainments, and combined that energy with ability which is certain to ensure success Added to this he had a profound knowledge of human nature, and was fully alive to the prejudices and pre-conceived opinions of the men-of-warsmen in reference to gunnery. But before any sound principles could be inculcated, it was indispensably necessary to eradicate the deeply rooted impressions of ignorance. He was fully aware that seamen thought that after they had rammed down the cartridge, the greater number of shot they could stuff into the muzzle of the gun the greater would be the damage inflicted; he therefore proposed one day that the seamen should man one gun, and he and the officers should man another, and they would then see which would do the most damage to the target. The men looked delighted, and were determined to show their captain what they could do.

As Sir Thomas expected, when left to themselves they rammed in as many shot as they thought the gun would safely hold, fired it off, and looked with intense anxiety to see the effect of their performance. The shot, of course, fell short, as the charge of powder was inadequate. He said, "Try again, my men! How is this?" They fired as before with exactly the same result.

Sir Thomas then said, "We will now try what we can do." Only one shot was put into the gun and fired; the target was struck and knocked to pieces. He then proposed to the seamen that they should try what they could do if they only inserted one shot, this they did, and were surprised to find that they had hit the target, and much damage was occasioned.

The lesson Sir Thomas Hastings sought to teach was eminently successful. The men were thoroughly convinced that they were wrong and their captain right, and from that day forward they placed implicit confidence in the soundness of the instruction they received, and it was soon discovered that a seaman-gunner displayed quite as much intelligence, and was as capable of acquiring knowledge, as the best artilleryman at Woolwich.

To show the necessity of establishing a simple and uniform system of gunnery drill throughout the service, Sir Thomas mentioned to me the following incident :—He had been reprimanding a petty officer for what appeared inattention, when he said, in a most respectful manner, "I beg pardon, sir, but this is the thirteenth gunnery drill I have been taught, and when I have had my dinner and a glass of grog, somehow or other, at times, the whole thirteen drills comes up at once, and my head gets bothered."

For many years past a good deal of dissatisfaction prevailed in the service, and it must be admitted that the complaints throughout the whole profession were well founded, for their grievances were alike numerous and just. The long war had crowded the Navy List to an overwhelming extent, and it was almost as difficult to obtain employment as it was to gain promotion.

Everything at this period depended upon the whim of the First Lord, who could make as many promotions as he thought fit, as no limit at this period was imposed upon the exercise of that prerogative.

On occasions, twelve or fifteen commanders would be promoted at once to the rank of captains, who came at the bottom of a list exceeding eight hundred.

Promotions were in like manner made to the ranks of

commander and lieutenant, the lists of which were equally overstocked; but what caused universal discontent was the reckless manner in which young officers of rank and influence were placed over the heads of officers who had proved their gallantry, gained their experience, and done good service during the long war.

Lieutenants of two and three years' standing, whose commission time was served in a 10-gun brig in the Mediterranean, were advanced to the rank of commander, whilst officers who had served as first lieutenants during the war had little or no chance at all of preferment

Young commanders who had served only a year or fifteen months in command of a 10-gun brig in the Mediterranean, or in a sloop on the North American Station, were promoted to be captains at an age varying from twenty-two to twenty-five years, many of whom had never served a day afloat from the date of their promotion until they obtained flag-rank and obtained the pay of retired admirals.

On the other hand, it is but just to state that many of these captains promoted at this early age rose through their gallantry and ability to the head of their profession, and filled with honour to themselves, and benefit to their country, the highest commands in the service, and finally the important position of First Sea Lord, and naval members of the Board of Admiralty.

Favouritism was equally apparent in the selection of captains to the command of line-of-battleships and frigates, and, as by the regulations no officer who had not commanded a line-of-battleship could be advanced to the active list of rear-admiral, political interest and family influence were brought to bear upon the First Lord and the members of the Board to obtain the appointment in question, as the commands were few and the candidates numerous. In regard to the frigates in the Mediterranean and upon the Pacific Station, they were commanded almost exclusively by captains who were noblemen or members of noble families : the former station being one of pleasure; the latter more lucrative, as their ships invariably brought home heavy freights.

A considerable amount of patronage had hitherto been accorded to commanders-in-chief on foreign stations, who had the privilege of promoting to all death vacancies as well as filling up all vacancies occasioned by the invaliding of officers, which vacancies were however to be filled from what was called the " Admiralty List," confidentially furnished from the private office. In addition, the commanders-in-chief had the privilege of recommending their flag-lieutenant for promotion to the rank of commander upon the hauling down of their flag.

In order to prevent the abuse of the last-mentioned privilege by commanders-in-chief upon the home station, a regulation was established by Sir James Graham to the effect that every lieutenant must actually serve two years in a sea-going ship before he could be considered eligible for promotion to the rank of commander, so as to ensure a certain amount of professional experience on the part of these favoured individuals, who were generally the sons, nephews, or near relations of the commander-in-chief.

To prove that old and meritorious officers had just grounds for dissatisfaction and complaint, I will mention an incident related to me by Sir Richard Dundas when First Sea Lord. As a naval cadet he was placed under the special charge of the first lieutenant of the ship to which he was appointed when first sent to sea. The lieutenant was a very zealous and efficient officer, as is evident from the fact that he was chosen to take charge of the First Lord's son; nevertheless, he still remained upon the half-pay lieutenants' list when Sir Richard as a young captain was appointed to the *Volage.* On commissioning that ship he took him as his own first lieutenant, and three years afterwards succeeded through his personal interest in obtaining for him his promotion to the rank of commander, which otherwise it is extremely improbable he would ever have received, notwithstanding his long and faithful services.

Every four or five years there was a general promotion in the navy and army, when a certain number of captains who had commanded line-of-battleships were advanced to the rank of rear-admirals upon the active list, but unfortunately the selection usually stopped so as just to exclude the most promising officers upon the list who, by the regulations then enforced, were consequently relegated to an additional five years' compulsory idleness upon the half-pay list, which certainly did not add to the efficiency of captains advancing in years.

Promotions took place in exactly the same manner in the subordinate ranks, and afforded a convenient opportunity for shelving old and meritorious officers, who, as they could not expect future employment, did not interfere with the private and political patronage of the First Lord. In a sentence, nothing could be more unsatisfactory than the crowded condition of the lists, and the course pursued in regard to both promotion and the employment of officers of all ranks in the Royal Navy.

But the difficulties, professional, political, and financial, were so great and numerous that it is not surprising that First Lords were disinclined to incur the responsibility of dealing with so vast and unpromising a task.

It is, however, very gratifying to see the manner in which this most difficult and intricate problem has been gradually brought to a felicitous solution, and to compare the state of the Navy List of the present day with that of the period to which I refer, so superior are the chances of promotion, of merit and service, and the certainty of employment, as compared with the nepotism and precariousness of a bye-gone age.

To Sir James Graham and his Board is certainly due the credit of taking the initiative in reducing the number of officers upon the active list, and adopting many salutary measures calculated to ensure the employment of deserving officers, thereby removing, to a certain extent, some of the discontent which at that time prevailed in the service to so painful and disheartening an extent.

The good example set by H.R.H. the Duke of Clarence, when Lord High Admiral, in sending the several guardships to sea on a summer cruise for the purpose of exercise and gunnery, was followed by Sir James Graham's Board. At this time the officer in command of the Channel Squadron was Vice-Admiral Sir Edward Codrington; he was a Trafalgar captain and the hero of Navarino. Unfortunately he had, about this time, involved himself in some unpleasantness by imprudently preferring certain charges against Captain Dickinson of the *Genoa* which he failed to substantiate.

The squadron being ready for sea, Sir Thomas Hardy asked Sir James Graham, just as the Board was breaking up, what orders he wished him to give to Sir Edward Codrington. He replied, "I think you had better send the squadron to cruise for three weeks or a month for the purpose of gunnery and exercise. Write a minute to that effect and give it to Mr. Briggs to bring to me." I went with Sir Thomas Hardy to his private room, where he wrote as follows: "Vice-Admiral Sir Edward Codrington to proceed to sea with the squadron under his command, and to cruise for three weeks for the purpose of exercise and gunnery off the 'Silly' Islands." I took the minute to Sir James Graham, and handed it to him with a grave face. He smiled upon reading it, and said, "A very proper place, Mr. Briggs, for that admiral to cruise. Nevertheless we had better insert the 'c' before it falls into the hands of the young gentlemen of the office."

The measure to which, perhaps, the country will attach greatest importance was the abolition of the Navy Office and Victualling Board, and the placing of the civil departments of the navy under the individual responsibility of five principal officers, respectively designated—

> Surveyor of the Navy.
> Accountant-General of the Navy.
> Storekeeper-General of the Navy.
> Controller of the Victualling, and
> Medical Director-General.

Each principal officer was to be superintended by a member of the Board of Admiralty.

Sir Thomas Hardy superintended the Surveyor.
Admiral Dundas the Storekeeper-General.
Sir John Pechell the Controller-General.
Captain Berkeley * the Medical Director-General.
Mr. Labouchere the Accountant-General, Public Works Department, etc.

Each Lord of the Admiralty had assigned to him certain specific duties, and each member at the meeting of the Board was to bring under its consideration such matters of import- ance, connected with his own department, as he deemed necessary for the collective decision of their lordships.

This division of duty was established on so sound a basis that, after sixty years, it still remains in full force, though of course certain additions have been made consequent upon the altered requirements of the service, attributable to the introduction of steam and the general expansion of the navy,

---

* Captain Berkeley succeeded Captain Barrington in April, 1833.—ED.

D

together with the placing of the transport service under Admiralty control, etc. The system laid down by Sir James Graham has proved to be not only sound in theory, but to have worked successfully when put to the test of practical experience. By this arrangement the whole business of the Admiralty was brought under the immediate eye of the First Lord, as well as the cognizance of every member of the Board, each individual being thus afforded an opportunity of giving expression to his opinion upon any subject in which he may feel either a personal, departmental, or professional interest. By this procedure every subject was well considered, and promptness and uniformity of action secured, and in the event of any details being required the principal officer was always near at hand to give the necessary explanations.

One of the most important benefits resulting from the consolidation, even thus far, under one roof of the various departments of the Admiralty, is the facility afforded for personal communications which prevent that endless correspondence which may be regarded as the futile cause of so much official procrastination, though the arrangement is not even yet complete. So convinced was Sir James Graham of the great advantages of inter-communication between the principal officers of State, that he habitually discussed the nature of the communication he proposed to write with the minister of the department before making the written communication, so that the decision was arrived at beforehand, and thereby much needless correspondence and misunderstanding judiciously avoided. It is to be regretted that this practice has not been followed in later years; for there is too much reason to believe that many measures proposed by the Admiralty and War Office, calculated to benefit both services, have met with obstruction on the part of subordinate officers of the Treasury, whose zeal for

economy was far in excess of their appreciation of the
benefits accruing to the services, and that the proposals did
not always come under the personal consideration of the
Chancellor of the Exchequer.

One of the greatest misfortunes of this country has been,
and still is, the want of communication between the various
departments of the State. There could be no more curious
illustration of this than is afforded by the correspondence
between the Admiralty, the War Office, Horse Guards,
Colonial Office, Foreign Office, and Treasury in reference to
the coaling-stations and their defences. It took seven years
to decide which stations were to be defended, the extent of
the defences, the nature of their defences, their armaments,
barracks, garrisons, and the never-ending estimates prepared,
reconsidered, added to, and cut down.

This correspondence ought certainly to occupy a very dis--
tinguished place amongst the curiosities of literature.

Sir James Graham, having placed the civil departments of
the navy upon an improved and permanent footing, then
proceeded to carry into effect a corresponding reform in the
control and management of the docks and victualling yards.
The office of civil commissioner was abolished at the several
yards, and a rear-admiral was appointed as Admiral Superintendent at Portsmouth and Plymouth. A captain, with the
rank of commodore superintendent, was appointed to Woolwich, and captain superintendents at the other dock and
victualling yards. By this arrangement the equipment of
all ships fitting out was greatly expedited, and great economy
effected in the expenditure of stores. It had, further, the
special advantage of placing all the vessels under the
immediate eye of a naval officer of high rank and experience.
It likewise ensured the vessels ordered to be placed in the
first and second-class reserve being provided with everything
necessary for maintaining them in a proper state of efficiency,

so as to be ready at the shortest notice to meet the requirements of any sudden emergency.

This measure may be regarded as the first step towards
that system of naval mobilisation which, under subsequent
governments, and more particularly under the able and
successful administration of Lord George Hamilton, is
rapidly advancing to a very high state of efficiency.

Amongst the many able and distinguished statesmen who
have filled the high and responsible office of First Lord of
the Admiralty, few have displayed greater ability, more
aptitude for business, or administrative capacity of a higher
order than Sir James Graham. He was never seen to greater
advantage than at the head of the Board-room table in
discharge of a duty which required so much temper, tact,
and delicacy.

Sir James was peculiarly happy in extracting from the
several members of the Board the particular information he
was desirous of eliciting, and then placing all the facts before
them in so plain, clear, and simple a manner as to carry
their opinions with him.

He frequently expressed a wish that the members of the
Board would state their views and opinions freely, frankly,
and honestly, which one member occasionally did, though
not always to his personal satisfaction, for Sir James Graham
read all papers, with their several enclosures, with such care
and attention, had so retentive a memory, was so accurate
in statement, powerful and conclusive in argument, that the
member in question was often proved to be mistaken, and was
seldom let off until he admitted he was so!

Sir John Pechell was unfortunately a martyr to the gout,
and it was with great difficulty that he could move, even
with the aid of crutches, and consequently found it somewhat dull sitting alone in the Board-room; he was therefore
anxious to persuade his colleagues that, instead of disposing

of their papers in their private rooms, it would be far better
to bring them into the Board-room, and talk the business
over previous to the meeting of the Board. At last a day
was fixed for the experiment to be tried. Very much to the
alarm of Mr. Barrow* and myself, who were naturally apprehensive that it would materially interfere with the opening
of the despatches, the distribution of the papers to the lords,
and the preparation of those to be read at the Board.

An hour before the usual meeting of the Board their
lordships made their appearance; and as all the members
of the Board of Admiralty were members of Parliament,
with the exception of Sir Thomas Hardy, it is not surprising
that the first subject discussed should be what passed in the
House the previous evening.

Party feeling at this time ran very high, as the Whigs
had only quite recently come into power. In the course of
a short conversation it was unanimously decided that Lord
John Russell had never made a more powerful or effective
speech, nor Sir Robert Peel (in the opinion of Sir John
Pechell) such a d——d bad one.

Sir John had in the course of the evening paired off, in
order to go to the opera to meet the lady who was shortly to
be Lady Pechell. He had been charmed with the personal
attractions of Mrs. Norton, whom he described as looking
perfectly lovely, adding, "And as for Lady Lyndhurst, I never
saw her make such an infernal guy of herself" The next
topic of interest was an inquiry as to the state of health of
several old admirals known to be in a somewhat shaky
condition, and the probable effect their demise would have
upon the Navy List, and to what extent their individual
interests might be benefited thereby. This occupied some
little time, and the rumoured marriage of a distinguished
admiral to a rich widow, who was reported to have been left

* Afterwards Sir John Barrow, Bart.

the choicest cellar of wine in all London, was exciting general interest, when the door unexpectedly opened and Sir James Graham made his appearance. At this point the several members snatched up their papers, and began minuting them, which up to this time had never even been looked at.

Sir James Graham advanced to the head of the table, and having made a stately bow to each member, took his seat, and as there seemed to be a great many papers, said, " We had better at once proceed to the despatch of business "

The reading consequently commenced, and at the expiration of about half an hour Sir James, observing that one or two of the lords were minuting their papers instead of attending to what was going on, said somewhat pointedly to Sir John Pechell, " What do you think we had better do in this case ? " Sir John coloured violently, and was obliged to admit that he had not been attending ! The First Lord with a laugh replied, " It is very strange, but do you know that is exactly what I was thinking ! " And then went on to say, " I must request the members of the Board to be so obliging as to minute their papers either before or after the meeting of the Board, but certainly not while the reading is going on, for it is a farce to meet for the despatch of business if the members do not attend. And, looking at the pile of papers Mr. Briggs has before him, I think he will have quite enough to do without having to read them a second time. What do you think, Mr. Briggs ? " But to the inquiry I made no answer.

The reading then proceeded, and everything went on very quietly until Sir John Pechell handed me a letter to read. It commenced. " Sir,—In reply to your letter of the 26th ulto, I have the honour to acquaint you, for the information of the Lords Commissioners of the Admiralty, that——" Sir James Graham, interrupting, said, "Have you the

former correspondence there, Mr. Briggs?" I replied in
the negative. He then said, "I think I have on more than
one occasion requested the members of the Board to obtain
from the Record Office all previous correspondence, as it is
impossible to deal with any case in a satisfactory manner
unless we have all the papers before us to refer to. But
very probably Sir John is master of the subject." It soon
became painfully evident that he was not, whereupon
Sir Thomas Hardy very kindly came to his assistance,
saying, "Don't be too hard upon a man in love, Sir James—
you really must not." "A man in what?" said the First Lord,
thoroughly astonished. "He is going to be married," said
Sir Thomas. "Then I beg you ten thousand pardons, Sir
John," said Sir James Graham; "it fully accounts for a man
being a little *égaré!* I offer you my sincere congratulations." And everybody present did the same until Sir John
was overwhelmed with good wishes, and looked anything
but grateful for them.

It is necessary to explain that the "Lover," as Sir Thomas
Hardy persisted in calling him, was between fifty and sixty
years of age, and suffered so much from gout that he could
not move without crutches, as has already been stated.
The Board shortly afterwards broke up, and I was left
alone with Sir John Pechell. For some time there was a
dead silence; at last he said, "What a devil of a temper
the First Lord was in to-day, Mr. Briggs; I cannot help
thinking that he must have dined at Bellamy's last night
off salt junk, which has given him a fit of indigestion." To
which I replied, "That is just possible, sir." And Sir John
Pechell seemed much pleased with his brilliant idea. At
this moment the head messenger came to me with a message
from Sir Thomas Hardy to say he wished to see me in his
private room. I accordingly went, and found all the naval
members with him. It struck me there was a peculiar

expression in the countenances of some of them, but I
thought nothing of it at the time. I was young in office, and
very anxious to carry into effect the exact instructions
I received. It never occurred to me as possible that distinguished admirals and Lords of the Admiralty would
indulge in any practical joke; I therefore, in the plenitude
of my innocence, delivered the message word for word,
which I was desired to convey to Sir John Pechell, namely:
"Sir Thomas Hardy desires me to give you these papers,
sir, as he thinks you are probably master of the subject." I
had scarcely uttered the words when Sir John Pechell said,
"I'll master the subject you, Master Briggs" He made two
ineffectual efforts to rise, and in the endeavour to get hold
of his crutch, let it fall I saw by the expression of his face
that mischief was meant. Anyhow, if I had no brains in
my head, I had quicksilver in my toes, for I instantly made
for the door, but found I could not get out. I tried another
with as little success, and so on with the whole four, when
suddenly they all opened at once, and an admiral at each,
shouting, "Go it, Pechell! Go it, youngster!"—at which
there was a general laugh, in which Sir John Pechell was
obliged to join. Sir Thomas Hardy then turned to me and
said, "I thought you were far too sharp a youngster to
deliver such a message as that, considering what passed at
the Board this morning!"

The proceedings of the day were, however, attended with
most beneficial results ; for it was the first and last time the
members ever met in the Board-room for the despatch of
business previous to the meeting of the Board.

Sir John Pechell was decidedly a very able man, a good
officer, and a first-rate artillerist; and though he had a stern
sense of justice, I must say he invariably took the kind view
of a case. But severe bodily sufferings rendered him at times
very irritable and wayward. Nevertheless, upon the whole,

I personally succeeded in getting on with him wonderfully well.

My duty, as reader, rendered it necessary that I should arrive at the Admiralty shortly after 8 A.M., so as to be there when the mails came in. Judge of my surprise when, one morning on entering the Board-room, I beheld Sir John Pechell seated in his usual place. He instantly asked me how soon might the newspapers be expected. I replied, "Almost immediately."

After a few minutes' silence he said, "I made a speech last night, and I declare I would rather go into action ten times over than go through again what I then experienced. I had my speech pat, I had repeated it the whole evening, and got up several times in the hope I might catch the Speaker's eye, but failed. I was repeating it for the last time, and was just in the middle of it, when I heard the Speaker call, 'Sir John Pechell.' I instantly rose, but when I saw two hundred pair of eyes fixed upon me, and all the naval chaps under the gallery grinning, and waiting to hear the words of wisdom that would drop from my official lips, I couldn't for the life of me remember a word of my speech. There I stood with everybody staring at me; I felt I must say something, but what I did say I don't exactly know, but I think it must have been very much to the purpose, and rather witty too, for there was a great deal of laughter when I sat down."

By this time the *Times* had arrived, and nothing could exceed Sir John's anxiety to ascertain how his speech had been reported. Imagine his feeling of anger and indignation when he read: "After a few words from Sir John Pechell, inaudible in the gallery, the House adjourned." It is not necessary to repeat here the complimentary epithets he applied to the *Times*.

It had been the intention of Sir John Pechell to give a settler to Captain Charles Yorke (afterwards Earl of Hard-

wicke), who was a fluent speaker of the Conservative side,
whilst Sir John was a Whig of a most uncompromising type.
Sir John Pechell had only just left when in came Sir Thomas
Hardy, saying, "So I hear Sir Samuel—I beg pardon, I
mustn't call him 'Sam'—made a speech last night ; pray give
me the *Times*," which I at once handed to him. He then
read out· "Inaudible in the gallery"—"Inaudible in the
gallery." "He has been here already this morning, sir," said
I. "The d—— he has! And I suppose the 'Lover' is not
in the best of humours with the *Times !* "

Sir Thomas went off intensely amused. And as there was
generally a little playful sparring between them, he could
not refrain when the Board met from congratulating Sir John
upon the decided success of his maiden speech.

Sir James Graham was a very powerful First Lord, and
conducted the responsible duties of the Board-room in a
manner that exhibited administrative qualities of the highest
order. When the Board met he took care that it was most
distinctly understood that it did so for the despatch of important public business. It is no easy matter for a First Lord to
keep the attention of the various members directed to the
particular subject under discussion. This can only be accomplished by occasionally putting questions to them, which,· if
they were not paying due attention to what was passing,
it would be impossible for them to answer. Sir James did
this with such cleverness and adroitness as to excite the
admiration of those ·who were silent listeners, and could
plainly perceive the force and object of the interruptions
when attention and interest were beginning to wane. He
instantly put a stop to all irrelevant discussions, especially
if the argument waxed warm, by requesting the members to
give expressions to their opinions in a written report, which
he hoped they would have the goodness to submit to the
Board the following day, ·and, at the same time, ·politely

intimating that this would be best effected by previously discussing the subject in their private rooms, as the matter did not appear quite ripe for a final decision. He also had a decided objection to anecdotes at the Board, and upon a distinguished admiral proposing to favour their lordships with an entertaining story, Sir James used to turn to me and say, "Are there not still a good many letters to be disposed of, Mr. Briggs?"—giving me a look which I knew how to interpret. I replied, "I'm afraid there are, sir." Sir James then said, "I fear, my dear admiral, we can't hear your story just now, but, as you dine with me to-night, you will have a good opportunity of telling this interesting anecdote after dinner, when we shall all be better able to enjoy it."

During the reading at the Board, Sir James Graham detailed to the Secretary the wording of every minute, and in most important cases drew up the answer himself, which he did with a rapidity and clearness of expression upon a sheet of note-paper which would cover, when copied, several pages of foolscap. The amount of work he would transact in the course of a morning was perfectly wonderful!

It has unfortunately happened that in more than one instance a First Lord, fully alive to the requirements of the service and the soundness of the representations made to him by his naval advisers, and convinced of the desirability of carrying into immediate effect what in his own judgment, and in the opinion of the naval lords was urgently needed, has failed in his endeavour to influence the Cabinet to obtain the necessary funds.

Sir James Graham, however, possessed that personal influence in the Cabinet of Earl Grey, and generally laid his case before the Ministry with such power and cogency of argument, that he rarely failed in bringing conviction to their minds, and carrying his point to a successful issue.

It not infrequently happens, much to the detriment of the

naval service and the best interests of the country, that the
First Lord of the Admiralty is the only member of the Cabinet
who is really acquainted with the actual condition of the navy
or takes any interest in it, so that he finds himself, at times,
placed in a somewhat painful and invidious position   And,
what is not less to be regretted, that until very recently the
strongly expressed opinion of the First Sea Lord and the other
naval members of the Board commanded so little attention as
to be virtually ignored.

The first administration of Sir James Graham may be
regarded as the one introducing those great and important
changes in the construction of our ships, the reorganisation
of the fleet, and the initial mobilisation of the navy which
have gradually brought it to its present state of efficiency,
and the placing of the civil department of the navy on so
sound and substantial a basis as to be regarded as a model
of administrative arrangement, departmental consolidation,
and individual responsibility, combining at the same time the
personal supervision of the First Lord.

The various important measures and reforms introduced
by this Board have left their mark upon the naval history
of the country, and reflect the highest credit upon the
administrative ability of Sir James Graham, the professional
experience and sound advice of Sir Thomas Hardy and the
other naval members of the Board.

Little could Lord Nelson's favourite captain have anticipated that his own grandson, Sir Evan MacGregor, as
Permanent Secretary of the Admiralty, would, at the end
of the century, assist in carrying into practical effect the views
he entertained and the opinions he expressed, as First Sea
Lord, of Sir James Graham's Board of 1830, and as his representative witness all those great and important changes which
he then predicted science and steam would render inevitably
necessary throughout every branch of the naval service.

CHAPTER IV.

THE ADMINISTRATION OF EARL DE GREY, 23RD DECEMBER, 1834, TO 25TH APRIL, 1835.

The first administration of Lord Auckland passed over—Observations in reference to Earl de Grey's personal attributes, also in regard to Lord Ashley (afterwards Lord Shaftesbury)—How science was viewed by the service—An anecdote to show the generosity of an admiral— Another in regard to private *tête-à-têtes*—How to uphold authority— " Didn't I make the First Lord laugh ? "

SIR JAMES GRAHAM was succeeded, in July, 1834, by Lord Auckland, who, upon this occasion only, held office a very few months, and it is therefore desirable to reserve for a future opportunity any remarks I may have to offer in reference to the naval administrations of this nobleman and popular statesman.

The accession of Sir Robert Peel to power, on 26th December, 1834, caused another change in the Ministry, and led to the appointment of Earl de Grey as First Lord of the Admiralty, with Sir John Poo Beresford, Bart., K.C.B., M.P., and Sir Charles Rowley, K.C.B., as Naval Lords; Lord Ashley, M.P., and the Knight of Kerry as Civil Lords, and Mr. Dawson as Secretary. Sir George Cockburn was offered the appointment of First Sea Lord, but, as the nomination was accompanied with a confidential intimation that the Government would in all probability be short lived, he prudently decided to retain his command as Commander-in-chief upon the West Indies and North American Station

Lord de Grey was a nobleman of considerable ability possessing sound judgment and discretion, liberal in his opinions, and free from party bias, and exhibited his good sense in adhering to the naval policy of Sir James Graham and Sir Thomas Hardy. Lord de Grey made an excellent First Lord, was a capital man of business, and managed his Board with tact and adroitness. It is much to be regretted that his brief tenure of office (only five months) prevented him from giving a practical proof of the benefits he would otherwise have conferred upon the naval service.

The Knight of Kerry was an Irish gentleman of most polished manners, and fully answered to the high reputation for which gentlemen of that nationality were, in days gone by, so pre-eminently distinguished.

Lord Ashley held office for the first time, and was deputed to bring forward the navy estimates in the House of Commons. For a novice in naval affairs to undertake and master the complex explanations contained in this annual exposition of proposed naval expenditure is a labour requiring no ordinary skill and ability, and so ably did Lord Ashley discharge the delicate and responsible duty assigned to him, notwithstanding the short time allotted, that Sir Robert Peel personally complimented him upon the marked success which had attended his entrance into political life. His lordship was a valuable member of the Board; but it soon became apparent that the peculiar ideas he entertained but little fitted him for the controversies of political life. His conscience was so tender that it was with the utmost difficulty he could be prevailed upon to make the slightest concession from anything he regarded as right, in utter forgetfulness of the fact that others had consciences as well as himself, and that the public services can only be efficiently conducted upon the principle of mutual concession. He therefore wisely determined to devote himself to those philanthropic labours which have obtained for him a reputation and reward far beyond the most brilliant success he could have hoped for in the arena of political life.

Mr. Dawson proved a valuable Secretary to Lord de Grey and performed the duties of the department with great efficiency, and was much esteemed by those who served under him.

The decision of Sir George Cockburn to retain his command in the West Indies threw increased responsibility upon the two remaining admirals. Sir John Poo Beresford was as popular in the service as he was at the Admiralty; he possessed a great deal of practical common sense and no small amount of Irish wit.

Sir Charles Rowley likewise was a very gallant naval officer, but both he and Sir John were decidedly of the old school, to which the following incident bears ample testimony.

Sir Charles superintended the *Excellent* and gunnery, and upon my presenting to him one evening the gunnery examination papers of a lieutenant, he said: "Do you know, it is very strange, but I don't understand all this. Pray, sir, what is the meaning of the word 'impact'?" I replied: "I rather think it means the force of a blow." He then said to Sir John Beresford: "What, in the name of good fortune, is meant by 'initial velocity'?" Sir John replied: "I'll be hanged if I know, but I suppose it is some of Tom Hastings' scientific bosh; but I'll tell you what I think we had better do—we'll just go at once to Lord de Grey and get that *Excellent* paid off. The Chancellor of the Exchequer is very anxious to get a reduction made in the navy estimates." And they both agreed it was a capital suggestion, and away they went to the First Lord.

It seemed to me desirable to give Mr. Dawson a private hint as to what was going on, and he consequently followed them into the First Lord's room.

About half an hour afterwards Mr. Dawson sent for me
and said he had been highly amused. The admirals gave
Lord de Grey a graphic account of their naval exploits, how
they had knocked away masts and yards, riddled hulls, and
all the damage they had done. Lord de Grey listened, with
the most exemplary patience, to all that was said, and rising
from his seat assured them that he thought their proposal
to pay off the *Excellent* was admirable, and doubtless would
be most acceptable to the Chancellor of the Exchequer;
and then, patting Sir John upon the back, added: "But
I am afraid, my dear Beresford, I cannot sanction it, for
you have no idea how d—— scientific that House of
Commons has become."

The above sufficiently illustrates the sort of estimation in
which science and gunnery were held by naval lords and
flag-officers of that date.

Little did they foresee what science would accomplish for
the country, and more especially for the navy, when they
gave expression to these opinions. Little did they imagine
that before the expiration of half a century the magnificent
fleets of three-deckers and 90-gun ships would be replaced
by ironclads of no less than 14,000 tons and 13,000 horse-
power, steaming at a speed of from 16 to 20 knots per
hour. Never did they realise that the 24 and 32-pounders
of that day would be replaced by guns of 47, 63, and 110 tons,
throwing a shot of 1200 pounds, and that with smokeless
powder It never occurred to them that the danger to which
vessels of war would be exposed would be from torpedo-boats,
rushing through the water at the furious rate of 25 or 30
knots an hour, and discharging their torpedoes under water
to the utter destruction of their ships. Little did they
imagine that all the heavy manual labour devolving upon
the ship's company would be performed by mechanical
appliances, and guns elevated and depressed by hydraulic

pressure; nay, more than this, that salt water would be distilled into fresh, and the dark and gloomy holds of their ships would be brilliantly illuminated by electric light. Such are some of the wonderful achievements of science which the highly educated flag-officers of the present day have happily learnt to fully appreciate.

One of the principal events which occurred during the administration of Lord de Grey was the unfortunate loss of the *Wolf* at the back of the Isle of Wight.

A great difference of opinion prevailed between the naval lords on the subject, and the discussion was conducted in a manner that afforded intense amusement to Lord de Grey. Sir John Poo Beresford took one side, and Sir Charles Rowley the other. The latter complaining of the way in which the ship had been run upon the rocks and the measures adopted after she had struck, which the former pronounced as right and seamanlike ; the discussion was both animated and prolonged. Sir Charles, however, laboured under this disadvantage, that he was very slow in his utterance, whilst Sir John spoke with that rapidity and volubility so characteristic of his nationality that he was enabled to pour in three broadsides to one of Sir Charles's, who, in his over anxiety to reply, began to stammer and stutter in such a manner that Sir John began to imitate him, to the immense amusement of all present, winding up by assuring Lord de Grey that old Chin-chopper knew nothing about the matter, and that, as he was senior officer, he must of course know best.

Sir Charles Rowley was a tall, dignified, and rather magnificent gentleman, with a decidedly fine profile, though his nose might have been rather prominent and his chin slightly protruding.

The expression of Sir Charles Rowley's countenance, when he heard himself designated old Chin-chopper, surpasses my

E

powers of description. But he, with admirable taste and good nature, joined heartily in the laugh against himself at Sir John's final outburst of eloquence.

Lord de Grey thought the discussion had now arrived at a stage when it would be prudent for him to interfere, and accordingly he said: "You know, my lords, what happens to the patient when doctors differ. I have listened with great attention to the arguments on both sides, which have been ably advanced and conducted with exemplary good humour, and, as this seems a matter far in excess of my knowledge of seamanship, I think perhaps your lordships will concur with me in opinion that the wiser course for us to pursue will be to suspend our judgment until we have the minutes of the court-martial before us, which will, no doubt, enable us to arrive at a more impartial decision."

Sir John Beresford might well be popular, for he was one of the most hospitable and genial naval lords that ever came within the Admiralty walls. He generally had half-a-dozen naval officers and others to breakfast, promised them ships, promotion, and almost everything they asked for, and sent them away full of bright hopes, but, alas! not very likely to be realised. Amongst other things, he had a beautiful Alderney cow which the dear old admiral gave to at least half-a-dozen different persons in the course of one morning, Mr. Taylor, the Director of Works, being one, who, like a sensible man, went straight to the stable and took it home. The consequence was that when the other claimants sent for their present there was no cow. Possession is nine points of the law.

One morning the reading of the Board was a little late, when Sir John Beresford asked me why. I replied that one of the lords had requested a private *tête-à-tête* with the First Lord, and had gone into his room. Whereupon he said, "I don't know what you think, but I don't see that

much good ever comes of these confounded titty-tatties, as
you call them, for nobody knows what is going on. I will
tell you how I should act if I were First Lord. I should
begin: 'Now, my lords, here you all are. You shall have
a clear deck, fair fight, and no favour. You may all talk
as long as you like, and I will take precious good care to
let you know when I have had enough.' Each of you should
have your say in turn, and, when I had heard all you have
got to say, I should say, 'Now, my lords, my opinion is so-
and-so, and do you, Mr. Secretary, make a minute to that
effect, and you, Mr. Reader, get along with something else as
quickly as you can.'

. "The fact is the First Lord must be captain of his ship.
I have been frequently asked by captains under my command,
'Don't you think so-and-so, sir?' My answer has been, 'No,
I don't; and, as I am senior officer, I must of course know
best.' This system may appear to you strange and very
ridiculous in theory, but you have no idea how well it works
in practice. It has many advantages. It upholds authority;
it prevents argument; it saves valuable time; and ensures a
decision. And let me tell you that is no slight thing."

One Sunday morning Lord de Grey and Sir John Beresford
entered the Board-room together, the latter inquiring of me
what steamers there were at Woolwich that could convey
men round to Portsmouth. The vessels available, curiously
enough, were named *Styx, Charon,* and *Rhadamanthus.* Sir
John then said, " Briggs, who was Styx ? " I replied, " Styx is
a river in hell, sir "—the question provoking a smile from the
First Lord. Sir John then said, " And pray who is Charon ? "
" He is the ferryman that rows the company across." " And
who is that other chap with the confoundedly hard name ? "
" He is the unjust judge, sir." Sir John then said to the
First Lord, "Lord de Grey, I cannot help thinking that our
friend Briggs has been to hell, or I don't see how he could

know so much about it; and, what is more, I have a shrewd
suspicion that he got tipsy, kicked up a row, and was brought
up before that beak with a hard name, and that is the reason
he is so spiteful against him."

Thus the joke which was at first against Sir John Beresford
was, by his ready wit, cleverly turned against me.

One of the greatest difficulties that Lord de Grey had to
contend with was Sir John Beresford's predilection for telling
anecdotes. He generally begun by addressing himself to the
First Lord, saying, "Now, my lord, I will tell you a capital
anecdote which occurred when I commanded the ——" He
seldom got farther than that when the First Lord interrupted
and said to me, "Have you not a great many papers to-day,
Mr. Briggs ? " in the same manner as Sir James Graham.

Upon one occasion Lord de Grey said, "It seems a light
day, and we will hear your anecdote, Sir John." The story
was told, and the First Lord laughed heartily, to the great
delight of Sir John, who, directly the Board was over, repeated
to me again for my especial benefit the story, ending, "Didn't
I just make the First Lord laugh!" The story was then told
to the chief clerk, who was immediately sent for that he might
hear how Sir John made the First Lord laugh! The story
was then repeated to two admirals, in the Admiralty courtyard,
and to three more between the Admiralty and the Senior
United Service Club; and to every member of the club whom
he met there he led confidentially into a corner as if he had
something very private and important to communicate, ending
on each occasion with, "Didn't I just make the First Lord
laugh!"

In fine, the permission to tell the anecdote and making the
First Lord laugh made the dear old admiral happy for at least
a week.

I much regret my inability to gratify my readers with
this particular anecdote, but it was my fate to be obliged to

listen to so many that I quite agreed with Lord de Grey that the business of the Board would get on a great deal better if it were not for these " confounded anecdotes."

Lord de Grey was admirably suited for the duties of the high office assigned to him. He possessed firmness and decision when necessary, and was affable and courteous in demeanour towards all with whom he came in personal contact. From the date of his appointment he was impressed with the conviction that his tenure of office could be but of short duration, therefore felt disinclined to take up any important reform, as it was improbable he would be able to carry it through.

I am consequently compelled rather to deal with what his lordship would have done than with what he actually achieved. But from all I learnt from Mr Dawson, and what I myself observed, there is no doubt, had it been permitted him, he would have proved a most valuable head of the naval department, as he was imbued with enlarged and enlightened opinions, and was quite free from party and professional prejudices.

CHAPTER V.

THE SECOND ADMINISTRATION OF THE EARL OF AUCKLAND,
25TH APRIL TO 19th SEPTEMBER, 1835.

Observations in reference to Lord Auckland's personal attributes—Changes
  in the composition of the squadron on the west coast of Africa—An
  admiral always in a passion—The time required to get together a
  ship's company and afterwards to reduce it to order and discipline—
  Making an example of a midshipman.

In 1835 Lord Auckland again came into office as First Lord
of the Admiralty, previous to proceeding to India as Governor-
General.   His lordship was a very able statesman, had a fine
and even temper, was calm, quiet and extremely patient, and
was remarkable for being silent; but when he spoke it was
always to the point, and sometimes displayed a dry humour
which had a most telling effect upon the naval members of
his Board.   One of his distinguishing characteristics was to
use his pen instead of his tongue; the minutes and reports
which he drew up were so well and cleverly expressed that
they saved an amount of valuable time which might otherwise
have been wasted in unprofitable discussion.   Lord Auckland's
Board was not particularly strong; for, though the naval
members were very distinguished officers and clever men,
they were far from being good men of business.   They were—

Rear-Admiral Sir Charles Adam, M.P. ;
Rear-Admiral Sir William Parker, K.C.B. ;
Captain the Hon. George Elliot, C.B , R.N. ;
Captain Sir Edward Troubridge, Bart., R.N., M.P. ;

The Right Hon. Archibald, Lord Dalmeny, M.P.;
First Secretary, Charles Wood, Esq , M.P.;
Second Secretary, Sir John Barrow, Bart.

Any deficiencies resulting from that cause was, however, more than compensated for by the great ability of the First Secretary, Mr. Wood, who discharged his duties with as much efficiency as he subsequently displayed when selected for the higher office of First Lord of the Admiralty, his administration being one of brilliant success.

Mr. Wood was at this time a young man of talent and energy, and had obtained the highest honours at Oxford.

Lord Auckland took the greatest interest in all that appertained to the navy and the efficiency of the service, but he was again prevented from undertaking any of the improvements he so ardently desired because of the shortness of his administration. However, in addition to the ordinary routine of the office, he effected in the brief period he held office one very important change.

It seemed to his lordship that the squadron stationed upon the west coast of Africa for the suppression of the slave trade consisted of ships of a far larger class than was required, and employed a greater number of men than was absolutely necessary upon that unhealthy station. He therefore determined to substitute 10-gun brigs and small steamers, with a complement of fifty men, instead of corvettes and large sloops, carrying from 220 to 125 men and boys. This judicious change in the composition of the squadron not only placed at his lordship's disposal a considerable number of seamen available for the general service of the fleet, but added greatly to the efficiency of the squadron. The gun-brigs and steamers, being of much lighter draught, were enabled to stand in closer to the shore and discover the lurking-places of the slave-raiders.

So inveterate 'was the indisposition to make any change or depart in the least from the usual routine, that Lord Auckland experienced no little difficulty in carrying into effect a measure so obviously beneficial to the navy, and so calculated to facilitate the capture of slave-traders.

It is much to be regretted that the attention of First Lords is not more frequently directed to the composition and distribution of the fleet upon our foreign stations. For years all that was deemed necessary was to replace at the end of three years the vessel whose term of service had expired with one of exactly the same type, without in the least considering whether there was any necessity for replacing her at all, or reflecting whether a larger or smaller vessel might not be more effective on that particular station. Now this is one of those questions in which sound economy might from time to time be effected, and the number of men voted for the year might be distributed more advantageously; but of course it should be considered previous to the preparation of the navy estimates, and not dealt with in a desultory and piecemeal fashion. It is astonishing what might be accomplished, both as regards economy and efficiency, by a thorough reconstruction of our squadrons at home and abroad, and by a careful selection of ships to discharge the duties of each particular station, which vary from year to year. But this is a great question for the naval lords, and, for obvious reason, requires very careful and delicate handling.

Sir Charles Adam was First Sea Lord, and was a gallant officer and a splendid specimen of a flag-officer of the old school. He was the most amiable and kind-hearted of men, and to look at him you would think he never could be out of temper; and yet he spent the whole day in a perpetual passion. He was constantly misplacing his spectacles and mislaying his papers, and could seldom speak without getting excited, talking loud, looking fierce, and thumping the table.

On one occasion he delivered a soliloquy for the benefit of the Board, got very angry, stood up, and said, "I say it is so" Whereupon Lord Auckland very calmly remarked, "I am not aware anyone has contradicted you." Sir Charles replied, "But I thought they might" "Oh! I understand now," said the First Lord; "you wish to have the last word in anticipation of the reply."

The whole Board could not refrain from laughing, in which Sir Charles Adam most heartily joined.

His change of countenance would be difficult to describe From everything that looked fierce and angry it became everything that was bright, beaming, and good-natured.

Sir Charles wrote a most wretched hand, which at times it was almost impossible to decipher. One day I was endeavouring to read one of his minutes, but failed utterly; he then got impatient, snatched the paper out of my hand, but did not manage it as well as I did. He then rang the bell violently, and in doing so pulled down the rope, sent for his private secretary, and desired him to read the minute immediately. This unfortunately exceeded his powers, thereupon Sir Charles dismissed him from that office on the spot.

This little episode afforded great amusement to Lord Auckland and his Board, and led to the gallant admiral perceiving the absurdity of his position and good-naturedly observing: "Dash my buttons! We naval chaps are a queer lot, are we not?"

Barring this little eccentricity he proved a very valuable member of the Board, for he possessed a very sound judgment, and generally made very shrewd remarks, though the *modus operandi* was at times somewhat circuitous.

It is difficult now, when ships proceed to sea within a few days of being commissioned, to bring the public to believe the utter want of method and system which prevailed, in the early days of my official career, in obtaining seamen for the fleet. In a time of peace it took from four to six months to get together a crew for a large frigate or a line-of-battleship, of which, when collected, two-thirds would be composed of merchant seamen who had never set foot on a man-of-war.

With such a motley ship's company it was at least six months before order or discipline could be established, it was not therefore surprising that in a Board-room full of admirals and captains, punishment and discipline should be a topic of frequent discussion, more especially where the delinquences of some midshipman or junior officer happened to be brought under their notice. But where the necessity of upholding the principle had been generally admitted, I must do the naval officers the justice to say that they were usually very lenient, and made every allowance for the indiscretions of youth

On a certain occasion the port-admiral at Portsmouth had made a strong representation to the Admiralty as to the imperative necessity of making a severe example of a young midshipman who had absented himself without leave, sending at the same time a private letter to Sir Charles Adam, complaining that it was becoming a growing habit which required a check.

Sir Charles, addressing the members of the Board, said, " I suppose after this representation of the admiral he had better be got rid of." There was a chorus of " Certainly. Discipline must be upheld ; there are plenty of young officers who would behave well," etc., etc., etc., and the order for his dismissal was made. I put the letter on one side, fully convinced the minute would be reversed before the Board broke up.

Scarcely twenty minutes had elapsed when a member said to me, " Is there any letter of complaint against Mr. ——— ? " I answered, " Why, you have just ordered him to be dismissed the service ," whereupon he said to Sir Charles, " You must not dismiss Mr. ——; here is a letter from his captain, who says he is the best midshipman in the ship." "The devil he is!" said Sir Charles. "It seems, after all, the boy has only absented himself for twenty-four hours to get a farewell kiss from his cousin, a confoundedly pretty girl! The fact is the admiral has a fit of the gout, the flag-captain has been put under arrest twice this week, and the poor secretary is afraid to go near him." There was a general opinion that dismissal was out of the question. Was he to be deprived of any time?

At last it was decided that a good jobation would be enough, which was soon translated into official phraseology. It was at this stage that Sir Charles Adam, turning to Lord Auckland, said, "I am the last man in the world who ought to have advocated his dismissal, my lord, for I was guilty of something of the same sort myself once" "And yet you were the first, Sir Charles, to propose it, and hustle the poor young man out of the service!" "Yes," he replied, looking the picture of good-nature, "I do feel rather ashamed of myself. The case stood thus, my lord. My frigate was lying off Belem at single anchor, with Blue Peter flying, under orders for England, when I thought I should like to have another kiss of an uncommon pretty Portuguese girl, one Donna Maria Angelina Sebestiana Victoriosa, etc., etc., di Ponjos. I arrived at the door, gave a loud knock, when to my utter astonishment who should open it but Lord St. Vincent himself! I bowed to the very ground, my cocked hat touching it, and said, 'My frigate is ready to start, my lord, at a moment's notice, riding at single anchor, Blue Peter flying, but I considered it my duty to come to your lordship at the last moment, thinking it just possible you might have some important despatches for the Admiralty' 'That d——d lie, sir,' said Lord St. Vincent, 'has raised you very much in my estimation; it proves to me that you are able to meet a sudden and somewhat unpleasant contingency with considerable adroitness; but you had better be off, or a court-martial might be the consequence.'" To explain the presence of Lord St Vincent, Sir Charles said that his lordship was rather sweet upon the mother, a young and attractive widow.

Everyone laughed, with the exception of Lord Auckland, who quietly observed, "You might well feel ashamed after what you have just told us to hustle a poor love-sick midshipman out of the service with such unseemly precipitancy when you, as a captain and in command of a ship, were guilty of a similar breach of discipline."

Lord Auckland's tenure of office was brief, as he accepted the high appointment of Viceroy of India, but I shall upon a future occasion refer to his administrative capacities, and direct attention to the benefits he conferred upon the naval service upon taking his seat, for the third time, at the head of the Board of Admiralty.

CHAPTER VI.

THE ADMINISTRATION OF THE EARL OF MINTO, 19TH SEPTEMBER, 1835, TO 8TH SEPTEMBER, 1841.

The success of the S S *Great Western*—How Mr. Wood (afterwards Lord Halifax) succeeded in getting a Dover packet—The opinions of Mr. Joseph Hume (member for Montrose) in regard to the United States—National debt and economy.

IN the year 1835, when Lord Auckland proceeded to India, the Earl of Minto was appointed his successor, but no change of policy of any importance was made upon his accession to office, the members of the Board continuing to retain their seats as before.

Several important events occurred during the administration of Lord Minto; but perhaps the most important of all was the successful voyage of the *Great Western* steamer to New York, occupying fifteen days, she being the first vessel that crossed the Atlantic by the power of steam alone. Several learned and scientific men, amongst them Dr. Dionysius Lardner, undertook to prove the matter to be of utter impossibility

The grand success which attended the *Great Western* imparted a great impetus to the introduction of steam, and led to a higher estimate being formed of its power and importance than had previously prevailed in the ranks of naval officers of the old school. Indeed, to the success of this vessel may be dated the mighty change that has taken place in the mercantile marine and in the Royal Navy, there being at the time not a single sailing-vessel upon the stocks in any one of Her Majesty's dockyards, so complete is the revolution that steam had effected.

When, as during Lord Minto's administration, nothing was heard of but proposals for reduction of establishments and diminution of expenditure, and when such politicians as Mr Joseph Hume were regarded as political leaders and popular patriots, it was as hopeless as it was a thankless task to endeavour to stem the tide of public opinion. *Apropos* of the economical, if not parsimonious, views of Lord Minto's Board, and the extreme lengths to which their party pushed political views, I may mention the difficulty which Mr. Wood (the Political Secretary) experienced in persuading the Board to sanction the expense of providing a new Dover packet, the packet service at this time having been transferred to the Admiralty.

Mr. Wood said to me one morning, " You will be glad to learn I have at last got my Dover packet, and how do you suppose I managed it ?   Well, I took up the Navy List, and said, ' Do you not think we ought to build two additional line-of-battleships to replace several that are scarcely fit for further service ? '   It was thought that frigates were more wanted.   It then became a question whether corvettes would not answer the purpose equally well.   A discussion then took place in regard to sloops and gunboats, when, having ·saved so much money, it was thought possible they might accede to my request for a Dover packet, which was all I really wanted "   Mr. Wood had many difficulties to contend with, but he always succeeded in carrying his point by the exercise of tact, patience, and good temper

How could those who desired an increase to the navy, however slight, hope to have any success in inducing the Board of Admiralty to make any addition to the fleet when Mr. Wood found it necessary to have recourse to so clever and ingenious an expedient to obtain even a Dover packet?

The policy of Lord Minto's Board was in strict accordance with the political and public feeling of the day, and that of the notorious member for Montrose. Economy was the order of the day, and Mr. Hume carried everything before him.

I remember being under the gallery of the House of Commons when the navy estimates were about to be discussed in committee. Everything that took place in the United States excited the admiration of the honourable member for Montrose. "That model Republic," as he was pleased to designate it, was held up as a pattern of perfection. He considered the people of the United States were far too sensible, far too prudent, possessed too much insight, and were too much alive to their own interests to be so foolish as to follow the miserable example of the mother-country and involve themselves in war. And thus, soaring to the heights of prophecy, and with a look of mysterious sagacity, he informed the Speaker that there was one thing he could assure him, yes, that he could, namely, that the United States would never be mad enough to incur a national debt. Now, so far from the predictions of the Scotch economist being verified, the United States not only went to war, but went to war with one another, and so far from not incurring a national debt, so successful were they in this particular, that they positively succeeded in amassing in four years an amount of debt which took this country a whole century to accomplish. So much for the prophetic wisdom of this economical monomaniac!

It is only those who have had a long official experience who are able to fully appreciate the difficulties interposed in the way of reform and improvement, so deeply rooted is prejudice, and so great the disinclination to introduce changes of any description; though this is a matter of far easier accomplishment now than in the early days of my official career. The English character is very conservative

The heads of the naval profession, gallant and distinguished as they were, had not, with few exceptions, attained to that high standard of education and literary ability which characterise the correspondence of such able officers as Sir Thomas Symonds,* Sir Geoffrey Hornby,* Sir George Elliot, Sir Edward Fanshawe,* and Admiral Colomb, and such gallant and promising captains as Lord Charles Beresford, Penrose Fitz-Gerald, and many others.

In the present day all the heads of the profession are in favour of progressive improvements. It was far otherwise forty or fifty years ago, when lords of the Admiralty, and commanders-in-chief at the ports, were from seventy to upwards of eighty years of age. Consequently it would be unreasonable to expect that science, steam and gunnery in its high development, were likely to be estimated at their proper value by these officers. Seamanship, in the opinion of the profession, was everything, and, naturally enough, its members dreaded the introduction of any change that would depreciate its value.

All experience goes to prove that officers advanced in years, and brought up in one school, cannot be induced to admit the superior advantages of another, although there were perhaps upon the flag-list a few distinguished admirals entertaining the same advanced views as Sir Thomas Hardy. Thus it was quite impossible for Sir James Graham and Mr. Wood to carry into effect those enlightened views which they so successfully accomplished at a later date.

What with the economical feeling prevailing throughout the country and in Parliament, combined with the strong professional prejudices existing amongst the distinguished admirals at the head of the profession, who deprecated every-

* Have all died since the above was written.—ED.

thing in the shape of change, and regarded every reform as a dangerous innovation, it would have been utterly impossible for Lord Minto, even had he desired, to introduce any of those salutary improvements into the naval service so urgently needed, and therefore he could only let things take their course and carry on the daily routine duties of the office.

I may here mention that it was during this administration, and through Lord Minto's kindness, that I obtained the appointment of reader to the Board, having held the appointment of deputy for several years, and discharged regularly the duties of reader for the twelve preceding months whilst Mr. Hay, my predecessor, was unavoidably absent consequent upon serious illness.

CHAPTER VII.

THE ADMINISTRATION OF THE EARL OF HADDINGTON,
8TH SEPTEMBER, 1841, TO 13TH JANUARY, 1846.

Small and handy frigates as compared with large ones and heavy ordnance
—Impressment and how it found employment for young officers—An
anecdote to illustrate the opinions entertained in regard to corporal
punishment—Another to show how Mr. Corry had admitted boys
into the Royal Navy—The interest taken at the French Admiralty
in our navy—The retirement of Sir John Barrow after a service of
forty-one years as Permanent Secretary—The efforts of Captain
Baillie Hamilton to diminish the sufferings of the Irish people during
the famine—A cross-examination in the Admiralty Board-room—The
abilities of First Lords—Further reference to the views and opinions
of Sir George Cockburn and Sir Thomas M. Hardy.

UPON the return of Sir Robert Peel to office, in 1841, the
Earl of Haddington was appointed First Lord of the
Admiralty.   The Board consisted of—

Admiral the Right Hon. Sir George Cockburn, G.C.B.,
    M.P ;
Vice-Admiral Sir William Hall Gage, Kt , G.C.H ,
Captain Sir George Francis Seymour, Kt , G.C.H., C.B.,
    R N. ,
Captain the Hon. William Gordon, R.N., M.P. ;
The Right Hon. Henry Thomas Lowry Corry, M.P. ;
The Hon. Sidney Herbert, M.P., Political Secretary;
Sir John Barrow, Bart., Permanent Secretary.

It was generally thought in naval circles that this Board

would be reactionary in its policy, but advanced views in naval affairs had, from various causes, begun to make progress. Sir George Seymour and Captain Gordon were of the movement party, in which they were supported by Mr. Corry and Mr. Sidney Herbert, as well as by Captain Baillie Hamilton (Lord Haddington's private secretary). This last appointment was a very popular one, as he was a naval officer and a general favourite, and destined to fill, at a little later date, the responsible post of Permanent Secretary, which duties he discharged with great ability during the Irish famine and the Crimean War.

There was great activity in the Admiralty during this administration, owing to the operations upon the coast of Syria, and by the excitement occasioned by the Pritchard affair, which will be dealt with elsewhere. Sir George Cockburn was very disinclined to depart from the preconceived opinions of his early career; he dilated upon the advantages of small and handy frigates, and evinced his dislike to heavy ordnance, which he declared tore the vessels to pieces. He invariably wound up with the superior economy of the small ones, to which he never failed to allude at the telling and appropriate moment. He argued in defence of the above views with an ability it was difficult to gainsay. Still he found it at times almost impossible to resist the strong representations made to him by Mr. Herbert and Mr. Corry. It was very amusing to see one on one side and one on the other rather persuading and coaxing than arguing the question. Yet you could perceive he was gradually giving way and conceding the point against his will and professional judgment.

On one occasion the Accountant-General sent in a return showing the extent to which desertion had been taking place in the fleet. The First Lord and several members viewed the matter in a very serious light, when Sir George Cockburn, to their utter astonishment, considered it rather a fortunate circumstance, giving as his reasons that if war broke out we should of course impress them, and thus find a number of men-of-warsmen ready at hand. Their places in the meantime would of course be supplied by merchant seamen who would have to be drilled and trained, and this would give ample employment to the young officers, and keep them well up in their various exercises and drills! Sir George Seymour said: "But what about impressment with a reformed Parliament?" Sir George Cockburn replied "There will be very little difficulty about that; only let some of our merchantmen be captured, and you would then hear but little of the radical talk about impressment, when seamen are wanted for men-of-war to protect our commerce and defend our shores."

The First Sea Lord had always a prompt and apt reply, although it did not always carry conviction with it.

It would have been difficult in those days to have persuaded Sir George Cockburn that the expression of public opinion had become so strong upon the subject of corporal punishment as ultimately to lead to its entire abolition Much credit is unquestionably due to the able articles which have, from time to time, appeared upon this painful subject in the columns of the *Times* and other leading journals of the day.

In illustration of the beneficent change which has taken place in regard to corporal punishment, I will adduce the following incident as proving the extraordinary opinions entertained upon punishment and discipline by some of the most distinguished and humane officers that ever sat in the Admiralty Board-room :—

The case stood thus. A young naval cadet, skylarking, whisked round a marine who was washing; the man exclaimed: "You d—— young rascal, what are you about?"

The marine was of fourteen years' standing, of good character, and was not aware that he was addressing a young officer at the time   Yet, for this unintentional offence, he was triced up and received forty-eight lashes for disrespect to an officer.

Lord Haddington designated the act as "tyranny," in which Mr. Sidney Herbert and every civilian in the Board-room cordially concurred; but the four naval officers were unanimously of opinion that such punishments were indispensably necessary for the maintenance of discipline

It was during the administration of Lord Haddington that Mr. H. Corry, who held the office of Civil Lord, drew up his able and elaborate report upon the deficiency in our dockyards in reference to slips for building, docks for repairing, and basins for the speedy equipment of our ships   This was accompanied by a detailed statement, setting forth the superior advantages possessed by the naval arsenals of France in these particulars, and the result was that, through his representations, some most important improvements were introduced, which have gradually led up to those grand works which have recently been completed at Keyham, Portsmouth, and Chatham.

Lord Haddington was a kind and courteous nobleman. A "Sir Charles Grandison" of the old school, and a rigid observer of everything appertaining to propriety and decorum He felt quite scandalised upon one occasion when, at an official inspection of the boys on board the *Victory* at Portsmouth, Mr. Sidney Herbert and Mr. Corry presented themselves in a yachting attire. It was in vain that Mr. Herbert endeavoured to explain to his lordship that he was really mistaken; that it was strictly nautical and quite *en règle*. But there was something more serious in store for them. They had very good naturedly, when members of Parliament had asked them to enter boys for the navy, merely inquired their names, and had written an order forthwith for their entry. On one side the deck of the, *Victory* was drawn up as fine a set of boys as anyone could wish to see, but on the other side was a line of boys who, were very far from answering to that description. These the first lieutenant had somewhat felicitously designated "Parliamentarians," and it was to these boys that Lord Haddington directed the particular attention of. Mr. Sidney Herbert and Mr. Henry Corry. When Mr Herbert returned to the Admiralty he told me he felt perfectly aghast when the inspecting officer handed to him his own minutes for the entry of these boys, for he assured me he had never set eyes on such a set of half-starved, miserable-looking urchins in all his life. Lord Haddington of course said they must be got rid of. "And how would you advise me to dispose of these boys, Mr. Briggs ?" " Oh! that is a matter of very easy accomplishment," I replied. " Give a general order that no boys are, for the future, to be entered for the navy who do not come up to such and such requirements. Age, height, and weight. Ascertain from the Medical Director-General what ought to be the average height and weight of a promising lad of fourteen years of age, and then order all those who do not come up to this regulation to be at once discharged. This will, I think, meet the difficulty and relieve you from all responsibility for the future" In accordance with this suggestion a circular was soon issued and the "Parliamentarians" were speedily got rid of.

One of the great Admiralty delusions in those days was the necessity of keeping everything secret, and that foreign Powers were to be kept perfectly ignorant as to the real state and condition of our navy, on the supposition that they were as indifferent as to what we were doing, as we unfortunately were, as to the altered views entertained in reference to naval affairs which had gradually taken place on the Continent.

Mr. Sidney Herbert and Mr. Corry found our harbours

blocked up with hulks and obsolete vessels which would never be sent to sea, and which they and the admirals at the ports were anxious to get rid of

I broached the subject to Sir George Cockburn and threw out a feeler, but to very little purpose ; he replied by saying, " You don't know the influence they exercise by having their names kept upon the Navy List, and the impression they produce upon foreign Powers." I thought it more prudent, however, to refrain from telling him what I knew to be the real truth. It so happened that I accompanied my father, who for many years held the appointment of Accountant-General of the Navy, when he was sent on a mission to Paris to inquire into the manner in which the public accounts were kept, and how the navy estimates of the French Admiralty were prepared.

I was consequently placed in personal communications with the French officials, and was not a little surprised to find that a complete register was kept of every ship in our navy. Her tonnage, armament, and complement, when she was launched, upon what station she had served, what repairs she had undergone, and whether she was fit for further service or not.

Such was the intense interest taken at the French Admiralty in regard to our navy that every scrap of information which appeared in the *Hampshire Telegraph* (a professional paper of high repute in those days) was cut out and placed under various heads of intelligence.

The impression all this made upon my mind was such that I only wished the First Lord, the Board, and Secretaries were as well informed of the real condition of our own fleet as were our friends on the other side of the Channel.

The hulks and obsolete vessels which the port-admirals wished to remove not only blocked up the harbours, but entailed a very large annual expense upon the country to

keep them in a state of proper repair for the habitation of
a number of warrant officers, boatswains, carpenters, and
gunners, who were appointed to take charge of them. Very
few were fit for active service, but they served a useful
purpose at a general election.

It was during the administration of Lord Haddington
that Sir John Barrow retired from the office of Permanent
Secretary, having received the honour of a baronetcy
(1835) as a well-merited reward for his long and valuable
services of forty-one years as Permanent Secretary. His
literary attainments likewise brought him a good deal
before the public. The interest he took in the various
expeditions to the North Pole under Sir Edward Parry,
Sir John Franklin, and other distinguished Polar navi-
gators brought his name in like manner prominently
forward. To his love of science and research is due the
formation of the Royal Geographical Society, of which he
was the first President, and which has since rendered such
substantial benefits and important services to the country.
Captain Baillie Hamilton, who filled the office of private
secretary to Lord Haddington, was appointed successor to
Sir John Barrow. Nothing could exceed the anxiety evinced
by Captain Hamilton during the Irish famine; his efforts
to diminish the sufferings of those unfortunate people were
deserving of all commendation; he laboured day and night
making arrangements for their relief. Meritorious as were
his exertions on that occasion, they were, if possible, sur-
passed during the Crimean War; for upon him, as Permanent
Secretary, the great bulk of the correspondence devolved. So
incessant were the calls made upon him, and so energetically
did he respond, that his health fairly broke down, and he was
therefore reluctantly obliged to quit an office the duties of
which he had so efficiently discharged.*

* He was Permanent Secretary from January, 1845, to May, 1855.—ED.

It was upon Lord Haddington's accession to office that I was for the first time placed in personal communication with Sir George Cockburn. At the first meeting of the Board he assumed towards me a very imperious and very overbearing tone. I soon observed that he was bent upon putting me through my facings by the numerous questions he asked and to which, fortunately, I was able to return correct answers; but to the last inquiry I replied with some hesitation and said, "I think, sir." Here he interrupted me, and in a very stern tone said, "I don't want you to think; is it so, or is it not?" I then addressed myself to Lord Haddington in these words: "I am sure, my lord, Sir George Cockburn is the last person who would wish me to reply without thinking, but the fact is, Sir George is so perfectly master of the Queen's regulations and Admiralty instructions, that it is not surprising that I should have some difficulty in bringing myself to believe that I can be right and he wrong, which is, however, the case in this instance." Lord Haddington then turned to Sir George and said, "Pray what have you to say to that pretty speech?" Sir George smiled and bowed graciously, and from that moment always treated me with the greatest politeness and kindness; he allowed me to discuss naval matters with him with a freedom which in after days surprised me; the more so when I bear in mind that my views upon naval subjects were almost always antagonistic to his.

I have always entertained a great respect for the First Lords of the Admiralty, not because they held the highest office in the department, but because, in the majority of cases, I found the First Lord the ablest man by far in the Board-room. There were, however, occasions when secretaries of the acknowledged ability of Mr. Croker and Mr. Charles Wood practically, if not nominally, exercised the paramount influence. In the administration of Lord Haddington it is not surprising that Sir George Cockburn, from his high professional position, should have been permitted to take a very decided lead in the discussion of the Board and in the administration of the navy.

The Earl of Haddington was a nobleman of liberal views, of refined and polished manners, had considerable literary abilities, and was, in a word, one of the most charming and benevolent First Lords that ever sat at the Board-room table. His knowledge of naval affairs previous to his appointment was not very extensive, so he wisely deputed their management to Sir George Cockburn, Mr. Sidney Herbert and Mr. Henry Corry.

Sir George Cockburn was fully alive to the advantage of having a Second Sea Lord who entertained the same opinions as himself; he therefore obtained the appointment for Sir William Gage, one of his old first lieutenants and a shipmate of Sir Thomas Hardy, as Second Sea Lord. The result was that, whenever a naval question was under consideration, he used to say, " My opinion on the subject is so-and-so. What do you think, Gage ? " Naturally Sir William thought exactly as Sir George Cockburn did. The inevitable sequence was that the question was decided in their favour

Although Lord Haddington courteously listened to all Sir George Seymour and Captain Gordon had to advance, he could not very well go against the opinions of the First and Second Sea Lord; notwithstanding the fact that both Sir George Seymour and Captain Gordon were very distinguished naval officers and always spoke to the point.

The contrast between Sir George Cockburn and Sir Thomas Hardy was to me, for several years, a most interesting study. I was incapable of understanding how anyone possessing such a powerful intellect, high attainment, worldly and professional experience as Sir George, could allow political feeling and personal prejudices to so completely blind his naturally sound judgment. How they could preclude him from seeing all the changes that had taken place, were taking, and must inevitably take place, not only in the political conditions of the country, but more especially in that particular profession of which he was at the time the executive and departmental head. Almost every opinion he expressed, every measure he devised, and every step he took, were retrograde in their tendencies. To a certain extent, however, he yielded to the zealous and untiring persuasions of Mr. Sidney Herbert and Mr. Henry Corry, both of whom displayed enlightened and advanced opinions upon naval subjects, in which they took an unusual interest. On the other hand there was Sir Thomas Hardy, who, without those superior gifts which characterised Sir George Cockburn, exhibiting on all occasions such a profound knowledge of the service, both present and prospective, that every measure he proposed was sound, well conceived, and progressive in its tendency.

CHAPTER VIII.

THE ADMINISTRATION OF THE EARL OF ELLENBOROUGH, 13TH JANUARY TO 13TH JULY, 1846.

Punctuality—The classical attainments of Sir William Gage—The despatch with which the business of the Admiralty was carried on—Reports as to a proposed railway to Greenwich, and how the instruments in the Observatory were to be affected—Observations as to the administrative ability of Lord Ellenborough.

LORD HADDINGTON, the peace-loving and gentle, was succeeded by the Earl of Ellenborough on the 13th January, 1846. He was a statesman of very opposite attributes from his predecessor; though, perhaps, on that account, better fitted for the head of a great war department.

His lordship's tenure of office was unfortunately very short, but there is no doubt that he entertained practical and advanced views, both upon naval and military affairs, being little in accordance with the economical opinions advocated by Sir Robert Peel, and prevalent on both sides of the House of Commons, and in the country generally.

The noble lord had held office on several previous occasions, and had only recently returned from India, where he had been regarded in the light of a great and grand Viceroy, his government being marked by some very brilliant military successes, in which he had taken a personal part, and had thereby acquired considerable notoriety. So highly appreciated were his services, that immediately upon his return Her Majesty was graciously pleased to confer upon him the dignity of an Earldom. Under these circumstances, it is not surprising that his apppointment as First Lord of the Admiralty excited great interest amongst the members of the Board, who were the same as in the administration of Lord Haddington.*

The lords and secretaries were duly assembled in the Board-room to receive the new First Lord. He entered as the clock struck eleven, with his chronometer in his hand, and, having bowed to their lordships, placed it upon the table, he then gave them to understand that he should expect them to be in their places for the despatch of public business by one minute past eleven—that being the rule laid down by the Duke of Wellington for all reviews and military inspections, and the course he himself pursued as Governor-General of India—and then, turning to Sir William Gage, who was upon his left, said, " No doubt, Sir William, you remember what Louis XIV. said in reference to punctuality—' *L'exactitude est la politesse des rois' ?* " Sir William smiled acquiescence, and whispered to me, " What was that the First Lord said about Louis Philippe ? " I was fortunately able to maintain my gravity, and in an undertone replied, " I will tell you after the Board, as I must read the Admiralty patent." This, however, I was saved the trouble of doing, as Lord Ellenborough thought fit to do it himself. After he had finished reading it, he remarked to Sir George Cockburn that there were only two men in the kingdom that were really capable of drawing up a legal document—" The Duke of Wellington and myself." The reading of the Board had not proceeded a quarter of an hour, when he was in full conversation about his battles in India. The reading was necessarily suspended whilst his lordship favoured the

* In February, 1847, the Hon. Henry Fitzroy, M.P., was appointed Civil Lord, the Right Hon. H. T. L. Corry becoming Political Secretary instead of the Hon. Sidney Herbert.—ED.

members of his Board with a most graphic and interesting description of a battle in which Sir John Littler took a prominent part. The noble lord himself, upon the back of an elephant, and under heavy fire, asked Sir John how long it would be before he took the position he was about to attack. Sir John, as he galloped off, replied, "About a quarter of an hour, my lord." "With that chronometer in my hand, I timed him," said Lord Ellenborough; "and, do you know, he did it in thirteen and a half minutes" The business of the Board was then resumed, and at its termination Sir William Gage inquired of the First Lord whether the *Stromboli* might receive her sailing orders—the admiral pronouncing the second *o* long instead of short. At this false quantity, Lord Ellenborough threw up his hands and exclaimed, "For God's sake, Sir William, have mercy on my Eton ears!"—to the utter astonishment of the dear old admiral, whose classical attainments were confined to the instruction received in the lower fourth of Westminster School at a very early age. Lord Ellenborough was First Lord in the real acceptation of the word. With such an excellent man of business at the head of the Board-room table, and Mr. Henry Corry with his ready pen at the bottom, the ordinary routine business of the day was despatched with such unusual facility and promptness, that it afforded the First Lord ample time to gratify himself and those present by relating anecdotes which were peculiarly agreeable to listen to, in consequence of the elegance of his diction and the charming intonation of his voice.

During his lordship's administration it became a great question between the *savants* of the day whether the valuable astronomical and nautical instruments in the Royal Observatory at Greenwich would not be seriously affected if the railway to Greenwich was permitted to pass in such close proximity to the Royal Observatory as that proposed in the plans. Professor Airey, the Astronomer Royal, had drawn up a very valuable report upon the subject, but it was deemed only right and proper by the scientific world that the other learned professors should be called upon to give expression to their opinions in regard to the matter. So thoroughly convinced was the First Lord as to the views embodied, that before the reading of the first report he turned to Sir George Cockburn and said, " I do not aspire to prophesy, but I think I may venture to predict that every one of these gentlemen will differ with the Astronomer Royal, and upon almost every point will have views at variance with his opinion ; further, it will be delicately hinted that the post of Astronomer Royal would be more advantageously filled by the writer of each report." And such proved to be the case to the very letter. Lord Ellenborough had seen enough of war on a grand scale to recognise our short-comings in one profession ; and he had those about him very competent to make known to him the pressing requirements of the other. It might be all very well to laugh at "his eccentricities," and to regard his sham fights, landing of troops, attacks on forts, and so forth as "tom-foolery," but he was certainly a remarkably clever man, and realised that efficiency in both services could only be attained by the experience gained in constant practice. He knew the day had gone by when the navy could be filled with idle boys who had run away from school in order to escape from their lessons, and that the young men who entered the army for the sake of a dashing uniform, and personal enjoyment, would find that they had duties to perform of a more arduous and serious character than they had been led to suppose.

It was most unfortunate for the country that the several First Lords who took the greatest interest in those branches of the service which were of such vital importance to the efficiency of the navy should have held office but for brief periods; but even had time permitted, their best endeavours would have been but little appreciated in the Cabinet, and would certainly have been regarded with utter indifference by the general public. All were profoundly ignorant of the real requirements of the naval service, and were so impressed with the conviction that our supremacy on the sea was incontestable, that nobody took any trouble to ascertain the facts upon a subject so important to national greatness and prosperity. The nation was, however, soon to be aroused from its apathy and lifeless monotony to see its defenceless and perilous position. On the 9th of January, 1847, the Duke of Wellington wrote his celebrated letter which, when published, caused a great sensation throughout the whole country.*

* *Vide* the Duke of Wellington's letter, p. 278.—ED.

CHAPTER IX.

The Third Administration of the Earl of Auckland, 13th July, 1846, to 18th January, 1849.

Great diversity of opinion amongst the members of his Board in reference to shipbuilding—Alteration in the design for an 80-gun ship— 'Different modes of managing business—Range of guns—The facility with which the French army embarked for Italy, and the change of opinion it effected in Mr. Ward—Prophecies in regard to peace.

Lord Auckland resumed his seat as First Lord of the Admiralty for the third time on the 13th July, 1846, shortly after his return from India; he held office until his death in 1849, which was a great blow to the service, as he was an able administrator, and was very popular, and took the deepest interest in the efficiency of the navy, especially in the construction, size, and armament of the line-of-battle-ships, in regard to which there was a great diversity of opinion amongst the naval members of his Board, who were—

Vice-Admiral Sir William Parker, Bart., G C.B ;*
Rear-Admiral J. W. D Dundas, C B., M P.;
Captain M. F. Fitzhardinge Berkeley, C B , R N., M.P.;
Captain the Right Hon. Lord John Hay, C.B , R.N.;
The Hon. William Francis Cowper, M.P.;
First Secretary, Henry G. Ward, Esq., M.P.;
Second Secretary, Captain W. A. B. Hamilton, R.N.

* Sir Charles Adam, K.C.B., succeeded Sir William Parker as First Sea Lord on the 24th July, 1846.

G

It has always been a question in my mind whether the public service is most benefited by a Board in which the members work harmoniously together, as in the two preceding administrations, or the reverse.   In the former case the First Lord was deprived of the great advantage of hearing all that could be adduced on both sides of the question, for when the senior naval members are distinguished officers holding high rank in the service, the junior members of the Board were professionally disinclined to give expression to any adverse views.   Lord Auckland, in this respect, might be regarded as more fortunate than his predecessors, though it is more than doubtful whether he himself held that opinion.   I will relate how not only doctors but admirals differ.   A design of an 80-gun ship was one morning placed upon the Board-room table for the inspection and approval of " my lords."   When Lord Auckland entered the room, Sir William Parker, kneeling on a chair with pencil in hand, was altering the lines of the bow; Admiral Dundas, in a similar position, was suggesting alterations in the stern, and marking them off; whilst the two other lords were engaged in making calculations as to an entirely new armament, and to the improvement of the rig.   Lord Auckland carefully examined the surveyor's design and listened patiently to all that each naval member had to advance in support of his particular amendment.   His lordship then desired me to hand him a piece of india-rubber, and after he had deliberately erased the pencil marks in question, he turned to the surveyor and dryly observed : " I really do not feel justified in introducing so many improvements "—with a strong emphasis on the word improvements—" into a single ship."   The original design was then approved, and the First Lord and naval lords affixed their signatures.   A few months after the foregoing incident an animated discussion was taking place between Sir Charles Adam and Admiral Dundas as Mr. (afterwards Sir Henry)

Ward, the Political Secretary, was passing through the Board-room on his way to his private room, and in an undertone, smiling, said to me, "How those admirals quarrel!" "Oh, dear, no, sir," I replied; "it is only their peculiar mode of conducting a naval discussion." Mr. Ward had scarcely left the room when Sir Charles Adam in a loud voice exclaimed, "I say it is so." Admiral Dundas replying, "That is exactly what I have been maintaining" "The d—— it is!" said Sir Charles; and then addressing himself to me, said: "Did you think, Briggs, that we naval chaps had been agreeing all this time? How do you account for our not having understood each other?" "Well, sir," I replied, "if I may venture to say what I think, it is easily explained; both talked and neither listened" Sir Charles then good-naturedly said · "Confound the fellow! I dare say what he says is not far from the truth."

After one of the meetings of the Board there was a desultory conversation between the members on a variety of subjects connected with shipbuilding and gunnery which lasted for some time. Lord Auckland made some remark to me which induced me to say in reply, "You will be surprised, my lord, to hear that a battery established at Ryde could completely destroy the buildings in Portsmouth Dockyard and many of the ships lying in ordinary in the harbour, so great is the improvement in the range of our guns" "I am indeed surprised to hear you talk such nonsense, Mr. Briggs."

At this point Sir Baldwin Walker kindly came to my assistance and said, "Mr. Briggs is quite right, my lord. It is only three miles across the Solent, and the range of our guns is far in excess of that." Lord Auckland then turned to Sir Thomas Hastings* and said, "What have you to say on the subject, Sir Thomas?" "I fully concur in what Sir Baldwin Walker says," was his reply.

* Storekeeper to the Ordnance; the office abolished in 1855.

The First Lord then asked "how many broadsides would be required to sink this new 80-gun ship we are about to build." The two naval officers considered for a moment, when Sir Baldwin Walker said "about three" Lord Auckland then inquired "how long that would take." Sir Thomas Hastings replied, "about the same number of minutes." Lord Auckland then exclaimed, "What an appalling state of things! To think of a vessel costing £100,000, with 600 or 700 valuable lives on board, to be sunk or destroyed in three minutes." But what would his lordship say if he were informed that in these days an ironclad costing not £100,000, but little short of a million, might be blown up by a torpedo in a few seconds, or sunk by a couple of shot from a 110-ton gun?

First Lords have all different modes of managing the business of their department. Some like to talk matters over in their private rooms, others prefer to transact everything in the Board-room. I am decidedly of opinion that a full and free discussion in the Board-room upon all professional subjects of importance is attended with the greater advantage. In the former case the First Lord places himself at this disadvantage—it is but natural that a distinguished admiral should consider that he knows more upon the subject than the First Lord, whom he regards in the light of a civilian. The adoption of this method has another disadvantage—discussions sometimes become warm, and there are misunderstandings as to what has been said; this could not happen in an open Board room because, in the first instance, there are witnesses, and, in the second, a certain amount of restraint is exercised and more deference and circumspection is observed I therefore think it more desirable for the First Lord to have all professional questions discussed in the Board-room by the naval lords, to hear all they have to say, and to let the subject be thoroughly argued out, when he will be better able to form a sound judgment upon the several bearings of the case, and thus arrive at a satisfactory and final decision This course generally enables a First Lord who possesses tact and ability to embody in his minute some of the points set forth by the different members, and so soften down any little differences. Thus, likewise, leads to a good understanding between the First Lord and the members of the Board, and tends to inspire mutual confidence. It has this further recommendation—that it induces the members to carefully consider the subject about to be discussed, and thereby prevent discursive and irrelevant controversy and waste of valuable time.

For instance, Sir James Graham conducted business after the following manner. Whenever any important subject was likely to come under consideration, and differences of opinion would probably arise, he availed himself of casual opportunities of joining members of his Board either in the Admiralty Garden or in St. James's Park, and entered upon the subject as a mere topic of conversation. He thus elicited their real views, so that when the discussion at the Board arrived, being master of the subject, he was able, by expressing himself as entirely approving of what was advanced by one member, and as strongly impressed with the very sensible remarks of another, to embody in his minute what satisfied both, and at the same time carried into effect his own views.

As I have already hinted, considerable differences of opinion prevailed amongst the several members of this Board, and the consequence was that papers were frequently allowed to stand over for some time. Upon one occasion, being in the First Lord's private room, I took the liberty of drawing his attention to a matter which had long been awaiting a decision, observing, " I am afraid it will lead to a difference of opinion among the naval lords," to which his lordship replied, " Surely, Mr. Briggs, you will not do me the injustice to suppose that

I could think it possible they were likely to agree ? However, we know the worst that can happen—look fierce, talk loud and thump the table "—and drily adding with a smile, " which is fortunately between them ! "

Lord Auckland's anticipations were fully verified the following morning, and he was never seen to a greater advantage, for the discussion, in parliamentary language, was both animated and prolonged ; and, judging from his lordship's frequent change of position, his bodily discomfiture bore ample testimony to the acuteness of his mental sufferings. At last patience and exhausted nature could endure no more, and quietly tapping on the table, he said, "I think, my lords, I have now heard everything it is possible to say upon this subject from both sides of the table, and that at least three times over." He then dictated to the Secretary the minute to go forward, whereupon an admiral jumped up, saying, " But I don't think so, my lord."

Lord Auckland calmly replied, " I am very sorry for you, but I do. Let the minute go forward, and you, Mr. Briggs, read something else."

After I had finished he very politely addressed himself to the admiral, saying, "What would you propose to do in this case ? Perhaps we shall agree better this time." The admiral, rising from his seat, said, " I really beg your pardon, my lord, but the fact was, my steam was up." Lord Auckland then said, " That was very evident, but I hope it has blown off now."

A member of the Board upon another occasion was about to bring forward a proposal, but before he had read three lines another member interrupted, saying, " I entirely differ, my lord ! " The First Lord then said, " That I was sure you would do, but we had better hear the proposal, for then you will be all the better able to differ."

As in the time of Lord Minto, so during the administration

of Lord Auckland—economy was the ruling passion of the day.

Lord Auckland himself, as a politician, was very moderate in his views, but the naval lords, and more especially Sir Henry Ward (then member for Sheffield) were unquestionably strong party men, and pushed economy to great lengths, with a view of keeping down the navy estimates, and postponed from year to year public works which were urgently required for the efficiency of the service.

Sir Henry Ward was full of dockyard reforms, dockyard accounts, and departmental retrenchments, all proper enough in their way, but I was impressed with the conviction that there were others of equal if not of greater importance, and on several occasions urged the necessity of increasing the fleet and providing for the defence of our own shores, because I knew the very unsatisfactory condition in which the department would be placed, in the event of war, from the want of all previous preparation.

All Europe was in a state bordering on revolution, and it was impossible from day to day to anticipate what unexpected events might unhappily arise. My opinions, however, did not coincide with Sir Henry Ward's, and one day discussing the question he said, " I am ready to admit you generally speak sensibly enough on most subjects, but when you hold forth on the increase of the navy and national defence, I would as soon hear you dilate upon the Apocalypse." · Such were the thanks I received—"*Chacun à son tour*"—and I had mine. Sir Henry Ward soon afterwards was appointed Lord High Commissioner of the Ionian Islands, and on the way to his government he arrived at Marseilles at the exact time the French army was embarking for Italy. When he beheld the facility and rapidity with which batteries of artillery, regiments of cavalry, and battalions of infantry, together with all the impedimenta required for a campaign were put on board troopships, transports, and men-of-war, it brought back to his recollection much that I had vainly endeavoured to impress upon his mind when Secretary of the Admiralty.

I must, however, do Sir Henry the justice to say that no gentleman holding high office ever offered a more handsome or ample apology than he did to me for the wrong he considered he had done. He went so far as to admit that conscience smote him for the very imperfect manner in which he felt he had discharged the more important duties of his office, and the mistaken views he had entertained in respect to them. He hoped I would never fail, in season and out of season, to impress my convictions upon his successors, and trusted, for the good of the country, they would pay more attention than had unfortunately been the case with himself; he further added that what he had witnessed had brought home most forcibly what might happen in the future, and especially when he considered the close proximity of the great naval arsenals of France to the shores of England, and the great change steam had effected in naval warfare.

It is astonishing how soon a little practical experience removes prejudices and imparts sound knowledge. I might as well have addressed myself to Mount Tabor among the mountains, or Mount Carmel upon the sea-shore, as to have hoped to make a convert of Sir Henry Ward to my opinions when in office. Yet a few days at Marseilles happily accomplished what I had tried in vain to effect. But whatever my opinions may have been upon the important subject of national defence, the period had not then arrived when they were likely to be listened to; for in 1851 the Great International Exhibition was held, and the whole nation seemed impressed with the belief that the era of peace was firmly established, that the millennium was at hand, and that the prophecy of Isaiah was in course of fulfilment, in which it is stated "they shall beat their swords into plowshares, and their spears into pruninghooks : nation shall not lift up sword against nation, neither shall they learn war any more." War was looked upon almost as an impossibility : arbitration, the skill of modern diplomatists, finance, philanthropy, improved education, nineteenth-century civilisation, and, above all, the advance of science as applied to war, would render the destruction of life so terrible as to ensure a continuance of peace.

Such were the wild ideas entertained at this period by all classes of society and by the leading statesmen of both parties.

Even that wise and sober minister, Sir Robert Peel, did not escape from the influence of the prevailing epidemic. Yet the grave had scarcely closed upon that great man when this pleasing delusion was rudely dispelled.

CHAPTER X.

The Administration of the Rt. Hon. Sir Francis
Baring, 18th Jan., 1849, to 2nd March, 1852.

The simplifying of the navy estimates and dockyard accounts—Difference
of opinion in regard to wasting time—The time and expense required
to prepare parliamentary returns—Reduction pushed to the very
verge of danger—Differences between England and France—No
protection for our home ports—All vessels on the coast of Syria—
Naval lords nervous and apprehensive at the rumour of war—The
deficiencies of the navy demonstrated by the vote of twenty-one
millions in 1889—Comparison in the interest taken after the vote in
naval affairs with the apathy displayed in the country during this
administration.

On the melancholy death of Lord Auckland in 1849 Sir
Francis Baring was appointed to succeed him at the
Admiralty, the members of the Board all retaining their
seats.*   Sir Francis was an able man of business, and
directed his special attention to the improvement and
simplifying of the navy estimates; he also added to them
much valuable information which greatly tended to the
convenience of the members of the House of Commons:
this being always a question that has annually engaged
the attention of the members of Parliament who take an
interest in naval affairs.   The navy estimates have certainly
been greatly improved from year to year; the vast changes
which are constantly taking place in all that appertains

---

* On the 21st May Mr. John Parker was appointed Political Secretary
in succession to Sir Henry Ward.—Ed.

to the navy render numerous additions and alterations indispensably necessary, and must constantly prove a never-
ending source of controversy as regards the subject-matter
to be introduced, the form in which it should be presented,
and the manner in which the references to its contents should
be compiled; the navy estimates must consequently be a
labour with no finality. Sir Francis Baring likewise directed
his personal attention to those complex dockyard accounts
which for years past engrossed the attention of so many
First Lords and secretaries, and regarding which there always
has been, and always will be, a great diversity of opinion
To clearly explain my meaning I will mention an incident.
One day when the late Sir Richard Dundas was visiting the
Woolwich Dockyard, in company with the captain-superintendent, his attention was directed to a man standing by
a piece of timber with his hands in his pocket, the captain-
superintendent remarking, " How that fellow is idling away
his time ! " Now Sir Richard Dundas had himself been a
captain-superintendent of a dockyard, and was consequently
well acquainted with the habits and abilities of the workmen,
and in reference to this particular man he doubted whether
he was really wasting his time, and going up to him said,
" What have you there, my man ? " " I was thinking, sir,"
was the reply, " how that piece of timber could be cut up to
the best possible advantage, and if you will allow me I will
show you what I propose to do with it; " and taking up a
piece of chalk he marked off upon the timber the various
pieces that might be appropriated to different vessels, and
so cleverly did he do it that there was not a bit wasted.
From this alone is easily seen the difficulty there is in
estimating and bringing into account the precise value of
the material employed, and placing each item into the
account of each separate vessel. Nor is this all An estimate
has to be formed of the increased value of timber, etc., in

consequence of it having become seasoned, as compared with its original value.

Dockyard returns are frequently moved for in the House of Commons and no opposition is raised, as the concession saves a great deal of discussion in the House and trouble to the Admiralty authorities, for if refused it would lead to a suspicion that there was something in the background it was desirable to conceal It may be all very well for political reasons to concede to the wishes of the members of the House, but there ought to be some check placed upon calling for returns , for it should be borne in mind that it entails incalculable labour upon the dockyard officers, and is attended with considerable expense to the country. To prepare these voluminous returns it is necessary to take from their work many of the best shipwrights and inspectors, and often the master-shipwright himself, who, instead of looking after the construction of his ships, is shut up in his office making or superintending the various calculations which the compilations of these returns involve, weeks and months being spent upon the work they entail. Reams of paper are covered with figures, which, when printed and laid before the House, present so appalling an aspect that the honourable members who called for them are perfectly satisfied that they have done their duty without in the least considering it incumbent upon them to scrutinise or verify their accuracy.

There was a painful similitude between the administrations of Lord Haddington, Lord Minto, Lord Auckland, and Sir Francis Baring in regard to economy. The navy estimates were framed upon the lowest scale and reduction pushed to the very verge of danger. The effects were visible by the depletion of stores, by the postponement of necessary repairs, and by the putting off to an indefinite period pressing works required for the efficiency of the public service; no expense was incurred that could be avoided, and the vote for seamen and marines was taken at the lowest number. Even from a financial point of view the course pursued was the reverse of economical, and ultimately led to wasteful and increased expenditure. Storehouses that should have been repaired fell into decay and new ones had to be erected   Great delay and expense were incurred from the want of basins, and then, when constructed, from the postponement of the erection of factories and cranes to facilitate the equipment of ships fitting out and the dismantling of ships paying off   The sums of public money wasted by this system were far in excess of any savings effected by the delay.   Indeed the sole object was to keep down the navy estimates for the current year to meet the convenience of the party in power, and to gain a little ephemeral popularity for economy, each political party vieing with the other regardless of the real interests of the nation.   The results of this disastrous system were only too apparent upon the outbreak of the Crimean War, which, fortunately for the naval service, was even more conspicuous in the total collapse of the military.

In 1841 we had a large fleet upon the coast of Syria, composed for the most part of the line-of-battleships usually kept at the home parts, which consequently left the shores of England utterly unprotected.   In 1844 serious differences arose between this country and France whilst M. Thiers was Minister for Foreign Affairs, and so grave were the apprehensions entertained by the Government at home—caused by the representation of our ambassador at Paris, and by the strongly expressed opinions of M. Thiers in reference to our proceedings in the East—that war seemed imminent   Great alarm and anxiety was felt from the want of adequate protection at home, and to such an extent had our home forces been reduced that the *Collingwood*, an 80-gun ship,

bearing the flag of Rear-Admiral Sir George Seymour, then
under orders for the Pacific, was actually detained at Spithead to protect the Solent, there being no other ship of the
line available; and, as regards the *Collingwood* herself, her
condition was so deplorable that her captain, Henry Eden
(afterwards a Lord of the Admiralty), told me that at the
time she had on board upwards of 200 merchant seamen
who had never been placed at a great gun. As far as our
military defences were concerned, it was doubtful whether
20,000 men could have been got together for the defence of
London. There was no Aldershot, no militia, no volunteer
force, and the condition of the artillery was such that
Viscount Hardinge, a couple of years afterwards, stated in
his place in the House of Lords "that there were not fifty
gun-carriages at Woolwich that could be dragged over a
ploughed field," which statement will be found in Hansard

Instead of those in power taking a grand and comprehensive view of their responsibilities, they allowed things to
drift from year to year. Even the Great Duke's pathetic
appeal was powerless to induce them to take measures to
improve the military defences of the country. It is not
surprising that the naval lords felt nervous and apprehensive
upon the very rumour of a war with France. The severe
strain that would have been placed upon the department
in providing protection for our dependencies, our commerce
all over the world, the defence of the Channel Islands, naval
arsenals, commercial ports, and our coast towns, gave sufficient cause. I can positively affirm that not a member
of the Board for years past could tell what ships in the
reserve were actually ready for sea, how they were to be
manned, or for what service they were respectively destined,
so grievous was the want of forethought, preparation, and
organisation.

It is passing strange how party politics cause a ministry

to flinch from the plainest obligations of national duty, when it becomes a question of public expenditure; but it is still more strange that, notwithstanding all our common sense in matters of business, there are no people in the world that benefit so little by past experience relating to the affairs of the country as we; the same mistakes are committed over and over again, and we cannot be induced to look calmly upon the future and systematically provide against those eventualities which in course of years will certainly arise, and : no one can tell how soon.

The opinions I entertained when I was forty years of age are identical with those I now give expression to at eighty-two. · It is only since the accession of the Marquess .of Salisbury and Lord George Hamilton to power, in 1886, that an effectual remedy has been applied to the naval and military defences of the Empire. One of the chief causes of the unsatisfactory state of naval and military affairs is not attributable to civilians being placed at the head of these great war departments, as some imagine, but in no small degree to the fact that there is no public record of the views and opinions of their professional advisers, which, for the good of the service, ought to be brought under the consideration of the Cabinet, and afterwards come forward with the navy estimates for the final decision of the House of Commons.

The deficiences of the navy in regard to ships would never have required a vote of twenty-one millions had : the representations of the naval members of various Boards of Admiralty received, from year to year, that attention they deserved, for in the majority of cases they were officers of experience and standing high in the service.* Neither would the War Office have needed four millions of money

* For example, in this Board at different periods there were officers of such high reputation and advanced views as Captain (now Admiral) Sir Houston Stewart and the late Admiral Sir G. Phipps Hornby.—ED.

for the construction of huts and barracks, nor would valuable
lives have been lost from typhoid and other fevers, had the
opinions of the Commander-in-chief and the staff at the War
Office been duly recorded and made public. The House of
Commons is not niggardly, neither is it disposed to withhold
what is right and proper from either of the services when
their requirements are fairly and honestly placed before it.

It is an extraordinary fact that the Duke of Wellington,
with all his glorious achievements, profound military knowledge, and great experience in actual war, failed to accomplish for the army what Lord Charles Beresford, a young
captain in the navy, has by perseverance, tact, and popularity
successfully effected for the sister service. It must be
acknowledged by all impartial observers that it is mainly
due to his forcible speeches in the House of Commons, based
upon his practical knowledge of naval affairs and to his
lucid statements of the absolute requirements of the navy,
that the shortcomings of our first line of defence have
received that attention which has brought it to its present
promising condition. Thanks to Lord Charles Beresford and
other distinguished naval officers, such questions as organisation, mobilisation, maritime defence, trade routes, coaling-
stations, steam tactics, and naval intelligence in all its
branches, have now become matters of daily interest and
subjects of discussion for all classes of the community,
contrasting most favourably with the apathy and sluggish
indifference of the period of Sir Francis Baring's administration.

CHAPTER XI.

THE ADMINISTRATION OF THE DUKE OF NORTHUMBERLAND, 2ND MARCH, 1852, TO 5TH JAN, 1853.

Those standing in need of advice adverse to accepting it—Admiralty minute ordered to go forward not in accordance with usage and Queen's regulations—An estimate for an additional five thousand men to the fleet—Differences of opinion in regard to filling up dockyard appointments between Sir Baldwin Walker and Mr. Augustus Stafford—Strong party feeling—Credit to the Duke of Northumberland for pushing on with naval construction and for obtaining five thousand men for the fleet—No resentful feeling on the part of his Grace to those who opposed his wishes.

THE Duke of Northumberland followed Sir Francis Baring as First Lord of the Admiralty in March, 1852, on the accession of the Earl of Derby to power. Few First Lords were more anxious to do what is right than was his Grace, but he had great difficulties to contend with, for he had neither parliamentary nor official experience. The members of his Board were unquestionably officers of great ability and distinction.

Rear-Admiral Hyde Parker, C.B., had the reputation of being one of the smartest and finest officers in the service, and had proved a most efficient admiral-superintendent at Portsmouth Dockyard.

Rear-Admiral Phipps Hornby, C.B., was an officer of judgment and experience, and one of the gallant heroes of Lissa, in which action each of the four British captains captured the enemy's frigate with which they were respectively engaged (13th March, 1811).

H

Captain the Hon A. Duncombe was the only member of Parliament, with the exception of Mr. Augustus Stafford, the Political Secretary, and Captain Alex. Milne, was the only member of the Board who had been in office before; therefore grave responsibility was thrown upon the Permanent Secretary, Captain Baillie Hamilton, who, fortunately, had occupied that position for over eight years and had filled the duties of his office in an able and efficient manner.

It often happens that those who stand most in need of advice, due to the want of official experience, are the very individuals who are most disinclined to accept it, however delicately and kindly proffered. They are so impressed with their own superior knowledge that oftentimes it requires unusual tact and judgment to prevent mistakes being made

In the whole of my long official career I never was placed in a position of so much personal perplexity and difficulty as during the administration of the Duke of Northumberland.

One morning his Grace's private secretary came to me, on his behalf, to inquire the monthly pay of an able seaman. I referred him to the page in the Navy List giving the information. Judge of my surprise, a few days later, when I was told that the Duke had formed an estimate of the expense of an additional five thousand men to the fleet upon my data, and that it had proved inaccurate; the one proposed by the Accountant-General of the Navy being far in excess of that which his Grace had laid before the Cabinet.

My bad luck followed me. The inexperience of the new Board entailed upon the Permanent Secretary such incessant and arduous duties that his health suffered, and he was obliged to seek temporary relaxation, and proceeded on leave for a limited period, which, in justice must be said, he did with the greatest reluctance. Captain Baillie Hamilton possessed every qualification for the delicate position in which he was placed; he had much natural ability, great tact, and was gracious and charming in manner, and with all exercised the prudence of the proverbial Scotchman. With the Permanent Secretary absent, and Mr Augustus Stafford young in office, my duties were greatly increased, and day by day my position became more and more embarrassing.

To be obliged to point out to official superiors that what they propose is at variance with the Queen's regulations and Admiralty instructions, and not in accordance with the established practice of the department, is an exceedingly disagreeable duty. When a First Lord has drawn up several reports, upon which he has bestowed much labour and care, and is informed, when he orders them to go forward, that there are certain formalities to be gone through before his instruction can be executed, he is naturally annoyed, and it is, indeed, a thankless and unenviable task for the individual upon whom this unpleasant duty is imposed, especially if the First Lord happens to be a naval officer, as in the instance of the Duke of Northumberland. One morning, soon after the Duke had entered the Board-room, he read the heads of several papers which he ordered to go forward, some involving a heavy outlay of money. I immediately handed them to Mr. Stafford, saying, "To go forward and obtain Treasury sanction," which was the proper official wording for the Secretary's minutes. His Grace turned to me and said, "Those were not my words, Mr. Briggs." I replied, "Your Grace will pardon me, but I think you will find the minute strictly correct, for, if I am not mistaken, your Grace stated to their lordships that the proposed expenditure was for £850,000, but as that sum has not been inserted in the navy estimates it is absolutely necessary to obtain the approval of the Treasury." The Duke said, "Am I not First Lord of the Admiralty, and as such cannot I give these orders?" "Certainly, my lord, but pardon me if I remind you that

H 2

the Chancellor of the Exchequer will have to provide the money and the House of Commons will have to vote it." His Grace then turned to the Secretary and said, " I order them to go forward "

Immediately after the breaking up of the Board I went to Mr Stafford and said to him, " Before you send the minute to be executed you had better see the head of the department, and hear what he has to say upon the subject." That gentleman fully confirmed the correctness of what I had stated—that as there was no money taken in the navy estimates, nothing could be done until the Treasury sanction had been obtained Mr Stafford found himself placed in a very awkward position, and consulted me as to the best course for him to adopt   I replied, " I am, of course, most anxious to assist you, but under the circumstances I scarcely like to offer advice, but as you have asked me, there appears only one course left open to you.   That is, take the papers at once to the Chancellor of the Exchequer, and explain to him the whole case." This he did, and Mr. Disraeli took them forthwith to Lord Derby, who put a stop to the whole proceeding

It was unfortunate for the Duke of Northumberland that neither he nor the members of his Board (with one exception) had ever held office before, and to that cause may be attributed whatever discredit was attached to his administration

His Grace was so impressed with the autocratic power and personal dignity of his high office, that it was only with the greatest difficulty he could be brought to believe that there was any limit to his authority, and that anything further was necessary than for him to issue his commands, quite forgetting the all-important fact that the Chancellor of the Exchequer had to provide the money and the House of Commons to vote it.

There were two gentlemen in the Board at the time who

had seats in the House of Commons, and I certainly think it was for them and not for me to have enlightened his Grace on the subject, or, at least, to have supported me in doing so. But I had by this time been long enough in office to have discovered that there are very few who will undertake the discharge of an unpleasant duty if they can by any possibility get another to do it for them.

In reference to the filling up of some dockyard appointments, a difference unhappily sprang up between Sir Baldwin Walker and Mr Augustus Stafford. I am satisfied that Sir Baldwin was actuated, from first to last, by no other motive than a conscientious desire to promote those men who had been represented to him, by the officers of the yard, as, from their merits, deserving of advancement, and that, too, utterly regardless of their political predilections, his only thought being the efficiency of the public service. I must, however, in justice to Mr Stafford, express my firm conviction that he had no intention of exercising more official influence than he had been led to believe, by interested parties, was the legitimate patronage of the Government of the day.

Captain Baillie Hamilton and I did all in our power to soften down these unfortunate differences, and to bring about, if possible, a more amicable understanding. We never failed to urge upon Mr. Stafford that he should attach no importance to the representations of the political agents at the outposts, as they saw everything through a party and perverted medium. We invariably advocated extreme prudence and discretion, and reminded Mr. Stafford of the strong party feeling prevailing. He generally agreed with us and promised to follow our advice; but we soon discovered that our recommendations were overruled by his private secretary and political friends. Frequently, differences arising out of trifles, and easily reconciled in the first instance, are often, from the injudicious interposition of third parties, brought to unfortunate issues, which, in this case, were increased by acts of indiscretion on the part of Mr. Stafford himself. At last, in so grave a light were matters regarded that a parliamentary inquiry was instituted, which, unhappily, brought some temporary discredit upon Mr. Stafford and upon the administration of his Grace.

Events of far greater importance than the promotion of shipwrights, the appointment of colour-loft women and oakum boys soon engrossed the attention of Parliament and the public. It became apparent that we were drifting slowly but surely into a war with Russia; and it was in the Crimea that Mr. Stafford subsequently gained, by his unremitting devotion and kindness to the sick and dying, the gratitude of our brave soldiers, and earned for himself a reputation which justly placed him amongst the great philanthropists of the age.

The Duke of Northumberland was full of good intentions, but did not see the difficulties interposed between his wishes and their accomplishment.

On my first introduction to his Grace, he said, "I wish, Mr. Briggs, everything to be done that is right;" but it never seemed to have occurred to the new First Lord that that is the identical point upon which there might be a diversity of opinion; and I am inclined to think that, if there is a public room in Her Majesty's dominions in which differences of opinion have existed, do exist, and will exist to the end of time, it is the Admiralty Board-room at Whitehall, and yet all who have been, and all who are, within its walls are actuated by a sincere desire to do what is right. The administration of the Duke of Northumberland was, from various untoward circumstances, somewhat unfortunate, but rather from a political than a departmental point of view.

The great measure of his administration was, unquestionably, the addition of the five thousand seamen to the fleet which his Grace had obtained in consequence of the strong recommendations of his naval advisers, who were ably supported by Sir Baldwin Walker and Captain Hamilton.

Great credit is also due to his Grace for pushing on with the vessels in course of construction, which would have been advanced still more rapidly had it not been for the economical tendencies of the day, and the unfortunate rivalry between the two great political parties of the State, to keep down taxation to the lowest possible ebb in order to produce a popular budget.

Another very important measure adopted by the Duke was to increase, to a considerable extent, the number of war steamers in commission, which, combined with the five thousand men added to the fleet, proved of such inestimable value to his successor—Sir James Graham—when, upon the outbreak of the Crimean War, it became necessary to augment the Mediterranean fleet and to organise a second for the Baltic Sea.

It too often happens that little mistakes are remembered, whilst valuable services are as frequently forgotten; and such, I fear, has been the case with the Duke of Northumberland. Those who take a large and liberal view, unbiassed by the trammels of party, will be more ready to see the good he conferred upon the country than to magnify the errors of official inexperience.

Although my official position obliged me, not infrequently, to interpose difficulties, and what might easily have appeared to those present as needless obstruction to the carrying out of his Grace's wishes, always intended for the good of the service, yet I cannot bring to my recollection a single instance when he exhibited displeasure at my conduct or evinced any ill-feeling towards me for it, though I know how personally distasteful my interposition was at times to his Grace. On the contrary, he most generously attributed whatever I said and did to a conscientious desire to faithfully discharge my public duty ; nay, more than this—he, on many occasions, gave substantial proofs of the kindly feelings he entertained towards me. I have ever regarded this as so noble a trait in his Grace's character that I am only too happy to have an opportunity to make public acknowledgment of the considerate kindness he extended towards me during the whole time he was at the head of the Admiralty.

CHAPTER XII.

THE SECOND ADMINISTRATION OF THE RIGHT HON. SIR
JAMES GRAHAM, 5TH JANUARY 1853, TO 8TH MARCH,
1855.

Frequent changes in the naval administration of the Admiralty being
good or bad—Diplomatic negotiations and naval preparations for war
—The interest Sir Maurice Berkeley took in manning the navy—The
transport service—Two parties in the State opposed to its best interest
—The fanatical party of peace and the party of ill-judged economy—
The duties which the Admiralty had not to perform during the Crimean
War, but which now would devolve upon the department—Mr. Bernal
Osborne a professor of economy—An indispensable requisite in a
member for Middlesex at this date—The advantages of fixed fortifications as compared with floating batteries—The two Commanders-
in-chief for the Baltic and Mediterranean fleets—Observations in
regard to Sir James Graham's abilities and natural gifts.

ON the 5th January, 1853, upon the accession of Lord Aberdeen to power, Sir James Graham returned to the Admiralty
as First Lord for the second time, succeeding the Duke of
Northumberland, who had held that post but for ten months.
It was a most fortunate thing for the country that so able
and experienced a minister was selected to discharge the
responsible duties which devolved upon the head of the
Admiralty at this eventful and critical juncture. The
members of his Board were—

Vice-Admiral Hyde Parker, C.B.;
Rear-Admiral M F F. Berkeley, C B, M P.;
Captain Hon. R S Dundas, C B, R N.;
Captain Alex. Milne, R.N.;

Hon. W. F. Cowper, M P. ;

R. Bernal Osborne, Esq., M.P., Political Secretary ;

Captain W. A. B Hamilton, Permanent Secretary.

The political changes that had taken place between Sir James Graham's first and second administrations had been very frequent, the office of First Lord of the Admiralty having been filled by no less than seven different Cabinet ministers during his absence of twenty years; including Lord Auckland's three administrations, the total is brought up to nine. It might be supposed that frequent changes at the Board of Admiralty would have tended to the detriment of the public service, but, strange to say, my official experience has caused me to arrive at the opposite conclusion. The simple fact is that an incoming Board is overflowing with zeal and bent upon all sorts of improvements; but before they have been very long in office they discover that many of the contemplated changes are attended with so much trouble, opposition, differences of opinion, and unpopularity, either in the service or out of doors, and, in addition, many of them cannot be carried into effect without an expenditure of money, not in accordance with the views of the First Lord, and still more rarely with the concurrence of the Chancellor of the Exchequer, that after a brief period things settle down again, and the ordinary routine business goes on as before. Soon zeal evaporates, and the contemplated improvements are indefinitely postponed, or carried into effect in a very modified form to that in which they were at first conceived

Again, on the eve of a change of ministry, the necessity arises to carry some measure to revive a waning popularity. A new Board replaces the old, and in turn feel bound to introduce some reforms which it is their pleasure to assume their predecessors have neglected; the result of the whole is that some good is achieved whenever a Board retires from office, and the same may be said on the accession of a new one.

These remarks do not of course apply to the greater questions, such as war organisation and to the defence of the Empire, considered as a whole, which, it is unnecessary to say, require time to work out and carry to a successful issue

The reorganisation of the business of the Admiralty, and placing it under five principal officers, each superintended by a Lord of the Admiralty, inaugurated by Sir James Graham during his administration of 1830, had been on trial for upwards of twenty years under different First Lords, and had been found to work smoothly and well during peace. It was now to be tested by the stern realities of war. It was a happy chance that the statesman who had devised the scheme should be placed in a position to personally super-intend its practical workings upon an occasion of such great importance. Sir James Graham's arrangement for the division of labour and responsibility proved of incalculable value to him during the Crimean War; for it brought under his immediate eye everything of importance that was going on, and led to each branch working in harmony with the other. Each member was cognisant of the proposals sub-mitted by the other departments, and consequently all those matters which were of pressing urgency received prompt attention.

The position in which Sir James Graham was placed at this time was one of extreme perplexity and delicacy. It was apparent to him, as it was to others, that we were drifting slowly but surely into a war with Russia, and must therefore be prepared for eventualities. Great preparations were to be made, whilst at the same time the greatest secrecy was to be maintained, so as to prevent apprehensions at home, and suspicions abroad. The Foreign Office was

carrying on diplomatic negotiations with the court of
St. Petersburg, and therefore any display of naval preparations was to be scrupulously avoided This required the
exercise of great tact and ingenuity. Never was a First
Lord placed in greater anxiety, nor a Controller of the Navy
in greater uncertainty, than Sir James Graham and Sir Baldwin Walker.

Weakness and vacillation were never more apparent in a
ministry than in that of Lord Aberdeen of 1852 to 1855.
One day the Foreign Office desired every possible exertion
to be made, and orders to that effect were sent out and were
promptly put in hand; then came a notification that negotiations were proceeding more satisfactorily, and a delicate hint
from the Treasury that no unnecessary expense was to be
incurred. A few days later a despatch arrived intimating
that a change for the worse had taken place, and that naval
preparations were to be pressed forward with all speed.
This was immediately followed by an order to suspend
proceedings lest they might have an injurious influence upon
the pending negotiations, and so precipitate a crisis. These
orders were scarcely issued when counter-instructions were
received to press on with vigour the preparations for war.

Under circumstances so trying, and instructions so con-
tradictory, no minister ever appeared to greater advantage
than did Sir James Graham, for no words can describe the
calmness and temper he displayed He was always cool
and collected; and thoroughly master of the subject under
consideration; all his arrangements were methodical and
his inquiries to the point At this anxious time he looked
so well at the head of the Board-room table! Quite the right
man in the right place. At one time Sir James Graham,
with Admiral Maurice Berkeley * and Sir Baldwin Walker,
would be going over the lists that might be prepared, the

* Admiral M. F. F. Berkeley was made K.C.B. in 1857.

Sampson Low Marston & Co. Ltd. F. Jenkins, Heliog. Paris

(iii)

ships in the reserve that could be put into commission on the shortest notice, the time that they would take to equip them for sea, and the expense they would incur. The vessels upon the stocks, their actual condition, and how soon they could be got ready for launching should their services be urgently required, were also subjects that engaged their lordships' earnest attention.

Numerous confidential communications were addressed to Mr. John Penn and other leading engineering firms as to the assistance they could render to the Controller of the Navy to expedite the work in hand and how soon they could provide the machinery, etc., for the vessels nearing completion. Arrangements were made for increasing the shipwrights and dockyard hands, but all had to be done in such a manner as not to attract public attention. How to provide ships' companies for the vessels that might be put into commission required much anxious thought, the continual-service system being then only in its infancy Into the difficulties of manning the navy Sir Maurice Berkeley threw himself heart and soul, had it not been for his perseverance, zeal, and energy the crews for the numerous ships put into commission would never have been got together. Sir Maurice had always taken the greatest interest in the manning of the fleet and the training of boys for the navy, and it is owing to the support he gave to Sir Henry Pennell, a predecessor of mine in office, that he (Sir Henry) was enabled to carry his scheme of continuous service for the navy, which has been such a conspicuous success.

Measures were taken by Sir Maurice for recruiting up the marine corps, which, from its high state of discipline and efficiency, has invariably rendered important service to the navy on the first outbreak of hostilities. When the *Excellent* was first established it was feared that a jealousy would arise between the seamen-gunners and the Royal Marine Artillery; but happily the apprehension proved unfounded, and it only led to a laudable rivalry between them. In such high estimation was the Royal Marine Artillery held by Sir James Graham and his Board that the corps was raised to a force of three thousand men. In military circles this corps, for stature and physique, is regarded as perhaps the finest in Her Majesty's service.

If one thing more than another bears stronger testimony to Sir James Graham's superior ability, forethought, and knowledge, it is the manner in which the transport service was organised. The valuable aid it gave to the army during the whole of the Crimean War is universally acknowledged, and the high reputation it acquired was well deserved. It is impossible to speak too highly of the various arrangements that were made for the conveyance of cavalry, artillery, infantry, and stores from the shores of England to the Crimea, and that for so protracted a period.

When heavy mails arrived from various foreign stations, pending the war, Sir James Graham has frequently sat, without leaving the Board-room, from eleven o'clock in the morning until six or seven in the evening, and seemed as fresh and ready for business as when he first entered. Often, after all the letters had been read and minuted, and everybody tired to death, he would ask me if there were no more letters to be disposed of, and upon hearing there were not he looked almost as disappointed as his colleagues appeared relieved.

It is not my province to give an account of the war—that has been ably done by others—but to direct public attention to the perils and dangers we have on so many occasions escaped, in the hope that the experience of the past may be turned to profitable account. A great Empire like ours ought not to play a gambler's game and trust to chance

The probability of a war with Russia was long foreseen, and we had ample time to make our preparations. Neither our shores, our commerce, nor dependencies were exposed to any immediate danger, but it would be far otherwise were we involved in a war with France. Negotiations may be of brief duration, as in the case between France and Germany in 1870, in which instance the advantages of preparation were so pre-eminently apparent. They enabled Germany to strike a blow, at the very commencement of hostilities, which ultimately settled the campaign. It is no less necessary for England than it is for Germany to consider calmly and dispassionately during a period of peace those various and complicated duties which are implied in national defence.

It is very easy to say, as I have often heard within the Admiralty walls, "But we are not going to war." Experience proves only too clearly how impossible it is, even for the ablest statesman, to foresee the future; and what the result of a great naval war would be no one can venture to predict There always have been, and probably always will be, two political parties in the country whose views are diametrically opposed to its best interests : the one, the fanatical party of peace at any price; the other, the pertinacious advocates of ill-judged economy. The first has already driven us into a war with Russia, and the other has, on more than one occasion, placed the Empire in positions of extreme peril which led to panic and profligate expenditure. Our rulers must from henceforth direct more and more attention to the military defences of the Empire; more care must be bestowed upon the composition and distribution of the fleet, and upon the adequacy and efficiency of the army. The difficulties Sir James Graham had to encounter in despatching fleets, properly equipped, to the Black Sea and Baltic, and in carrying on a war three thousand miles distant, sink into

insignificance when compared with those which will devolve
on the First Lord of the Admiralty in the next naval war. Sir
James Graham was not called upon to provide within forty-
eight hours protection for the Channel Islands, commercial
ports, the towns on the south coast, commerce in the Narrow
Seas, the homeward-bound trade, coaling-stations, and, what is
perhaps of the most importance, the Suez Canal. Neither
had Sir James Graham to commission flying squadrons to
keep the mother-country in touch with her dependencies and
with the squadrons stationed in all parts of the world   The
foregoing gives but an idea of all that a First Lord of the
Admiralty, holding office at the commencement of hostilities
in the present day, would have to provide for, and that at
the very beginning of hostilities.

The Political Secretary in this administration had made
his mark in the House of Commons, and had established a
reputation for being an able speaker and a ready debater.
No doubt Mr. Bernal Osborne possessed great natural talent,
wit, and knowledge of the world, but was too much a man of
pleasure for the arduous and never-ending labours of official
life, though in justice to him it is but fair to say that his
presence was as much required in the House of Commons as
at the Admiralty. Like most of his party, he was a professor
of economy—in those days an indispensable requisite in a
member for Middlesex—but in his private affairs he was
generous to a fault. He had a remarkably fine temper; once
only did I see it ruffled, and I was, most unfortunately, the
cause. He was a strong advocate for floating batteries as
opposed to forts. My opinion was asked which of the two
would be the best for the defence of our important position.
I expressed myself very decidedly in favour of forts, as I was
thoroughly convinced that, on the first pressing emergency
that arose, the floating battery would be removed from the
important point it was meant to protect.

Mr Osborne then protested very energetically against more money being spent on the construction of forts, and directed attention to the large sums of money that had been thrown away upon those at Portsdown, saying, "They had been made so strong that nobody with any sense would dream of attacking them." To this I replied, perhaps somewhat injudiciously, that by his own showing money could not be considered as wasted upon forts when they so completely accomplished the object for which they were constructed. To be proved wrong by his own argument somewhat irritated him, and for this I felt very sorry.

Both Sir James Graham and Mr. Osborne, when they came into office, were convinced there was some job at the bottom of the large expenditure required for the works carried on at Keyham; but, after a strict investigation of the matter, they found they were mistaken, and Sir James, as soon as he could, doubled the vote and pressed the works forward.

Military matters and political questions are seen from a totally different point of view by those upon whom the responsibilities of office devolve, and by the same individuals sitting on the front opposition bench clamouring for economy and retrenchment.

It is no less singular than true that there are times in the lives of the most wise and cautious when acts of grave indiscretion and imprudence are committed.

It is almost impossible to believe that so sagacious and experienced a statesman as Sir James Graham could have been guilty of so palpable an act of indiscretion, when announcing, at a public dinner, the names of the two admirals respectively appointed to the Mediterranean and Baltic fleets, as to have rendered it only too apparent that the selection had been made solely upon party and political grounds, irrespective of professional claims, which on im-

I

portant occasions, such as this, ought, for the honour of the
service and the interest of the country, to outweigh all other
considerations. Both appointments proved unfortunate.

Sir James Dundas had for years been the Liberal representative for Greenwich. He was most popular with his
constituents and in the House of Commons. His manner
was manly and open, and he was most kind and hospitable
to his brother-officers and to all with whom he came in
personal intercourse, and to none more than to myself. He
had been a Lord of the Admiralty for many years, and at
the date of his appointment to the Mediterranean command
was Second Sea Lord, a position he had occupied for some
time.

From a very early date in my official career I found it
imperatively necessary to study the individual temper and
disposition of those with whom I was thrown in daily contact
and to find out their distinguishing characteristics.

When I heard of Sir James Dundas's appointment I lost
no time in offering him my congratulations; but it was not
without inward misgivings that this command would not
afford him the gratification he anticipated, for I knew he was
advanced in years, had recently re-married, and was full of
the pleasures of Malta and Naples, and of extending hospi-
talities to his brother-officers and personal friends, and,
unhappily for him, viewed too lightly the lowering aspect of
the political sky.

I was well acquainted with all the good traits in his
character, but I could not conceal from myself that he
possessed what may be designated firmness in a good case
and obstinacy in a bad one. He was by nature very im-
pulsive and at times dictatorial in his manner, and disinclined
to listen to argument or reason.

No Commander-in-chief was ever placed in a more favourable position for learning the opinions entertained at head-

quarters than Sir James Dundas. Captain Baillie Hamilton and I never failed to keep him fully acquainted with the state of public feeling in the country and at headquarters, and the probable course events would take. But, alas! it was all in vain, the simple truth being that what was taking place was diametrically opposed to his personal wishes. I never lost an opportunity of placing before him the gravity of his position, and what I knew would be expected from him; and, to spur him on, went so far as to assure him that he had only to act with energy, and then he might pick up the coronet which would be at his feet. But all I got in reply to my urgent representations and entreaties was, "My dear Briggs, you are all wrong—it will be peace." And to such an extent did he allow his wishes to get the better of his judgment that, at the very time the troops were landing in the Crimea, he was in momentary expectation of the arrival of a vessel bringing him instructions to suspend all further operations, and announcing peace.

Sir Charles Napier was likewise a Liberal member of parliament, and was very popular at all the seaports throughout the kingdom. He was an officer of remarkable courage, and in his early days had gained a reputation of being a lion-hearted hero. I have often heard Sir George Cockburn bear testimony to his coolness under the heaviest fire, and I never saw Sir Thomas Hardy so excited as when he read the account in the *Times* of the gallant style in which, from his frigate, sword in hand, he boarded and took a line-of-battle-ship during the revolutionary war in Portugal. The splendid achievements of Sir Charles, as a Commodore, on the coast of Syria, obtained for him a great reputation; but years and responsibility exercise a very taming influence, and he clearly proved, in his own case, the soundness of the opinions he himself had often expressed with more force than delicacy—that officers advanced in years are very different individuals from

I 2

what they were when they achieved those brilliant successes which obtained for them honour and distinction   Hence the necessity for *young* officers being placed in responsible command.

Nothing is more distressing than for officers of acknowledged ability and high professional character to be placed in positions demanding qualifications incompatible with advancing years and the decline of mental and physical powers, and to be called upon to discharge duties which would be more efficiently executed by younger men.

It is as impossible to make a gallant admiral believe that he is past work as Gil Blas found it to convince the Archbishop of Granada that his sermons smelt of apoplexy.

Mr. Childers, by his well thought-out scheme of naval retirement, has prevented for the future flag-officers from being placed in positions so invidious.

It must have been most gratifying to Sir James Graham to have found that his reorganisation of the naval department, upon which he had bestowed so much thought and labour when at the Admiralty in 1830 to 1834, should have worked smoothly, not only in peace, but had been able to bear the severe strain and test of a naval war, combined with military operations on a grand scale, carried on at a great distance from home. Sir James was undoubtedly a capable minister, and was ably assisted by the members of his Board; indeed, I may say that every individual connected with the Admiralty at this critical time, from the highest to the lowest, worked with a will; but the First Lord was the ruling power.

It may be asked how is it that a statesman possessing such administrative ability as Sir James Graham, with all his powers of eloquence, splendid natural gifts, rare and varied attainments, failed to secure for himself that position which his three political contemporaries, Lord John Russell,

Lord Stanley, and Lord Palmerston, respectively attained It was because he lacked the courage of his opinions, was vacillating and timid, and was over anxious to gain a popularity he never acquired; for he was unquestionably unpopular in the House of Commons and in the country, but was seldom liked by those who served with him or about him.

CHAPTER XIII.

THE ADMINISTRATION OF THE RIGHT HON. SIR CHARLES
WOOD,* 8TH MARCH, 1855, TO 8TH MARCH, 1858.

The personal qualities and noble character of Sir Charles Wood—After
the war, ships hurriedly paid off and marines disbanded—The outbreak of the Indian Mutiny and the efforts made to get back the
seamen and same marines—The troops going through the Suez Canal
and the Emperor's friendly feeling—Sir Charles Wood and his Board
equal to meet the difficulties caused by the Indian Mutiny—The
fleet of magnificent three-deckers and 90-gun ships exhibited to the
Sovereign and to the country—An anecdote in reference to widows'
pensions—Another to illustrate how boys for naval cadet-ships were
examined—A curious incident to Captain Horatio Austin—Reference
to a letter from Lord Halifax (Sir Charles Wood), written on his
eightieth birthday, lamenting the disappearance of the beautiful
masted vessels which it had been the labour of his life to bring into
existence.

SIR JAMES GRAHAM'S second administration was followed on
the 8th of March, 1855, by that of Sir Charles Wood,* whose
valuable services, as Political Secretary during the administration of Lord Minto, have already been referred to.

Sir Charles exhibited, in his own person, the identical
qualifications lacked by his predecessor, though he did not
possess his more showy and imposing attributes. Still he
was a minister of very great ability, indomitable courage,
and decision of character, and never failed to inspire confidence in those about him, and impress them with the
conviction that, if they only did their duty, he would fight for
them and stand by them to the very last. In a word, he was
a fine and noble character, beloved, respected, and trusted

* Created Viscount Halifax, 1866.

Sampson Low, Marston & C. Ltd.   F. Jenkins, Helig, Paris

Halifax

by all who were so fortunate as to be officially associated with him *

The appointment of Sir Charles Wood proved a most judicious selection, for he energetically carried on the policy of Sir James Graham, and brought to a successful issue all that remained of the arduous duties connected with the winding up of the Crimean War. The war had been scarcely brought to a close before imperative orders were issued by the Government to reduce expenditure in every possible way. Consequently ships were hurriedly paid off, seamen discharged, marines disbanded, and stores of every description summarily disposed of, and the whole fleet was dismantled with far more haste than prudence, as the Government only too soon found out to its cost. Although many years have elapsed, I still entertain a perfect recollection of my fruitless endeavours to prevail upon Sir Charles Wood to induce the Chancellor of the Exchequer to reverse the order for the immediate disbanding of a thousand Royal Marines. I stated that the loss in wear and tear at that time amounted to between sixty and seventy men per month, and that it would be much better to discharge all those of bad or questionable character, all invalids, and call in all recruiting parties, by which means the corps would soon be diminished in numbers. I further reminded Sir Charles that it took at least four years to make an efficient marine, for he had first to learn the duties of an infantry soldier, then of an artilleryman, and, lastly, to acquire the habits of a sea life, I set forth, to the best of my ability, the value of these men, the time it would take, and the difficulty there would be, in replacing them. But all to no purpose; the Treasury would not listen to any such proposal from Sir Charles; they were as usual

---

* There was no change in the Board with the exception that Rear-Admiral Henry Eden took the place of Rear-Admiral Hon. R. S. Dundas. On the 14th March Sir Robert Peel was appointed Civil Lord.—Ed.

more intent upon their economical arrangements than the efficiency of the navy.

The order was no sooner carried into effect than news arrived of the outbreak of the Indian Mutiny. This appalling intelligence created great national alarm, and the greatest excitement prevailed throughout the kingdom. So urgent and serious did affairs appear, from the very first, that the Cabinet were impressed with the conviction that not a moment was to be lost The panic was so universal that economy was entirely disregarded The War Office and Admiralty felt the necessity to be so pressing that they strained every nerve to get back, with all possible speed, the soldiers and marines so hastily and imprudently discharged but so short a time before, and actually offered no less a sum than £15 bounty to induce them to return, and a like sum to any stunted lad that could be prevailed upon to enlist into any arm of the military service.

Public alarm was greatly intensified by the apprehension that a difficulty might be interposed by France to so large a body of troops as that required to quell the Indian Mutiny passing through the Suez Canal. The question was violently discussed in the Parisian press, but the Emperor Napoleon, remembering with gratitude the hospitality extended to him by this country when in exile—much to his honour be it said—expressed himself strongly on the subject, and would allow no obstacles to be interposed Had the Emperor evinced a less friendly feeling, it is impossible to say what might have been the ultimate result of the Indian Mutiny or the fate of this country. The European forces in India were utterly inadequate to the defence of that great empire, and the home army had for years been so starved, and reduced to so low a standard, as to be quite unfit to discharge the duty of protecting the country in any sudden emergency.

Sir Charles Wood and his Board proved quite equal to

meet the difficulties which the outbreak of the Indian Mutiny suddenly threw upon the Admiralty, and on the occasion nothing could exceed their energy and zeal. The arrangements made for the embarkation of troops at the home ports, and for those on foreign stations, to arrive at their destination at the earliest possible moment, were admirable in the extreme, and were attended with the greatest success. The transport service upon this occasion, as during the Crimean War, proved most efficient, and richly deserved the high encomium passed upon it by the Indian and Home Governments.

The brilliant services rendered by Sir William Peel and his naval brigade at the siege of Lucknow, of which Lord Clyde gave such splendid accounts in his public despatches, should also be mentioned in this connection, as also the assistance rendered by the officers and men of H.M.S. *Pearl*, under the command of Captain (afterwards Sir Edward) Sotheby, who received the thanks of both Houses of Parliament and the Viceroy of India for his brave and gallant conduct.

It fortunately happened that the termination of the war with Russia placed a considerable military force at the disposal of the Government, which was despatched as reinforcements to India, and, but for this coincidence, would not have been immediately available. The arrangements and preparations, which were luckily adequate to meet the demands created by the Crimean War and Indian Mutiny, would be utterly useless in any future emergency. The merchant seamen and raw recruits were, in days gone by, turned to very profitable account, but their utility now is very differently estimated. Men-of-warsmen and soldiers can no longer be extemporised; time and training alone render them efficient, and unless they are well drilled and highly trained they are unfit to be entrusted with the deadly

weapons placed in their hands, and those who are not equal
to their work are only in the way. To prevent the shores
of England being again left in the condition they were
during the Indian Mutiny, when nearly the whole military
force of the country was abroad, it is necessary that there
should always be large numbers of highly trained seamen and
soldiers in the reserves. Until quite recently there was
more difficulty experienced in this great and wealthy country
to obtain a vote of five thousand men for the navy, or a
slight numerical increase to the army, than a minister on the
Continent found in obtaining an addition of fifty thousand
men to augment the army.

At the termination of the Crimean War Sir Charles Wood
had the proud satisfaction of exhibiting before his Sovereign
and the country one of the grandest spectacles the world has
ever seen. It consisted of the most magnificent three-deckers
and 90-gun ships that ever floated upon the crest of the
waters, and in the creation of this grand fleet Sir Charles
had, during his long connection with the Admiralty, taken no
small part. In later years he was fated to see these fine
vessels converted into receiving and training-ships, and into
coaling hulks. So great have been, and so constant are, the
changes in naval construction, that First Lords and secretaries
are often placed in doubt and difficulty as to the proper
course to pursue. To remain inactive is impossible, and yet
to decide the rate of progress is most embarrassing, for the
expenditure to be incurred is great, and improvements in
every branch of naval architecture follow each other in rapid
succession.

During Sir Charles Wood's administration two curious
incidents occurred, in one of which I took a rather prominent part. One day, after the reading of the Board, the
First Lord turned to me and said, "Here is a very distressing
case, Mr. Briggs, in which I wish you could assist me, for the

head of the pension branch tells me there is no precedent. It seems the chaplain of the *Calypso* has died of yellow fever at Halifax, which he caught at Jamaica, and has left a widow. By the regulation she ought to have been married a full year to entitle her to a pension, but, unfortunately, a month is required to complete the prescribed period." A similar case instantly came to my recollection. I suggested to Sir Charles that he should send to the Record Office for the papers referring to Mrs. Dodd, widow of the chaplain of the *Blonde*, about the year 1835. After a messenger had been sent to fetch the paper, Sir Charles complimented me upon my memory, to which I replied that his compliments were unmerited, for I had a personal interest in the case, and with his permission I told the story. When I was a Westminster scholar there was a poor woman in the Abbey one Saturday afternoon at service who had St. Vitus' dance; her grimaces and twitching movements so tickled my boyish fancy that I laughed outright. I had scarcely left the Abbey when my particular friend, who had sat next to me, announced, with a beaming face, that as Dodd (one of the masters) wanted to see me, he thought I was in for a six cutter. Upon making my appearance before him, he said, "You shouldn't have laughed in church, Briggs; but if anything is said to you about it, just say that I have given you a good jobation upon the impropriety of doing so;" and then, with a good-natured smile, added, "Really, the contortions of that poor woman were enough to give any schoolboy the giggles." This act of unexpected kindness so completely overpowered me that I felt for the moment I would rather have gone in for the six cutter.

In 1834, when I was in the commission branch, I heard Mr. Dodd request the head of that department to try and get his appointment changed from the West Indies to the Mediterranean. I instantly recognised my old friend; I told my story to the head of the branch, and got the change effected, for which, I need hardly say, Mr. Dodd was very grateful. He married just before his ship sailed, and whilst in Greece he caught a fever and died, leaving a widow and child, having been married but eleven months By the regulations, if rigidly enforced, this poor lady was not entitled to a pension, but, fortunately for her, I was acting as reader for Mr. Hay on the day her .petition came before the Board. At first it was decided that nothing could be done, but I pleaded her case as strongly and pathetically as I could, and stated the grounds upon which I was so personally interested—to the no little amusement of the members of the Board. I also felt that I had been chiefly instrumental in getting his appointment changed. Lord Ashley and Sir John Barrow supported me very warmly, and in the end the Board was pleased to direct that Mrs. Dodd should have a pension, and that I should draw up the memorial to Council under my own hand.

I had scarcely finished telling my story to the First Lord when the original document made its appearance, which, after perusal, was considered satisfactory, and quite met the case in which Sir Charles Wood was interested. The widow of the chaplain of the *Calypso* got her pension, as did also two other unfortunate ladies similarly situated, who had previously been refused, and they were awarded the back pay as well No First Lord of the Admiralty was ever more anxious to help the widows and orphans of the officers of the navy than was Sir Charles Wood This anecdote proves to demonstration "what great results from trifling causes spring." Never, perhaps, did the remission of punishment to a schoolboy lead to consequences more important.

The second incident to which I have referred was that of a father who complained to the Board of the hardship of his son being rejected at the examination for a naval cadetship because he did not know the capital of Madagascar. Sir Charles Wood, turning to the First Sea Lord, said, " I am sure I don't know what it is called, do you ? " He did not, neither did any of the naval lords. Sir Charles then turned to Mr. Phinn, Q.C.,* Permanent Secretary, and said, " You are a first-class man, perhaps you can tell us ? " But he, too, was obliged to reply in the negative Sir Francis Beaufort, the hydrographer of the Admiralty, was then requested to step into the Board-room. Upon the question being put to him he looked very embarrassed, and said he would make inquiries; but no one in his department could tell him. Some half-hour afterwards a scrap of paper was handed to me with the word Antananarivo, the information being privately furnished by Sir Roderick Murchison !

The Board was greatly amused at the circumstance, and Sir Charles said, " Telegraph instantly for that boy's imme- diate admission, for it would be too bad to refuse it because he did not know that which the Lords of the Admiralty, the secretary, and the hydrographer himself, were unable to answer.† The examining officers ought never to have put such a ridiculous question to a boy of twelve or fourteen years of age, and regard it as a fair test of his geographical knowledge." Upon occasions, it really appears that, instead of endeavouring to ascertain what the boys actually know, questions are put by the examiners as if to confuse and stump them

At the risk of wearying my readers with anecdotes I will

---

* Thomas Phinn, Esq, appointed Permanent Secretary 22nd May, 1855, in succession to Captain Baillie Hamilton, who retired in ill health consequent upon the heavy duties entailed upon him during the Irish Famine and Indian Mutiny.

† Since 1855 Madagascar has come very much to the front, and the name of its capital is now well known to everybody. How it occurs that none of these gentlemen thought of looking on a map, or whether there was no map at the time in the Admiralty giving the required information, the author does not say

relate one which, at the time the incident occurred, caused
some innocent fun amongst the higher officers of the naval
service. Captain Horatio Austin, a very gallant and zealous
steam officer, was captain-superintendent at Deptford; he
was very popular in the service although somewhat eccentric
in manner. Whilst strolling upon the quay one day he
suddenly inquired of the marine sentry why he did not
challenge him. The sentry respectfully replied, "Because
I know you to be the captain-superintendent, sir." Captain
Austin then said, "It is your duty to challenge everybody;"
and gave to the sentry a full and detailed description of the
course to be pursued even to the position in which he should
stand in front of the prisoner. The marine determined to
carry out his instructions to the letter. In the evening
Captain Austin went out to take another turn on the quay;
he was instantly challenged and the countersign demanded;
this the captain had for the moment forgotten, whereupon
the old marine put into practical effect the orders he had
received in the morning. He seized the captain-superintendent by the neck, shoved him into the sentry-box,
sounded the alarm, and stood over his prisoner in the exact
position Captain Austin had shown him. In a few minutes
up came the drummers with a lantern, the officer of the
guard with a sergeant of marines and two privates, all at
the double. When the officer of the guard saw the captain-
superintendent he was perfectly astounded. And when he
heard the story from the old marine the prisoner was of
course released. The next day Captain Austin applied for
a month's leave on urgent private affairs, and was not seen
at the "Senior United Club" for weeks; whilst the marine
found himself a corporal within a few days.

The naval administration of Sir Charles Wood was in
every respect a marked success, and in recognition of his
public services he was raised to the Peerage in the year

1866 and assumed the title of Viscount Halifax. On his eightieth birthday his lordship addressed a letter to me from Hickleton Hall couched in somewhat desponding and touching terms He deplored the great change which science had caused in the construction of our vessels of war, and the removal from the active list of those splendid structures which had been the labour of his life to bring into existence, and which had given such a good account of themselves before Sebastopol and in the Baltic. Well might Lord Halifax lament the disappearance of those stately three-deckers and full-rigged vessels which Mr. Canning in the first quarter of the century, upon visiting Plymouth, described with such unrivalled eloquence and poetical imagination. With their departure all the beauty, poetry, and romance have completely vanished away from the navy.

CHAPTER XIV.

The First Administration of the Rt. Hon. Sir John Pakington, 8th March, 1858, to 28th June, 1859.

The personal qualities of Sir John Pakington—Fortunate in his secretaries —No money to be got to increase the fleet—Anecdotes about doctors —The bravery of the non-combatant officers—Admiralty contracts— The difference in the business routine at the Admiralty and War Office.

Sir John Pakington succeeded Sir Charles Wood as First Lord of the Admiralty on the 8th of March, 1858, which appointment he held but for a brief period.* He possessed many statesmanlike qualities, was liberal-minded, very impartial, remarkably free from all prejudices, and took a keen and lively interest in everything connected with the naval service, in which he was ably supported by the naval members of his Board, and more particularly by Sir William Fanshawe Martin, the First Sea Lord †

This Board was one of the strongest under which I ever had the honour of serving, both as regards its naval and civil members, all of whom were ably seconded by very efficient secretaries. It consisted of—

Vice-Admiral W F. Martin;
Vice-Admiral the Hon. Sir R S. Dundas, K.C.B ;
Rear-Admiral Alex. Milne; ‡

* From the 8th of March, 1858, to the 28th of June, 1859.
† Vice-Admiral W. F. Martin succeeded his cousin, the third baronet, in 1863.
‡ Rear-Admiral Alex. Milne was made a K.C.B. in 1859.

Captain the Hon. Jas. R. Drummond, C.B , R N.;
The Rt. Hon. Lord Lovaine, M.P.;
The Rt Hon. H. T. L. Corry, M P , Political Secretary;
W. G. Romaine, Esq., C.B., Permanent Secretary.

Sir Fanshawe Martin obtained post-rank at a very early age, being the son of the late Admiral Sir Byam Martin, a naval officer of high reputation and distinction, who for many years filled with great ability the then very important post of Controller of the Navy. Sir Fanshawe, previous to his appointment at the Admiralty, had acquired the character of being one of the smartest captains and one of the most efficient officers on the flag-list As captain he had held several most important commands, and obtained great credit for the very efficient manner he discharged his duties as Admiral - Superintendent of Portsmouth Dockyard. He brought to the Admiralty not only a great knowledge of his profession but a clear conception of what the navy required.

Sir Fanshawe Martin was the First Sea Lord who fully realised the grave responsibilities attached to his professional position. He saw at once the imperative necessity of making increased preparations to meet the numerous calls that would be made upon the Admiralty in case of war. His advanced and statesman-like views fortunately coincided with those of the Second Sea Lord, who zealously supported him in his endeavours to give practical shape to his scheme of defending our shores and protecting our yearly expanding commerce. They commenced by going into the actual condition of the ships in the first-class reserve, and the distribution of the ships that would soon be available; but the more they went into the matter, the greater the difficulties which presented themselves. They were truly in earnest, and were determined to do their best to overcome all obstacles, when, unfortunately for the navy, a change of ministry prevented the First Sea

K

Lord from carrying out his good intentions, and removed him from a position he was so admirably fitted to fill.

This Board was distinctly a progressive one. Strong representations were made by the naval members to Sir John Pakington as to the necessity of increasing the fleet, and were well received by him, who submitted their views to the Cabinet, and expressed himself as entirely coinciding; but, as usual, the Cabinet regarded the moment as very inopportune, and any increase to the navy estimates as quite inadmissible. Without money, ships could not be built, stores repleted, nor men added to the navy. Sir John Pakington was as fortunate in his secretaries as in his naval advisers. Mr. Corry had gained great official experience in regard to naval affairs from having previously held the appointments of Civil Lord under Lord Haddington, and Political Secretary under Lord Ellenborough; whilst Mr. Romaine possessed to a remarkable degree all those peculiar qualifications required in the one who fills the post of Permanent Secretary at the Admiralty.

I should here remark that the grave responsibilities which devolved upon Captain Baillie Hamilton, during the Irish Famine and Indian Mutiny, had so completely shattered his health that he was compelled to retire—much to the loss of the public service and to the heartfelt regret of all those who were in any way officially connected with him. He was succeeded in the office by Mr. Thomas Phinn, Q.C., a barrister of high standing, but who unfortunately did not take kindly to official life. Its restraints were irksome to him, and at variance with his previous habits. To so great an extent did he give expression to his feeling of discontent and dissatisfaction that he hinted his wish on several occasions to resign. Sir Charles Wood at length became so weary with his complaints, that one day he unexpectedly took him at his word and appointed Mr. Romaine in his place; and a more judicious selection Sir Charles could not have made, as eleven years of faithful service in that post bear ample testimony

As the financial resources of the country, according to the representation of the Cabinet, did not permit of any increase to the navy estimates, Sir John Pakington and his Board were obliged to content themselves with reforms affecting the *personnel* rather than in those relating to the *matériel* of the navy. In Sir John Pakington the medical officers of the navy found a good friend. He entertained a high opinion of their professional attainments and valuable services, and exercised his influence to the utmost to improve their position in the service, in which he was successful to a considerable degree.

It is perhaps natural, though unfortunate, that the combatant officers of the navy should not always view the civilian branches of the profession, in regard to rank and emolument, in as liberal and friendly a spirit as the good of the service requires. For many years scant justice was extended to the medical officers of the profession; assistant-surgeons (gentlemen from twenty-five to thirty years of age) who had passed high examinations and the degree of M.D. were consigned to the cockpit, compelled to mess with the midshipmen and naval cadets, and to bear with good humour the practical jokes of their young associates.

This might well be regarded as a legitimate grievance, as they had no place for study, and were exposed to incessant interruptions The ward-room officers objected to having them, and difficulties were interposed in the way of providing them with suitable cabins; but at last the objections were happily overruled, and suitable accommodation was provided.

During the administration of Sir John Pakington many memorials were presented to the Board in reference to the relative rank, uniform, pay, and emoluments of the medical officers, which were found very difficult to bring to any satisfactory solution.   The medical officers were far more popular amongst the officers holding flag-rank than they were in the ward-room.   Being gentlemen of good education, they frequently rendered great assistance to captains and commanders in writing their despatches on the slave trade, political questions, or what not, for which the naval officers received the commendations from the Admiralty and Foreign Office.

The combatant officers are frequently placed at this advantage: they are in many cases men of good family, single, and possess ample private means, consequently they are at times too much given to hospitality, with a view of upholding the honour and credit of their profession, when in company with ships of foreign nations, and in return for civilities extended to them by consular agents and leading merchants at the different ports they visit.   This is not always in accordance with the financial convenience of the civilian officers, who are more often married men, and have to provide for wives and families at home; and on such occasions the doctor is regarded as leading the opposition, and by his vote and influence sometimes secures an adverse majority.

The doctors have also from time to time been unfortunate in getting the naval cadets into scrapes by being late when the boats were strictly ordered to regain their ships at a certain time; they likewise preferred frequent complaints against them to their superior officers because they were not treated with proper respect; and by other such trifles they rendered themselves unpopular.   Some years ago a young cadet of the *Algiers* had incurred the displeasure of the doctor by refusing to order the men to "toss oars," of which complaint was made to the captain, who reprimanded the cadet   In talking over the matter with the commander, the smart little officer pointed out that the doctor had only relative rank on shore and was not entitled to the honour. The young cadet was therefore considered to have proved his case, and was accordingly exonerated. One day the same cadet received positive orders from the first lieutenant to push off the moment the clock struck twelve and to wait for no one. To the delight of the youngster and the amusement of the coxswain, the doctor was seen running down the hill, but upon the last stroke of the clock off went the boat in spite of the frantic gesticulations of the doctor, who was obliged to incur the expense of a bumboat to take him to the ship. This led to another complaint, but the captain calmly remarked, " It was a pity you were not in time, doctor. Mr ——'s orders were emphatic."

The coxswain had observed that the doctor was ill at ease when the boat carried sail, and it was determined on the next occasion to make the doctor feel still more uncomfortable There was a stiff breeze blowing, and they were carrying full sail, when the boat gave a lurch and some spray came into it ; the doctor jumped up and involuntarily exclaimed, " Oh ! " The cadet gave instant orders to shorten sail, as the doctor seemed nervous. On their arrival on board the first lieutenant sternly inquired why the boat was behind time again. The cadet replied, " I beg pardon, sir, but the doctor was so nervous we were obliged to shorten sail " The result of this was that the doctor was chaffed out of his life by the repeated inquiries as to the state of his nerves. At last he thought he was getting the worst of it, and, in his broad Scotch accent, said, " Don't you think, Mr. ——, it would be better for both of us if we were to make friends ? " " Certainly," was the reply ; " that is easily done if you don't complain so often about me. However, here is my hand."

There is no profession in which there are not some

individuals who are apt to exhibit the weaknesses of human nature in some form or other, and to bring upon themselves more ridicule than pride and vanity deserve. Relative rank on shore and afloat are better understood in the service than they are ever likely to be in the outside world.

An amusing incident occurred in the West Indies in the case of a doctor belonging to a frigate in which there happened to be several lieutenants of high rank and good family connections. The doctor, in an unguarded moment, was heard to complain that when on shore, with the exception of the Lieutenant-Governor, the Bishop, and the Chief Justice, there was no one of his own social rank with whom he could associate; this occasioned great fun in the ward-room; the officers expressed themselves as highly flattered that he could condescend to be on social terms with such humble individuals as themselves. The doctor found himself so ridiculed and tormented by the profound deference and respect paid to him, that he invalided. On his invalid certificate was written, " Invalided on account of his rank ! " Upon the story getting wind at the Admiralty, and his health proving perfectly sound, it was decided that a medical officer entertaining his peculiar views, instead of being employed afloat in a beautiful frigate, could not be better placed than in a shore appointment, where he could enjoy his "high rank" and social position to his heart's content. He was, therefore, appointed as medical officer to the hospital at Hong-Kong.

To show that there are medical officers who know how to take care of themselves, and uphold their rightful position, I will relate a circumstance, in this connection, that occurred to the late Admiral R A. Yates, a popular and well-known officer in the service. When serving as a young commander in the *Espiègle*, stationed in the West Indies, he one day invited his brother-officers to dine with him. When the

soup came up, it was soon discovered that the black cook
had greatly overdone the Cayenne pepper. It was so hot
that it quite burnt their throats. It was suggested for fun
that after dinner cookie should have a good taste of his own
soup, and accordingly he was sent for and made to swallow
a large quantity. All the time it was being forced down
his throat he was yelling and screaming, and making the
most frightful grimaces imaginable. This was regarded as a
capital joke, and the evening passed off pleasantly enough
A little after midnight there was a tap at the commander's
door, who was informed that Dr. McArthur wished to speak
to him. "What can that d—— Scotch doctor want at this
hour of the night?" was the not very polite inquiry that
came from within. "He says the black cook is very ill
and must see you, sir," was the reply. Dr. McArthur,
having heard all this, came forward, and in his Scotch accent
said, "I think it my duty to tell you, Captain Yates, that
the cook is in a very critical condition; I doubt if I shall
be able to save his life." "Good God, you don't say so!"
exclaimed the captain. "But I do," replied the doctor,
looking very serious. "His mucous membrane is in a
frightful state of inflammation, I can assure you," he continued. I am afraid I cannot do justice to the mental
sufferings and unpleasant forebodings of Captain Yates, but
I will do my best to relate them as he described them to me.
He had visions of a court-martial, he dreamt that Mr. Joseph
Hume had given notice that he was going to ask the
Secretary of the Admiralty in the House of Commons
whether there was any foundation for the report which had
appeared in the *Times* as to an act of cruelty towards a black
cook serving in a ship-of-war in the West Indies. He
pictured to himself all the articles that would be written in
the papers if the man should die. At last he determined to
send for the doctor in the hope that he would relieve his

mind by telling him that the patient was progressing favourably.

Precious little comfort could he get out of Dr. McArthur; in fact, he did nothing but dilate upon his critical condition, and rang the changes pretty evenly between that and the condition of his mucous membrane This state of things went on for three whole days;. on the morning of the fourth, as Captain Yates and his first lieutenant were walking up and down the quarterdeck, the doctor made his appearance and walked slowly up to the captain and whispered in a mysterious undertone, "I think I have saved the man's life." "My dear doctor, I cannot thank you sufficiently for all you have done," exclaimed the grateful captain "So I am 'dear doctor' now, captain," replied Dr. McArthur. "I hope you will not call me again that 'd—— Scotch doctor,' for Scotch doctors have their feelings as well as other people," said the doctor in an ironical tone "No, that I will not, for I shall always regard you as the best friend I ever had," replied Captain Yates, giving the doctor his hand ; and from that day he never spoke but in praise of the medical officers of the navy, and especially of the Scotch doctors.

It is a curious fact, and generally admitted by the combatant officers themselves, that amongst the ship's company, on trying occasions, there is no class of men that exhibits more personal courage than the civilian officers—doctors, chaplains, captains' clerks, etc.   The Rev. Dr. Cole, of Greenwich Hospital, gained for himself immortal glory for pulling off his coat and taking his place at a great gun in one of the naval actions, which he did amidst the cheers of the bluejackets, who were stimulated by the example of the parson to increased exertion.

During this and other administrations the Admiralty have, from time to time, been placed in awkward positions in regard to contracts.   Amongst the economists and the party in opposition there is always a suspicion that undue favouritism has prevailed if the lowest tender be not accepted; and a feeling of jealousy is produced between the rival firms anxious for the orders if one is preferred to the others. In many cases, however, the lowest tender has proved anything but the most economical. For example, complaints had been proferred that the tender of Mr John Penń had been accepted when it was higher than those of other firms; but the reason for this is easily explained. During the Crimean War the engines supplied to the line-of-battleships by that firm were punctually delivered and found to work with such perfect success, that the only trials deemed necessary before proceeding on active service were those that took place in the short run between the Nore and the Downs, merely to ascertain whether their bearings heated or not; whilst the *James Watt*, a line-of-battleship with a complement of between 600 and 700 men, with engines supplied from another firm at a lower tender, was precluded from proceeding to her station for several months in consequence of the defective and unsatisfactory condition of her machinery; and this was at a time when her services were urgently required on active service. Another instance may be adduced in the case of Messrs. Brown and Lennox, cable-chain manufacturers, who supplied the cable-chains to the *Retribution*, which was the only vessel that rode out of that terrific storm off Balaclava in November, 1854, which occasioned such a fearful loss of life and destruction of ships The valuable life of H.R.H. the Duke of Cambridge was spared to the country in consequence of the excellence of Messrs. Brown and Lennoxs' cable-chains, and of the excellence of the engines supplied by the firm of Messrs. John Penn and Co. The Admiralty, with such precedents before them, have no right to accept the tenders of an inferior or unknown firm in order to effect some little saving; to employ unworthy firms

brings discredit upon the Admiralty, and often does great
injustice to the officers of the various yards. A large contract for flannel was entered into with a Manchester firm,
but on delivery was condemned by the Deptford officers as
not in accordance with the sample approved. A long correspondence took place and representations were made to
the Admiralty as to the respectability of the firm by various
members of Parliament and others. In the end it was
decided that the bales of flannel did not come up to
the sample, and the terms of the contract were very properly
enforced. The bales subsequently sent by the firm were
accepted; afterwards the firm boasted that the bales rejected
by the Deptford officers in the first instance were the identical
ones accepted in the second. When this came to the
knowledge of Sir John Pakington and the members of his
Board, they considered it a curious proceeding on the part
of the Deptford officers and could not account for it. I
respectfully reminded their lordships that it was only one
bale in ten that was opened and examined, and it was
therefore quite possible, in the delivery of such a large
number, to include a few of the rejected bales, just sufficient
to enable the firm to make the discreditable statement and
to throw unmerited odium upon the Deptford officers. The
lords saw the force of the observation, and a note was made
for the non-employment of that firm upon any future
occasion.

In consequence of a change of ministry a circumstance
occurred which showed the different manner in which public
business is conducted at the War Office as compared with
the Admiralty. When Mr. Sidney Herbert was appointed
Secretary at War, he requested Sir John Pakington to send
him some information he was anxious to obtain at once
(the Admiralty patent appointing the new Board with the
Duke of Somerset as First Lord not being ready). Sir John

Pakington had the information despatched immediately, the letter containing it being conveyed by a gentleman of the office to ensure its safe and prompt delivery, and not in the ordinary way by a messenger. Three days after Sir John received a second note from Mr. Herbert renewing the request, and showing some annoyance at this apparent neglect. Shortly after· a third note was received explaining the matter and offering an apology. The practice of the War Office, it appeared, differed from that of the Admiralty, the routine commencing in the reverse order. At the Admiralty all important letters directly they were received were opened by one of the Secretaries, or the reader, and if necessary instantly forwarded to the First Lord. At the War Office, as it seemed from the explanation, the letters were first registered, then sent to the branch to which they belong, passed through the hands of several clerks, and then forwarded to the Under Secretary, and by him to the Political Secretary, or laid before the Secretary of State. Thus three days elapsed before Mr. Sidney Herbert received the letter from Sir John Pakington, which was despatched from the Admiralty within half-an-hour of the receipt of the request contained in Mr. Sidney Herbert's first note.

CHAPTER XV.

'THE ADMINISTRATION OF THE DUKE OF SOMERSET, K G.,
28TH JUNE, 1859, TO 13TH JULY, 1866.

Progress in the construction of ironclads—Further improvements in the
ratings of petty officers—The sudden death of two naval lords—
Further efforts to increase the navy—The advantages of having
the professional opinions of the naval advisers made public—How
impossible it is to get at truth—Regulations amended in awarding
punishments at courts-martial—The interest taken in the "Woolwich
gun"—Lord Clarence Paget and the "missing two millions"—The
proposal to turn the marine corps into marine artillery to garrison
Malta and coaling-stations—The compassionate fund—The levelling
spirit of the age.

IN June, 1859, The Duke of Somerset was appointed
First Lord of the Admiralty. His Grace was a statesman
held in very high esteem, and had acquired· a considerable
reputation in the House of Commons as Lord St, Maur. He
had been chairman of several important committees, for
which he had been selected on account of his well-known
ability, sound judgment, and impartiality—qualities which
he displayed during his long tenure of office at the Admiralty,
where they are so much required. His promotions afforded
general satisfaction, which, considering the claims of the
many and the rare opportunities of meeting them, may be
regarded as a most unusual circumstance.

On the Duke's accession to office he was very ably supported by the naval members of his Board, who were—

Vice-Admiral the Hon Sir R S. Dundas, K.C.B.;
Rear-Admiral the Hon. F T. Pelham, C.B.;

Captain Charles Eden, C.B., R.N.;

Captain Charles Frederick, R N ;

Samuel Whitbread, Esq , M P.;

Rear-Admiral Lord Clarence Paget, C.B., M P., Political
Secretary;

W. G. Romaine, Esq , C B , Permanent Secretary.

Most of his Grace's naval advisers had had the recent
experience of active service, and had won distinction in
battle—at Sebastopol, Bomarsund, and elsewhere.   They
were therefore competent to give sound advice to the First
Lord.   Marked progress was made during this administration in the construction of ironclads, as will appear from the
following list :—

			Tons.
Launched 1860.	*Warrior*	. . . . .	9,210
„	1861.	*Black Prince*	9,210
„	„	*Defence*	6,270
„	„	*Resistance*	6,270
„	1862.	*Hector*	6,710
„	1863.	*Minotaur*	10,690
„	„	*Achilles*	9,820
„	„	*Valiant*	6,710
„	1865.	*Agincourt*	10,690
„	„	*Bellerophon*	7,550
„	„	*Lord Warden*	7,840

, His Grace also added three armoured floating batteries
(now designated coast-defence vessels), named *Prince Albert,*
Scorpion, and *Wivern,* as well as three armoured gunboats,
named *Water Witch, Viper,* and *Vixen.*   Slowly and steadily
were the great changes made in the navy which have entirely altered, not only the nature of the fleet, but the character of the naval profession.   Beautiful and imposing as
was the three-decker, with her stately masts and yards, three
tiers of cannon, and manned by a thousand gallant sailors,
she was, nevertheless, compelled to give place to a terrific and

unsightly monster, cased in iron and propelled by a moving
power which forces her through the water at the furious rate
of some twenty knots an hour, and discharges from a single
gun a weight of metal equal to that of the whole broadside
of the *Victory* at the battle of Trafalgar.   Great, indeed, are
the innovations wrought by science which have necessitated
a corresponding change in the training, education, and duties
of the naval officers of the present day.   The difficulties
encountered in effecting these great alterations were of no
ordinary character, requiring alike firmness and tact; for it
can be easily understood that all these changes were diametrically opposed to the prejudices and interests of the
heads of the profession, who were naturally indisposed to appreciate a system which tended to cast into the shade that skill
and seamanship which had obtained for them their professional
reputation.   Nor was this all; for, after the necessity for the
change had been reluctantly admitted, there was a great
diversity of opinion, not only amongst naval architects but
between experienced flag-officers, as to the construction of
ironclads, their size, protection, speed, and armament, which
has continued uninterruptedly up to the present date ; and,
therefore, when large sums of public money are to be
expended and warm controversy is the order of the day, it
behoves those in power to act with prudence and circumspection.   There were, however, several subjects unconnected
with expenditure which had for years engaged the attention
of the members of various Boards of Admiralty.   Many
valuable and important measures were introduced to ameliorate the naval service, especially the seamen, during the
administrations of Sir Charles Wood, Sir John Pakington,
and the Duke of Somerset.   Numerous salutary regulations
have been introduced from time to time tending materially
to improve the ratings and position of the working petty
officers, and, amongst others, may be enumerated good-service

badges, carrying an increase of pay; medals for long service
and good conduct have been more liberally distributed, the
position of the seamen-gunners had likewise been improved
in several respects, and more frequent indulgences in the
way of leave to go on shore to see their friends had been
extended, and, what is of still greater importance to the
seamen themselves, punishments had been reduced to a
consistent and uniform system, to which I shall more
particularly direct attention a little later

Sir Richard Dundas, like Sir Fanshawe Martin, had been
for years impressed with the grave responsibility which
devolve upon a First Sea Lord in the event of war, and
was directing his attention to the important subject of
meeting the great demands that would be made upon the
Admiralty in such an eventuality, when the navy was
suddenly deprived of his services by death. His loss was
greatly deplored throughout the service, and by everyone
connected with the Admiralty. After the briefest period the
Duke of Somerset sustained the further loss of his Second
Sea Lord, who died after a short illness. The melancholy
demise of these two distinguished admirals, following so
closely upon each other, cast a gloom over the department,
for they were much respected; and the efficient manner in
which they had taken up their responsibilities was recognised and appreciated by all those who entertained
advanced views upon naval affairs.

The vacancies thus created in the Board of his Grace were
filled up by the appointment of Rear-Admiral the Hon. Sir
Frederick Grey, K.C.B., the advancement of Captain Charles
Eden to be Second Sea Lord, and Captain the Hon. J. R.
Drummond again found a place at the Board as Fourth
Lord.*

* In 1863 the Marquess of Hartington (afterwards Duke of Devonshire)
was appointed Civil Lord.

The new First Sea Lord was as fully impressed with the inadequacy of the fleet, and the imperative necessity of making great additions to the navy, as had been his predecessor, and consequently many were the representations made to the Duke of Somerset as to the urgency that existed for an increased vote to place the navy on a footing equal to the duties that would be required of it in case of war Sir Frederick Grey was well supported by his naval colleagues and also by Mr. Romaine, one of the highest authorities upon naval affairs in the kingdom at the time. The Duke, I have every reason to believe, entirely concurred in their opinion, and, in accordance with their wishes, brought them under the consideration of the Cabinet; but his Grace always found the subject very distasteful to his colleagues, and especially to the Chancellor of the Exchequer. The Lords of the Admiralty naturally felt their position very invidious, as the state of Europe was very unsettled at the time, and war might have been declared at any moment; they knew the fleet had fallen far below the standard at which it should be if it was efficiently to discharge its duties, and they were well aware that, in case of failure, they would be held responsible for it by the country. It was not only in ships that the navy was deficient, but also as regards men and organisation. It is really for the interest of the country that some, measure should be adopted by which the responsible naval advisers of the Admiralty should have their opinions made known; either by embodying them in a report to the First Lord, to be submitted by him to the Cabinet with his views annexed, the final decision of course resting with the ministry, whose objections should be explained by the First Lord or Political Secretary to the House of Commons when the navy estimates are brought forward, or by some other method that would ensure their recommendation receiving proper attention. If some such course were pursued, it would lead to a more careful consideration of the real requirements of the service by the naval lords, whose proposals would be duly weighed and revised by the First Lord, and again approved, modified, or rejected by the Cabinet, as the case might be, and then the responsibility would be thrown upon those who were really to blame.

My official experience justifies me in stating that nothing is so difficult to obtain as really accurate information; the country never gets it, the House of Commons very seldom, and it is doubtful whether the Prime Minister himself is honestly furnished with what he requires. There is so much political, so much professional, so much departmental, and so much personal feeling brought to bear upon all occasions, and such a desire to conceal what is known to be unwelcome, and to present everything in the most favourable light, to meet the exigencies of the moment, that the information sought after, when supplied, bears little resemblance to facts. During the administration of Sir Robert Peel some circumstance occurred which led to his inquiring what steam-vessels could be got ready for sea on the shortest possible notice, and he wrote a confidential note to a member of the Board soliciting this information. Private instructions were given to me to prepare the return. I included every steam-vessel in it which appeared to me could, by any possibility, be got ready for sea on short notice. When I presented the list I was told that that was not at all what was wanted. I was then directed to prepare another from the Board-room book, enumerating the names of every steam-vessel in the navy, with tonnage, horse-power, etc. This list was at once despatched to Sir Robert Peel. Half-an-hour afterwards his private secretary came to the Admiralty with the return in question, and explained what the Prime Minister really required. I was again sent for, and reproduced my original return, which contained the information actually asked for;

L

but, in order to make a better show, I received positive directions to include not only vessels standing in need of extensive repairs, but several building upon the stocks, for which neither boilers nor machinery had even been ordered. I ventured a protest, but was assured, with a smile, that if they were really wanted for service they could soon be got ready if pressure was put upon the dockyards. This was a Tory Board, but to my certain knowledge Lord Palmerston, when Prime Minister, was some years after furnished with a return equally inaccurate and misleading.

It would really appear that in politics and diplomacy veracity was regarded as a superfluous and inconvenient virtue. One of the most serious complaints that can be brought against our system of administration is that we do not tell the truth to the English people; the Prime Minister himself cannot get at it, however anxious he may be to ascertain it. Misrepresentations such as these might lead to the most disastrous consequences. Foreign powers are kept well informed as to the minutest detail of everything that is taking place in all our naval ports by their naval attachés, the English people only being kept in ignorance.

During the administration of the Duke of Somerset some very valuable and much-needed regulations were drawn up by Sir Frederick Grey and Captain Eden * at the suggestion of Mr. Romaine, who had carefully read over all the minutes and sentences of the naval courts-martial, and, upon doing so, observed many grave irregularities and acts of injustice in the awarding of punishments for the same kind of offence, in some cases the sentences being unduly severe, and in others far too lenient. In fine, there was no order or system, the awarding of punishment all depending upon the view taken by the president of the court-martial on discipline and punishment;

* Afterwards Admiral Sir Charles Eden, K.C.B.

some flag-officers regarding drunkenness as the greatest of all crimes, and punished accordingly; others thought no crime equal to absence without leave, or not returning punctually at its expiration, others, again, considered disrespect in the light of mutiny, though the saucy answer might have come from a half-drunken man.

Men were sometimes tried for desertion and *found guilty of drunkenness*, and sentenced to be punished for an offence with which they had not been charged. A seaman at Devonport would be sentenced to three months' imprisonment with hard labour in Lewes Gaol. Another seaman at Portsmouth, guilty of the identical offence, would get off with only having his grog watered and his leave stopped for a week or ten days. These and other similar acts of uneven justice were brought under the especial notice of the several Commanders-in-chief at the home ports, and, in consequence, a code of rules was framed defining the amount of punishment to be awarded for the various offences prevalent amongst the seamen, so that each man distinctly understood the nature and the amount of punishment to which he was liable for any given offence. Thus, under this administration, a uniformity of punishment and a strict adherance to justice and fairness was established for the fleet at all the home ports. From time immemorial the crime of drunkenness has, unhappily, been one of the predominating vices of the naval service, and with a view to its repression may be traced many of those severe corporal punishments which excited so much adverse criticism. Sir James Dundas, who always had the good of the seamen at heart, when First Sea Lord,* succeeded in prevailing upon the Board of Admiralty to reduce the allowance of grog and substitute other articles of a wholesome and nutritious nature in its stead—a measure which has been attended with the most beneficial results, both as

* In Lord Auckland's administration, 1847.

regards health and discipline, and, contrary to expectation has given the greatest satisfaction to the seamen themselves.

The Duke of Somerset possessed very high scientific attainments, took great interest in gunnery and in the construction of heavy guns, and especially in the one known as the Woolwich gun. He also directed his attention to the state of the dockyards, and the system of dockyard accounts, which, from all time, seem to have been kept in a manner which would have puzzled the brains of so great an arithmetician as Michael Cassio himself, so impossible was it to understand them or put them on an intelligible basis.

Previous to Lord Clarence Paget's appointment as Civil Lord he had acquired great popularity in the House of Commons by taking up this very subject; he had been connected with the great shipbuilding firm of Green, where, it was assumed, he had gained a great insight into the manner in which the details and interior economy of so important a private establishment were carried on. His lordship undoubtedly possessed considerable ability, a keen knowledge of the world, and a still more acute perception of the prevailing humour of the House of Commons, and he was determined to befool it to the top of its bent. He had great tact, charming and persuasive manners, and an apparent sincerity of purpose which took with the House. He professed to have deeply studied the navy estimates, and, to the delight of that august body, he assured them that after a careful examination of naval expenditure he had arrived at the conclusion that two millions of money remained unaccounted for, under the head of dockyard and naval construction. There is nothing like doing things on a grand scale! His lordship undertook to explain by a series of statistics, tables of prices, etc.—which everybody found it convenient to believe, and no one felt called upon to investigate—how he had arrived at such a result.

Fortunately for Lord Clarence, a change of ministry took place about this time, and he was appointed Political Secretary of the Admiralty—a nomination which was regarded by the House of Commons as ample security that everything would be done that was right in that department.

What may be thought a piece of good fortune for Lord Clarence, and to which his cleverness fully entitled him, was regarded in a very different point of view by Sir Baldwin Walker, the Controller of the Navy, who felt that, in the eyes of the country, he was responsible for the missing two millions! Everybody that had the slightest acquaintance with Sir Baldwin knew him to be a public servant of great probity and ability, the very soul of honour and honesty, as well as a very gallant and distinguished naval officer. So ridiculous was the charge preferred against him that the very mention of two millions provoked a smile upon the countenance of everyone who knew anything of the subject.

I have, in the course of my life, witnessed some amusing comedies, but a more perfect burlesque than to see Sir Baldwin Walker, with a very grave face and a huge bundle of papers under his arm, requesting to be informed when it would be agreeable to Lord Clarence Paget to enter upon the investigation of the case, I never saw. His lordship constantly assured him that it was not at all a pressing matter—it was a very complex one, and would take up a great deal of time: it was not one that could by any possibility reflect personally upon Sir Baldwin; nevertheless, as he seems so much to desire it, he would go into the matter at once. At this juncture, strange to say, Mr. Charles Kempe, that able and most experienced of diplomatic private secretaries, made his appearance, and with a look of vexation handed to his chief a summons to the effect that the presence of Lord Clarence Paget was instantly required to make up a House. His lordship then, with a smile and shrug of the shoulders, said, "I have no alternative; I must obey the summons, as you know, my dear Walker, although it is very provoking," and then walked off, looking as disappointed as Sir Baldwin himself Provoking it certainly was to Sir Baldwin, for he did not regard the affair of the two millions in the same light-hearted and playful manner as the Political Secretary , and so the Controller once more retired with his bundle of papers under his arm, feeling vexed at this further postponement of his explanation, which had already been delayed several times. A similar summons has been useful to many a member of the Board at an inconvenient moment.

Lord Clarence Paget was Political Secretary during the seven years the Duke of Somerset was at the head of the Board of Admiralty, and, notwithstanding the fact that our views were diametrically opposed on naval affairs and public expenditure, Lord Clarence being a rigid economist and firm believer in the maintenance of a perpetual peace, he was one of the most amiable and agreeable Political Secretaries I ever had the honour of serving with There was one proposal made by Lord Clarence Paget in which I heartily concurred, and which, I trust, may eventually be carried into effect. I refer to his suggestion to convert the whole of the marine corps into marine artillery, and that several batteries may be stationed at Malta and Bermuda, and detachments told off for our coaling-stations and sea defences of our several dependencies It is artillery the navy stands most in need of, not light infantry.

The Duke of Somerset, in consequence of several strong representations made to him by the members of his Board, succeeded in prevailing upon the Treasury to make a considerable annual increase to the compassionate fund. Perhaps no public grant confers more real and substantial benefits upon its recipients, nor is more wisely or judiciously administered, than the funds placed at the disposal of their lordships. Few persons can form a remote conception of the very distressing and pitiable cases which are brought under their notice, or the depths of misery and suffering to which the widows and daughters and near relatives of distinguished naval officers who have rendered valuable services to their country are very frequently reduced. The cases are so numerous and so sad that the great difficulty is to decide which has the priority of claim. There are the claims of age and infirmity, as well as the sufferings of youth, and of those who, in the laudable effort to assist themselves by needlework, drawing, copying and teaching, injure their health and eyes to such an extent that they are threatened with a serious illness in the one case, and total loss of sight in the other, if they are unable to secure for a short time absolute secession from their arduous labours. Other cases occur in which widows of officers are left in such a state of pecuniary distress that they positively are unable to meet the expenses the funeral of the departed entail, provide decent mourning, or defray the bills for medical attendance.

I will mention one of the many melancholy instances which came under my own observation. Two orphan daughters of a captain in the navy, who kept a little school, had for a long time successfully struggled against many difficulties, when a visitation of scarlet fever broke up the school, carried off one of the sisters, leaving the other ill, alone, and involved in pecuniary troubles, and, had it not been for a small contribution opportunely received from the compassionate fund, this poor lady would never have been able to extricate herself from her financial difficulties.

I cannot speak too highly in praise of the trouble and pains taken by the members of the Board when investigating the claims of the numerous applicants, together with the services of the officers to whom they belong, so that the claims of the one may be weighed with the merits of the other. No politics, no private interest, nor favouritism of any kind, direct or indirect, have ever been permitted to influence a decision, each case being decided upon its own intrinsic merits.

Amongst the many lords of the Admiralty and naval officers none took a more lively interest in the administration of this admirable charity than the late Sir Charles Eden, who always stood the friend of the widow, the orphan, and all those in trouble and adversity. I never witnessed a more touching sight than that presented by those dear, kind, admirals devoting a whole morning to the consideration of the various claims submitted for their decision, and that, too, at a time when they felt they ought to be directing their attention to other duties of more public importance. Nothing could exceed their anxiety to turn to the best possible account the means placed at their disposal, so as to afford the greatest relief to all those in distress and sorrow.

It was during the administration of the Duke of Somerset that my duties as reader were brought to a close, his Grace being pleased to advance me to the office of chief clerk, a position of superior rank and emolument, but not so congenial to me as that of reader to the lords. It was with much sincere regret that I vacated a post the duties of which I had discharged for some thirty years, and which had placed me in close personal communication with many of the most distinguished statesmen of the day and the heads of the naval profession, from all of whom I had always received the greatest kindness and consideration, and which I shall ever bear in grateful recollection. Many great social changes had taken place during those thirty years, but the one I observed with most concern was the levelling spirit of the age, which had forced its way into even the Admiralty Board-room itself. Nothing could be more marked than the contrast between the respect and deference paid to Sir James

Graham, Lord de Grey, Lord Ellenborough and Lord Auckland, and to other First Lords of the Admiralty who held that high office at an earlier date. A more dignified or more courteous nobleman than the Duke of Somerset never presided at the head of the Board-room table, and yet I have seen his Grace enter the room for the despatch of public business with no one in waiting to receive him but the Permanent Secretary and myself.

CHAPTER XVI.

The Second Administration of the Rt. Hon. Sir John Pakington,* 13th July, 1866, to 8th March, 1867.

The advantages of the foreign policy and naval requirements being placed beyond the range of party strife—The continuous service system found to work well—The efficiency of the secretariate.

In 1866 Sir John Pakington again resumed the office of First Lord of the Admiralty, the duties of which he had so ably and satisfactorily discharged when his party was in power in 1858. Sir John Pakington entertained the same views in regard to naval affairs as the Duke of Somerset, and, consequently, there was no marked difference between his policy and that of his Grace which calls for special notice.

The members of his Board were—

Vice-Admiral Sir Alexander Milne, K.C B ;
Vice-Admiral Sir Sydney Dacres, K C.B.;
Rear-Admiral G. H. Seymour, C.B., M.P.;
Rear-Admiral Sir J. C. D. Hay, Bart., C.B.;
Charles Du Cane, Esq , M.P.;
Lord H. G. Lennox, Political Secretary.
W. G. Romaine, Esq , C B., Permanent Secretary.

There had been a growing conviction amongst the leading statesmen of both parties that it would greatly contribute to the best interests of the country if they could come to

* Created Baron Hampton in 1874.

some understanding upon the foreign policy of the nation. There is no doubt that we have been placed at a great disadvantage, by frequent changes in the ministry, in consequence of having no continuity of policy at the Foreign Office, which has raised grave doubts as to whether agreements entered into with one party might not, from political motives, be overthrown by a change of ministry in England. Stability is the only basis upon which diplomatic relations can be successfully sustained. Not less important would it be if the two political parties could be brought to consider the question of national defence from the point of view of efficiency both as regards our naval and military forces, free from all political controversy, and discover some means by which an agreement could be entered into for the permanent maintenance of this important object, and so prevent that painful exhibition of exaggeration and misrepresentation as evident on the one side as on the other.* The opposition invariably denounce the demands of those in power as extravagant, unnecessary, and tending to a warlike policy. This naturally excites undue apprehension both at home and abroad, disturbs the finances of the country, checks commercial enterprise, and greatly increases the difficulties of those in office, who, under the most favourable auspices, are at all times disinclined to incur any expenditure which they can, with any degree of propriety, avoid.

It is deplorable to be compelled to admit that, for party purposes alone, charges and counter-charges of the most wild and baseless character, and comparisons of the most ridiculous description, are bandied about from one side of the House of Commons to the other until the thoughtful and sober-minded public feel themselves utterly incapable of understanding the real position of affairs.

Sir John Pakington found the Cabinet of Lord Derby,

* This seems now to be the case.—En.

quite as disinclined to incur increased expense on behalf
of the navy as the Duke of Somerset experienced when
representing to the Cabinet of Lord Palmerston the strongly
expressed opinions of his naval advisers.

Until the country is really made acquainted, year by year,
with the proposals of the naval members of the Board of
Admiralty, and the distinct grounds upon which their
suggestions are offered, there cannot fail to be, from time
to time, those spasmodic panics which occasion mistrust and
lead to hasty and injudicious expenditure. Although no grand
and comprehensive measure had been brought forward to
place the fleet in a condition to meet the requirements that
the advance of science had wrought, or to ameliorate the
congested state of the navy lists, still many improvements
had gradually been introduced. The continuous service
system had been found to work with marked success; ships
were commissioned, prepared for sea, and provided with
efficient crews with an alacrity unknown in the days of
Sir George Cockburn and Mr. Croker. Great progress had
been made, through the untiring efforts of Sir Charles Eden,
of bringing into practical utility at short notice the seamen
of the coastguard, and to render the naval volunteers more
efficient, especially in gunnery. Thus a reserve was formed
capable of making an addition to the seamen of the fleet
upon any pressing or sudden emergency. The training of
the boys for the navy was likewise attended with very
beneficial results. None but lads of superior physique,
promising intelligence, and good character were admitted
into the service, an entry to which was regarded as a piece
of good fortune by their relatives and friends. The consequence of all this has been that the continual service
system has reared up a class of men-of-warsmen so respectable, intelligent, and well-conducted, that all those punishments and restrictions upon leave and other indulgencies

can be safely dispensed with, as now every confidence can be placed in their integrity and good behaviour.

The Secretary's office had always been considered as in a very efficient state in the days of Sir John Barrow and Captain Baillie Hamilton; but, without entering into comparisons, it was never in a more satisfactory condition than whilst Mr. Romaine was Permanent Secretary. This efficiency may be attributed solely to his personal supervision of everything that took place in the office; there was not a letter that came into it that he did not read through with its enclosures, nor one to which he affixed his signature which he did not first peruse.

He was generally at his post by half-past eight in the morning, in order to open the more important despatches, and seldom left before six or seven in the evening, and, not unfrequently, would sit up in his own house until one or two o'clock in the morning, going over voluminous minutes of courts-martial, the results of which he would summarise and bring under the consideration of the naval lords.

Sir John Pakington, on leaving office, entertained so high an opinion of the valuable assistance he had received during his two administrations from Mr. Romaine, that he left a memorandum on record of a most flattering character, expressive of his satisfaction of the highly efficient state of the secretariate, and the promptness with which all questions were answered and papers produced.

The duties of the Permanent Secretary of the Admiralty are at all times of a most responsible and laborious character, demanding unremitting attention and the sacrifice of all personal enjoyment, as it is impossible to anticipate the events which, in a department like the Admiralty, suddenly present themselves.

CHAPTER XVII.

THE ADMINISTRATION OF THE RIGHT HON. H. T. L. CORRY
8TH MARCH, 1867, TO 18TH DECEMBER, 1868.

The want of basins, docks, and building slips—Rigid economy quite as
urgently enforced by one party as by the other—Confidence should
be placed in the First Lord of the Admiralty—Disinclination to trust
to steam-power alone—The conflict between the ship and the gun an
excuse for not spending money—Mr. Corry's knowledge of dockyards
—The disadvantages of having officials located in private houses that
have been turned into public offices—The lack of fine public buildings
—An anecdote in reference to the National Gallery—The Prince
Consort's interest in South Kensington Museum.

MR. CORRY, upon the accession of Mr. Disraeli to power, was
appointed First Lord of the Admiralty on the 8th March,
1867. It will be seen, by reference to these pages, that
Mr. Corry, in the early days of his official career, had
exhibited great zeal and ability as Civil Lord, under the
administration of the Earl of Haddington, and directed his
special attention to the want of proper basin accommodation,
docks, and building slips in our several naval arsenals. As
Political Secretary he rendered valuable services during the
administration of the Earl of Ellenborough, and in the same
capacity under the administration of Sir John Pakington.
The members of his Board were the same as in the preceding
administration.*

(Now that Mr. Corry had at last attained to the height of

* In September, 1868, the Hon. F. A. Stanley (afterwards Lord Stanley
of Preston, and now Earl of Derby) was appointed Civil Lord in succession
to Mr. Charles Du Cane.

his ambition, and to which his long service and intimate acquaintance with the Admiralty management of naval affairs so fully entitled him, he looked forward with sanguine hopes to the realisation of the various measures he had so long wished to see accomplished. But it unfortunately happened in his case (as in that of many others) that, at the very moment the opportunity he had looked forward to arrived, unexpected and insurmountable difficulties presented themselves to baffle and defeat his plans. Mr. Corry soon discovered that the Cabinet of Mr. Disraeli regarded rigid economy quite as essential for the retention of office as the Government they had just succeeded; for both parties had vied with each other as to the imperative necessity of reduction in the two great spending departments, so that any change of policy in that particular could not be advanced with any degree of consistency. It is greatly to be deplored that the two great leading statesmen of that day, possessing so many grand qualifications for their high office, should have permitted party feelings to predominate to such an extent as to blind them to the necessity of placing the naval power of this great kingdom upon a footing more commensurate with its augmented wealth, increased Colonial Empire, and an expanding commerce of unprecedented magnitude. But, alas! so it was; and Mr. Corry for some time experienced a persistent opposition on the part of the Treasury to the most moderate and reasonable demands, made upon the recommendation of the naval members of the Board over which he presided.

So systematic were these refusals becoming, to both the Admiralty and War Office, that Mr. Corry found it necessary to address himself to the higher authorities on the subject, as he had every reason to believe that the representations made by their lordships were never brought under the personal notice of either the First Lord of the Treasury or

the Chancellor of the Exchequer, but were dealt with, after
a somewhat summary fashion, by official subordinates anxious
to obtain for themselves a character for zeal and economy
from their departmental superiors by keeping down the
estimates and reducing expenditure.

The complaints then preferred by the Admiralty and War
Office are identical with those more recently made by various
departments of the public service; and the *Times* has, in
several admirable leading articles, set forth the well-grounded
dissatisfaction expressed by influential and experienced public
servants as to the scant attention paid by the Treasury to
their well-considered representations in regard to the improvement of their several departments. Mr. Corry was
quite as anxious as any other Cabinet minister to meet the
views of the ministry in respect to economy, and was
disposed to enforce it, both in the Admiralty and dockyards;
but, as First Lord of the Admiralty, grave responsibilities
devolved upon him; and both he and his colleagues felt
certain that there were some measures essential for the
efficiency of the navy to which no reasonable objection could
have been raised by the Treasury on the score of expense
if the recommendations had been duly considered.

It is but right and proper that a certain amount of
confidence should be placed in statesmen filling the high
offices of First Lord of the Admiralty and Secretary of State
for War, as they represent the opinions of the most distinguished officers of the two services, purposely selected to
act as their professional advisers, for it cannot be expected
that either the Prime Minister or the Chancellor of the
Exchequer can spare the time to master all the numerous
and complicated naval and military questions, and the solid
grounds on which they are based; but certainly it is not in
order that the submissions of their respective departments
should be refused upon the mere reports of subordinates in

the Treasury, who are utterly ignorant of the importance of the recommendations, the rejection of which might seriously effect the best interests of the naval and military establishments of the country. This has been frequently done without even an opportunity being given to the First Lord or the Secretary of State for affording any explanation.

At this period opinion in naval circles was very much divided. The young and scientific naval officers (who knew from practical experience the value of steam and the importance of modern projectiles) had not then attained to that rank and position in the service which gave that weight to their opinions which they really deserved.

Mr Corry was placed at this disadvantage in consequence of the various views entertained by the leading members of the profession, not only as to the intrinsic value of ironclads, but as to their mode of construction, thickness of plating, and points of defence, as well as to their size, horse-power, and coal endurance.

The officers of the old school were compelled to admit, from the force of public opinion, that ironclads might be valuable in time of war, but, at the same time, they were very disinclined to trust to steam-power alone, and consequently insisted on the employment of masts and yards as indispensable adjuncts to their equipment and safety, seamanship naturally enough being always uppermost in their minds. Hence the construction of the *Captain*, the disastrous loss of which ultimately settled the question

, The next difficulty interposed to onward progress was the long-disputed conflict between the ship and the gun Armour-plates of augmented resisting power were manufactured in rapid succession by various energetic and enterprising firms; whilst, on the other hand, corresponding efforts were being made to increase the size and piercing power of the gun; so that the relative advantages trembled

M

in the balance, and a final decision was necessarily deferred. Nor was this all; so great was the revolution in the construction of our ships, that it became only too evident that the period was fast approaching when the whole fleet must be replaced by another more in accordance with the requirements of the day. To suddenly effect such a change would have involved an immense increase of expenditure, and, considering the various views entertained, sound and rational grounds were afforded for postponement, as all parties admitted that the more prudent course to adopt would be to cause further experiments to be made, both as to the resisting power of the armour-plates and the piercing power of the guns, which latter were being as rapidly improved as the armour-plates were being strengthened The discussion on these points waxed warm. It was maintained that the armour-plating was insufficient to render the security of the ship complete; whilst others argued that the rotatory motion of the turret would be impeded by a single shot. But when an experiment was made upon the *Royal Sovereign*, and though no less than four shots were fired at the turret at right angles at a distance of two hundred yards (all of which struck), yet not the slightest injury was inflicted to the rotary movement of the turret, so great is the difference between practice and theory. Naval experts also expressed their opinions very freely in reference to target practice. To fire at a target on shore, with backing and earthworks behind at right angles, was not considered a satisfactory test as to the amount of injury likely to be inflicted upon a floating body yielding to the force of a blow which would, in all probability, hit the vessel obliquely, especially if steaming at great speed; in addition to which there is extreme difficulty in accuracy of aim when taken from a floating body as compared with a stationary battery.

The relative value of guns of great size, worked by

hydraulic pressure, was found to combine so many difficulties in ensuring correctness of aim, that there always has been a great diversity of opinion upon the subject amongst the most skilful and experienced officers of the *Excellent* and *Cambridge,* a controversy which remains unsettled to this day

The question of expense weighed heavily with the ministry, as it was evident the construction of ironclads of increased size, with powerful machinery and modern armaments, must necessarily lead to an ultimate expenditure the extent of which it would be impossible to forecast, and that at the very time when political considerations demanded a reduction of taxation which was incompatable with an increase to the estimates. It was impossible to deny that, if the necessity for this great change was once sanctioned, it must year by year lead to a compulsory demand for more ships, more costly machinery, more guns and ammunition of a far more expensive nature ; therefore it was decided to stave off the evil day to a more convenient season.

Many distinguished admirals at this period still held to the opinion that, after the efficiency of ironclads had been fully tested, it would in the end be found necessary to revert again to the construction of wooden vessels for the purposes of war.

Such were the financial, professional, and scientific difficulties which presented themselves to Mr. Corry upon his accession to the office of First Lord of the Admiralty; but so brief was his tenure of that office that, notwithstanding his earnest desire to bring these questions to a satisfactory solution, he was reluctantly compelled to bequeath to others what he himself had so anxiously hoped to achieve.

Few First Lords were more intimately acquainted with the internal management of the dockyards than Mr. Corry , for, from his earliest introduction to the naval department, as Civil Lord, and subsequently as Secretary, he had made it his especial study, and so personally was he acquainted with the dockyard officers and many of the artificers, that his appointment to office was regarded by them with as much satisfaction as his retirement from it was deeply regretted. He was recognised by all as a minister who thoroughly knew what was required for the good of the service, and would forward, to the best of his ability, the substantial interests of those who were zealous and efficient in the discharge of their respective duties.

Lord Henry Lennox, who was Political Secretary with both Sir John Pakington and Mr. Corry, took almost as great an interest in the shipbuilding programmes, and the condition of the artificers and workmen in the establishments under Admiralty control, as even the First Lord himself

Mr. Corry, during his long Admiralty experience, had felt the great inconvenience of the subordinate departments being so far distant from the Admiralty at Whitehall, and the delay which took place in communicating with the principal officers at Somerset House and elsewhere. He was thoroughly convinced, from the rapidly increasing business of the Admiralty, that the time had arrived when a building should be erected capable of embracing within its precincts all the various branches under Admiralty control.

Few people have any idea of the fearful waste of time which was, and in a less degree is still, occasioned from the want of intercommunication between the different branches of the Admiralty, and the constant and well-founded complaints preferred by those who are sent from place to place to obtain some information of pressing importance ; and as to the disadvantage of locating the officials of a great department in private houses converted into public offices, I can bring my personal testimony to bear as to the ill effects it has upon the health of the Government *employés*, which is chiefly due to the want of those sanitary arrangements that cannot, from their construction, be expected in buildings erected for the use of private families. Nothing can be more fatal to health, efficiency, discipline, and comfort than the makeshift system pursued twenty-five years ago, and which exists, to some extent, to this very hour. The sums of money which have been annually expended in providing temporary accommodation for officials who cannot be located in the offices to which they respectively belong, would have been more than ample for the erection of suitable buildings, and that upon a scale commensurate with the requirements of the public services in a great maritime and commercial country like this. Why is it that London should be the ugliest, dirtiest, and worse-managed capital in all Europe, although it is admitted to be the largest, the most populous, and the wealthiest, of them all ? Why is it that London is deficient in all those public buildings which not only add to the splendour of continental capitals, but contribute so materially, at the same time, to the convenience and comfort of the public at large ?

It is because successive governments have been more deeply interested in maintaining themselves in office, and pandering to the never-ending and senseless cry of reduced estimates, than bringing forward measures which they know to be indispensably necessary for the honour and safety of the country, and the dignity and beauty of the capital. Recent events have gone far to prove that, when a ministry has the courage of its opinions, and fairly and honestly places before the country what is required for its best interests, there is no lack of response either on the part of the public or their representatives. Party spirit soon disappears, and a better and more patriotic feeling prevails, and a liberal grant is soon forthcoming. A bold stroke of policy is always admired and appreciated by Englishmen. It is impossible to suppose that it is the wish of the people of this country that, at the end of the nineteenth century, England should still be without an

Admiralty deserving the name, or a War Office, a Treasury, or other public buildings absolutely necessary for the efficient discharge of the duties of the public service. Such public buildings are to be found in nearly all the capitals of second-rate Powers, and are as remarkable for external beauty as for internal convenience.

Perhaps the National Gallery exhibits the most melancholy specimen that could be adduced of ill-judged parsimony, and has occasioned for years more adverse criticism than any other edifice in the metropolis. An amusing anecdote was told to me in reference to a practical joke played upon Lord Althorp (the late Earl Spencer) when Chancellor of the Exchequer His lordship was fully aware of the very unfavourable criticisms passed upon his well-intentioned and economical makeshift. Mr. Croker, in those days, had the reputation of being among the few who were regarded as men of taste. A wag assured Lord Althorp that Mr. Croker had spoken in eulogistic terms of his architectural bantling, and upon Lord Althorp meeting Mr. Croker at an evening party, he said, with his characteristic simplicity, " I am told that you are one of the few who admire my National Gallery ; is it so ? " " Certainly," replied Mr. Croker ; " I admire it above all things, for I regard it as a most successful architectural embodiment of the views of your party. It is low, mean, and withal, presumptuous ; low in stature, mean in architecture, and presumptuous from its impertinent intrusion into a position it could never have been intended to occupy." I think it may fairly be assumed that Lord Althorp never again requested Mr Croker's opinion upon any of his achievements. And there it remains to this day, a standing monument of ugliness, bad taste, and misplaced economy.

It is necessary to explain to the uninitiated that this unsightly structure was erected for the sole purpose of turning to profitable account the old columns of Carlton

House, and in order to save these half-dozen columns, the beauty of the finest site in all London has been destroyed, and now, fifty years afterwards, this miserable and unfortunate precedent is being followed in regard to the Admiralty, in this instance, as in the former, under the pretence of economy. The hideous wing of the old Admiralty, which, as reported, cannot last more than seventy years, and has its foundation upon the mud of the Thames, is to have an addition made to it in flaring red brick, quite out of keeping with all its surroundings.* This economical arrangement will have the double advantage of disfiguring St. James's Park and preventing all improvements in Whitehall. But there is, unhappily, another building in London which no Englishman can behold without a feeling of shame, and with a sense of deep ingratitude to one of the most illustrious and enlightened Princes this country has ever known. I need scarcely say I refer to the late Prince Consort and the external appearance and surroundings of the South Kensington Museum. When we consider the many national benefits that have accrued from this magnificent school of art, it is to be deeply deplored that the labours of its illustrous founder should have been so imperfectly recognised, and that the unrivalled contents of this grand institution should still remain without an edifice worthy of their reception †

* The new Admiralty buildings have since been completed. The stone facings tone down the red to a certain degree.

† It is a pity that the Government could not see their way to finish this building as a national memorial for Her Majesty's long reign commemoration. It would have been a compliment to the Prince Consort and gratifying to the Queen.—ED.

CHAPTER XVIII.

THE ADMINISTRATION OF THE RT. HON HUGH CHILDERS, 18TH DECEMBER, 1868, TO 13TH MARCH, 1871.

A memorable administration—Naval retirement scheme, the difficulties encountered—Ships sent to relieve others as a matter of course —A change in the composition of two squadrons on foreign stations which added three thousand men to the fighting strength of the fleets—Efficient ironclads as coastguard ships instead of obsolete vessels—The formation of a training squadron for boys, and the sending it to sea during the winter months—The advantages of reviving, as an Admiral's command, the Brazilian station—The difficulties caused by the injudicious composition of the Board and the distribution of business—The amalgamation and consolidation of the civil department of the Admiralty—The superiority of Sir James Graham's system—A plan suggested to put a stop to dissensions which did much towards bringing on the illness which ultimately compelled the First Lord to retire—The old nomenclature of the regiments of the army—The retirement of the author from the Admiralty.

MR. GLADSTONE, on his accession to power in 1868, placed Mr. Childers at the head of the Board of Admiralty. The members of his Board were—

Vice-Admiral Sir Sydney Dacres, K.C B ;

Vice-Admiral Sir R. Spencer Robinson, K.C.B. ;

Captain Lord John Hay, C.B.. R.N., M.P. (Controller of the Navy);

G. O. Trevelyan, Esq., M P. ;*

W. E. Baxter, Esq , M.P., Political Secretary ;

W. G. Romaine, Esq., C.B., Permanent Secretary.

* The Earl of Camperdown succeeded in 1870, as Civil Lord, Mr. G. O. Trevelyan (afterwards Sir George O. Trevelyan).

This administration will be for ever a memorable one, for it marks a great era in the naval history of the country, by drawing the line of demarkation between the system that had so long prevailed and the one which has, in spite of many difficulties, reached the happy consummation that now characterises the navy and all that appertains to it

Mr. Childers' great and comprehensive scheme of naval retirement effected the most benificent and complete change throughout the whole service, and to it can chiefly be traced those important changes which have been so successfully introduced during the last few years.

It not infrequently happens that measures which confer substantial good upon the country, and permanent benefits upon a profession, are but imperfectly appreciated by the former and insufficiently recognised by the latter, the good to the country being rather prospective than immediate; and in regard to the advantages conferred upon a profession, no measure that could be devised could possibly be gratifying to all alike.

Admirable and successful as Mr. Childers' scheme of naval retirement has proved to be, it was at first very distasteful to many distinguished officers, whose personal interest was somewhat affected. But they who remember the feeling of general discontent which for years was chronic throughout the service, consequent upon the slowness of promotion, want of employment and favouritism, which was evident in the selection of officers for commands, will, I am sure, bear their voluntary and impartial testimony to the general improvement and contentment which happily now prevails amongst the officers in the Royal Navy.

Mr. Childers fully realised the money difficulties and other objections he would have to encounter in his endeavour to carry to a successful issue his contemplated plan, coming not only from the heads of the naval profession, and, in no slight degree, from the Treasury, but from the members of his own Board, who, when considering proposals in regard to it, looked at them from two points of view; first, how they would affect their own personal interest, and, secondly, how they would interfere with the advancement of their friends.   Many preceding administrations were fully impressed with the necessity of bringing forward some plan of naval retirement, but all had shirked a duty which they knew would certainly entail great unpopularity upon themselves, and prove very displeasing to the distinguished Admirals at the head of the list.   Mr. Childers plainly foresaw that until some scheme of retirement was put into force, which would diminish the crowded state of the Navy List, it would be impossible to remove the cause for those numerous and well-grounded complaints, and the general discontent which was known to exist.   Moreover, he well knew, from his previous Admiralty experience, that until the higher ranks of the profession were filled with younger officers, better able to appreciate, from their recent practical experience and scientific attainments, all those innovations and improvements which had become so imperatively necessary to meet the requirements of modern warfare, no satisfactory progress could be achieved.

So fully impressed was Mr. Childers with the paramount importance of carrying his measure into practical effect, that until it was accomplished he felt that it would be futile for him to attempt to introduce the various other reforms which he contemplated for the good of the service.

It is now over twenty years since this invaluable measure was carried, and the substantial and lasting benefits it has conferred upon the country, and more especially upon the service, are as yet but partially understood, and its advantages are but imperfectly appreciated by the profession which has so greatly benefited by its liberal provisions.   On all such occasions much is heard of grievances, real and imaginary, whilst a prudent reserve is strictly maintained by those who reap the harvest.

Too much praise cannot be awarded Mr. Childers for the energy he displayed, the opposition he knowingly encountered, and the firmness with which he carried this great measure to a successful issue, and it is only they who were officially associated with him at the time who are able to form an approximate estimate of the difficulties with which, from first to last, he had to contend, and know the unpopularity it occasioned   The next subject to which Mr. Childers directed his especial attention was the composition and distribution of the fleet, one of as great national importance as his scheme of naval retirement; for upon its composition and distribution so much depend, both as regards the protection of our commerce and the safety of our shores and maritime ports; and it is much to be regretted that, until Mr. Childers' accession to office, it was a matter which did not sufficiently engage the attention of naval administrations; in fine, little or none was paid to it.   No arguments were needed to convince the First Lord of the inadequacy of the naval protection for the Channel and home ports, or the insufficiency of the navy to meet any sudden emergency.   He was often struck by the system of routine, which seemed to have become a confirmed official habit.   At the expiration of three years ships were relieved, as a matter of course, by vessels of exactly the same type, without any inquiry being made as to whether they were absolutely necessary, whether a squadron might not be improved in some instances by vessels of a superior force, or whether those of an inferior type might not with benefit be substituted, so as to render, if necessary, an additional number of seamen available.

For many years a 130-gun ship, with 1100 men, was stationed at Malta, and had war broken out must either have sought protection under the batteries of Malta, or run the risk of being captured or sunk by a modern ironclad in her endeavour to reach a home port As this flagship was seldom at sea the younger officers had few opportunities of improving their nautical knowledge, which they should have done instead of imbibing those expensive habits and tastes for pleasure too evident at the military messes of the garrisons in the Mediterranean. The *Caledonia* was accordingly ordered home and put out of commission, her crew providing ships' companies for no less than three ironclads. Four large 50-gun frigates were likewise stationed in the West Indies, performing a duty very gratifying no doubt to the vanity of the consuls and vice-consuls, and were unquestionably of use at the time when slavery was first abolished and insurrections anticipated; but as their services were no longer required in that locality, they too were ordered home and paid off, their duties being since efficiently discharged by the steam-vessels on the station paying occasional visits to the several islands. This change effected upon these two stations alone placed nearly 3000 men at the disposal of the Board of Admiralty.

Mr. Childers had been long enough in official life to know that money or financial grants were not obtainable, so he considered how he could best augment the fighting power of the navy with the ships and means placed at his disposal. Modern ironclads, as a rule, do not require anything like the number of seamen that were necessary for sailing line-of-battleships and frigates; therefore, by commissioning the former, the men go much further and greatly add to the numerical as well as to the real fighting efficiency of the fleet. With a view to strengthen the Channel fleet, and to render it really effective at the outbreak of war, Mr. Childers took the initiative in introducing that judicious arrangement of substituting efficient ironclads at the several coastguard stations instead of the obsolete vessels then employed—a system now brought to great perfection by successive Boards of Admiralty, as year by year the ironclads of an earlier date have been gradually replaced by vessels of the most approved and powerful type; so that now some ten or twelve battleships could be added to the Channel fleet in the course of a few days.

Another most important measure introduced by Mr Childers was the formation of a training squadron for the practical instruction, in navigation and seamanship, of the junior officers of the navy, as well as the ordinary seamen and boys, so as to accustom them to the duties and habits incidental to sea life ; and so useful has it proved that it justifies its existence to this day. The squadron has hitherto been composed of four powerful corvettes under the command of a commodore, and has doubtless much to recommend it in various ways To enumerate a few: it imparts, to a certain degree, tactical knowledge in naval evolutions, and inspires an amount of rivalry in the several vessels which causes emulation, and so prevents that apathy and indifference which sometimes occur in ships sailing singly ; whereas, those in company are kept alive by the knowledge that, both night and day, they are under the immediate eye of a superior officer, who will direct attention to any vessel not keeping the exact position she ought to maintain, no matter what that formation may be. The exercises carried out on board the squadron are of the most varied and interesting character, embracing every branch of the service, from practical seamanship to gunnery and torpedo-firing, as well as the broadsword exercise and the use of the rifle and revolver. The result is that, when officers and men are drafted from thence into sea-going ships, they have passed through an apprenticeship which qualifies them to discharge, to a certain extent, many of the duties they would be called upon to perform. This cruising squadron, in addition, has many other advantages: it generally visits, during the winter season, the Tagus, Gibraltar, the Balearic Islands, Tangiers, and Morocco, proceeding from thence to the Azores, and stretching to the West Indies, and after visiting the several islands returns home early in the month of May. The squadron is always within cable communication with the Admiralty, and can therefore be utilised in any little emergency which may unexpectedly arise, and put in an appearance where least expected.

As masts and yards are so rapidly disappearing, and seamanship year by year diminishing in importance, it now becomes a question for consideration whether it is not more advisable to substitute four of our most efficient second-class steam-cruisers in the place of the four steam and sailing corvettes now composing the training squadron   Surely, for purposes of instruction, it would be far better to train the officers and men in those especial duties they will be called upon to perform, and in the class of vessels in which they will in future be required to serve.   It is not so much seamen who are required in these days as engineers, artificers, stokers and coal-trimmers, torpedo-men, seamen-gunners, and, last but not least, signalmen; for it is only on board steam-vessels that a knowledge of these duties is obtainable, and there cannot be a doubt, in any unprejudiced mind, that in the event of war four powerful steam-cruisers, always in a high state of efficiency, would be of far greater service for any pressing duty the Admiralty might be called upon to provide for than the steam and sailing corvettes now in commission. But this only leads up to the consideration of a question of greater moment.   The expansion of the navy is becoming year by year a growing necessity.   The system inaugurated by Mr. Childers is one that admits of fuller development.   The composition and distribution of the fleet should, previous to the preparation of the navy estimates, be carefully revised,

not only with a due regard to the men asked for, but with
reference to the requirements of each station, and the class of
ships best suited for the performance of the various duties
belonging to each particular station, so as to meet those
changes which must arise in the course of each succeeding
year, and thus ensure, as far as possible, those two most
desired objects, namely, economy combined with efficiency.
When the composition and distribution of the fleet is under
discussion, it would be very desirable to ascertain what
tactical combinations could be made, so as to ensure the ships
upon one station being able to render prompt support to
those upon another, and to make such arrangements as would
secure the arrival of a concentrated force where needed and
when least expected. The difficulties of former years have
disappeared, as the Admiralty is in direct cable communication with all our foreign naval stations, and changes can now
be effected both promptly and secretly. The reduction of
the squadron on the south-east coast of America, and its
abolition as an Admiral's command, has long been regarded
by able and experienced strategists as a mistake, and there is
a growing opinion in naval circles that its revival is very
necessary for reasons readily recognised. British interests in
the Brazils and the south-east coast of America are very
great, as has been most unfortunately demonstrated in the
recent revolutions both at Rio de Janeiro and the Argentine
Republic. Therefore, the stationing of a few powerful steam-
cruisers at Rio could not fail to be of the greatest possible
advantage to the political as well as commercial interests of
this country. There is no station that occupies so central
and commanding a position as Rio; cruisers could be despatched from thence, at a moment's notice, to the Pacific,
China and Australia, as well as to the Cape, the east coast
of Africa, India, and the Strait Settlements by cable from
Whitehall with as much secrecy as despatch. It is not at all

necessary for British interests that foreign powers should know the exact position and movements of all our ships-of-war or the combinations the Admiralty may be able to make with them. It is a subject upon which greater reticence might be advantageously maintained.

The re-establishment of the Brazil station as an Admiral's command is a policy I have earnestly advocated for years. It was abolished, in a fit of economy, to the great detriment of the commercial interest of the country.

From my personal knowledge of Mr. Childers, I am perfectly satisfied he did the utmost in his power (as I have already stated) to increase the fighting strength of the fleet in commission, although he was unable to obtain a vote for an additional number of seamen, or for the construction of iron-clads, still he so far prevailed upon the Chancellor of the Exchequer as to obtain an annual vote for those grand works which were recently completed at Portsmouth and Chatham under the supervision of that distinguished and able engineer officer, Sir Andrew Clarke. These fine works, in the event of war, would prove of incalculable value by facilitating the equipment of several vessels at the same time, which otherwise might have become a tardy and difficult process.

The naval administration of Mr Childers was unquestionably a most important one, and will be long remembered by the many statutory reforms, long needed, which he carried to a successful issue. He had previously served as Civil Lord under the Duke of Somerset, and in the discharge of the duties of that office displayed great ability and aptitude for business. It was at this time I became personally acquainted with him, and many opportunities were afforded me of discussing with him Admiralty and naval affairs. A few weeks before his accession to the office of First Lord, he published a pamphlet, and paid me the compliment of sending me a copy, requesting at the same time that I would offer any remarks that might occur to me in reference to its contents The pamphlet struck me as a remarkably able one. I expressed my opinions very freely, and threw out several suggestions which met with his approval, and when he was, a few weeks afterwards, appointed First Lord he bore them in remembrance.

I also drew up for his perusal (after he had taken his seat at the head of the Board of Admiralty) a memorandum on the organisation of the navy, which, as it bears somewhat on the deficiencies complained of in the Duke of Wellington's letter of twenty years before, and also tends to confirm the statements in Lord Charles Beresford's confidential memorandum of twenty years after, I will reproduce it.

MEMORANDUM ON THE ORGANISATION OF THE NAVY.

THE most important events in this world are generally alike unexpected and sudden.

No better illustration of this truth can be adduced than in the occurrences of the last twelve years, and in those of the most recent date.

Whether we look across the Atlantic or nearer home, the events themselves, and their results, have been totally at variance with the preconceived opinions of the wisest statesmen and the most able commanders.

In America, the Southern States have not achieved their independence ; whilst in Europe, the military power, held by professional officers in the highest repute, succumbs, after the briefest of campaigns, before a Prussian army, heretofore estimated by military men as little better than a well-drilled militia.

The war in America demonstrates the advantages of numbers, the inestimable importance of fortified cities, and the value of the spade in all military operations, whilst the late war in Europe has set forth the superiority acquired by

N

departmental organisation, and the prompt adoption of the most approved arms of precision.

The needle-gun may have done much, but it is unmistakably evident that the grand success of the campaign was attributable to the excellence of the Prussian organisation.

It is to this very question of organisation I beg to be pardoned if I venture to direct your lordship's attention, not as relates to the army, as that is not in my province, but in reference to the navy, upon which, for the present at all events, the nation must mainly depend for national defence.

In stating this, I do so advisedly, for our fortifications are for the most part unfinished, and those which are completed are without their armament and garrisons. Our standing army is numerically insignificant, our militia is untrained, and our Volunteers devoid of that very organisation which is so much needed to render the force available at the moment of danger.*

The navy is, and ever has been, our national and our popular defence, but it is no longer the navy of which our forefathers had so much reason to be proud.

Then the navy of Great Britain held the supremacy of the seas, and would have given battle to the combined fleets of the whole world ; now she may have to contest that question with a single power

Whilst the navy of England has been decreasing in numbers and power, other nations have only been too successful in the augmentation of their navies, and have assumed a position, dangerous, if not threatening to our naval superiority.

The returns with which you have been furnished, or can have ready access, too fully confirm the correctness of my statement.

I shall not, therefore, distract your lordship with a mass

* *Vide* Duke of Wellington's letter, p. 278.—ED.

of elaborate statistics in reference to the past and present navies of this country, or of those of foreign nations, but content myself with instituting a comparison between the navy of this country in the month of February, 1860, and at the present date.

That your lordship may be put in possession of the requisite information to arrive at a correct and impartial judgment, I enclose the monthly lists of ships in commission and in the several classes of reserve at the date specified, and will only solicit your attention to the details given under the following heads :—

1 Channel Fleet.
2. Unappropriated and fitting out.
3. Coastguard, and
4 First Class Reserve as constituting our home force, ready to meet any sudden emergency.

I would likewise request you to notice the amount of naval force upon the Mediterranean station in February, 1860, as compared with that at the present date.

I abstain from passing any comments, as the returns speak for themselves, and I do not wish to complicate the subject by the introduction of any questionable estimate as to the increased or relative value of the ironclads.

It is sufficient to state that it is a debateable point whether England or France has the advantage as regards ironclads, either in numbers or efficiency.

The returns in question are, I humbly submit, sufficient to establish these facts :—

1. That our present force in commission and reserve is quite inadequate to meet any sudden emergency at home, by which I mean to give battle to the fleet of a powerful enemy, defend the Channel Islands, protect our naval arsenals, and afford security to the commercial ports and our

homeward-bound commerce, arriving hourly from all quarters of the globe with specie and freights of incalculable value

2. That our force in the Mediterranean and at Malta is insufficient to either uphold British supremacy upon that sea or to defend Malta

3. That our naval armaments being unable to meet the foregoing requirements, our colonies and shipping upon the high seas must be left to their fate.

In order to arrive at any sound decision as to what measure should be adopted by the naval administration of this country,* it is necessary, calmly and dispassionately, to consider the great changes which science and time have effected since 1815.

The introduction of steam, the substitution of ironclads for vessels of wood, the progress of gunnery and the use of shells, to which must be added the increased facilities afforded by the railway and electric telegraph in the transport of men and stores, and the transmission of orders and news—one and all must and will tell in the exact proportion to the value attached to these discoveries, and the practical purposes to which they are applied.

In striking the balance as to the advantages or disadvantages accruing to this country from these great changes, I fear that the impartial judge must give his verdict against us

Steam has bridged the Channel and rendered the blockade of the French ports a matter of impossibility

It enables the enemies' cruisers to leave their ports at pleasure, to prey upon our commerce, and keep up perpetual alarm along the whole length of our island.

It renders easy the embarkation and transport of troops for purposes of national invasion or desultory warfare.

But, above all, steam, in time of war, not only imperils our

* *Vide* Lord Charles Beresford's Confidential Memorandum, p. 229.

wealth upon the seas, but under certain circumstances might deprive us of the necessaries of life.

The exploits and depredations committed by the *Alabama* and *Amazon* upon the commerce of the United States teach a lesson which it would be unpardonable to disregard.

With reference to guns, I will only observe that it seems a questionable policy whether it be wise to leave forts without guns, and ships without armaments, whilst committees of artillerists are seeking for perfection

No country has derived greater advantages from the railway and the electric telegraph than Great Britain in time of peace; but during war, that nation which has the most complete organisation, and commands the largest number of men, is the nation which must benefit to the greatest extent *

Success in war depends upon the concentration of an overpowering force upon a given spot in the shortest possible time, and as the attacking power has the privilege of selection, the advantage is generally on that side.

And so would it be with France unless our organisation, both naval and military, were very different from that which it now is.

France possesses another advantage too often overlooked.

She is able to concentrate her whole naval force at pleasure, either in the Channel, or in the Mediterranean, and, by means of her railways, transfer her seamen from the British Channel to the Mediterranean, and *vice versâ*, with incredible rapidity; indeed, she can almost man two fleets with one set of men, which gives France a superiority at the outbreak of a war.

Such are the advantages enjoyed by France

Against these it is right to bear in mind those especially possessed by this country in respect to coal, iron, machinery, and in the numerous private establishments which can be

* *Vide* Lord Charles Beresford's Confidential Memorandum, p. 229.—ED.

rendered available for the construction of ironclads and gunboats, or indeed, vessels of every class and description.

To the advantages already specified must be added those of her mercantile marine and her reserve of seamen.

But the great question to consider is the course which, in all human probability, France will adopt towards England upon the great outbreak of hostilities; and this is the danger against which the Board of Admiralty is bound to provide.

It would be worse than childish to assume that France would not be perfectly well informed as to the state of our naval and military preparations, and regulate her proceedings in reference to the probabilities of success.

I am strongly impressed with the conviction that, whenever the fatal period arrives, France will display an ability and promptitude not even second to that of Prussia, and that not a day will be permitted to elapse, after the declaration of hostilities, without attacks upon Malta, the Channel Islands, our naval arsenals, and long line of exposed coast unless one and all are far better protected than at present, whilst a swarm of swift cruisers would be despatched in all directions to capture and destroy our shipping.

The position of Malta and the Channel Islands deserves serious attention, for it is the navy which the country expects to defend her and not the handful of troops which constitute her feeble garrisons.

France will not waste her strength upon our distant possessions, but bring the horrors of war to our own homes—a work of far more easy accomplishment now than formerly.

Let us now examine our present means of defence

Our standing army is so reduced in numbers that it would not provide adequate garrisons for our arsenals.

Our militia is untrained and unready

The Volunteer force is well drilled, but devoid of all military organisation.

Our forts and batteries are incomplete, unarmed, and without garrisons; whilst the enclosed returns make only too plainly manifest to your lordship the extent to which economy and naval reduction have been carried.

To designate the few ships under the command of Admiral Yelverton as a "Channel fleet" is ridiculous; and diminished in numbers as "our home squadron" now is, there are, nevertheless, no ships in first-class reserve to augment its strength.

I hope and believe I have placed the case fairly before your lordship, and I must leave you to judge whether I have misrepresented facts or exaggerated dangers.

Deem me not presumptuous if, after an experience of forty years, I venture to offer a few suggestions with a view to avert (if possible) the recurrence of dangers, happily escaped, and to prevent the repetition of mistakes which, once made, ought not again to occur.

· The proposed remedies are very simple, for they are comprised in *due preparation* and *improved organisation* *

1. The first measure I would suggest is the completion, for service, and the arming of all our ironclads, which, until their numbers be increased, I am humbly of opinion ought to be reserved for the defence of our naval arsenals, the Channel Islands, and Malta.

2. The next step in advance is the repairing and equipping for first-class reserve every gunboat worth the expense.

3. To bring forward for first-class reserve a considerable number of frigates and corvettes.

It is possible that these vessels might not be able to contend successfully with ironclads, but they would be of the greatest utility in preventing the transport and disembarka-

* Compare with Lord Charles Beresford's Memorandum, p. 229.—Ed.

tion of troops, in protecting our commerce, capturing the merchant ships of the enemy, and in affording succour and support to our distant colonies

4 The last subject to which I would direct attention is the necessity of a more perfect understanding between the naval dockyard and military authorities, as to the proper measures to be taken by them for the defence of our naval arsenals

Unless the heads of departments act in concert and, to a certain extent, anticipate and provide against the dangers which must inevitably occur upon the outbreak of war, delay, confusion, and failure must be the certain consequence.

In any future war little time will be left for inquiry by telegraph as to the movement of ships or vessels, how the Channel Islands are to be defended, or what artillery and troops should be despatched to the Isle of Wight, or how the anchorage of Spithead is to be protected   Surely these are not questions to be discussed with the enemy on this side of the Channel.

Yet, during my official career, I have witnessed two, if not three, escapes from the risks and dangers already described.

Why such was the case, and probably will be so again, I will explain.

The ministry hopes for peace to the very last moment; and whilst the Admiralty and the Horse Guards are urged to make every preparation and warned of the threatening danger, they are nevertheless instructed to take no steps which intimate a hostile intention; in plain language their hands are tied, and they are prevented from adopting just those identical measures which professional experience and prudence would suggest.

· Nor is this the only disadvantage under which the country labours at such a crisis. Whilst in France the strictest secrecy would be observed, on this side of the Channel the public press makes known the movement of every regiment and the sailing of every ship.

To ensure security it is necessary at a period of profound peace to adopt those prudential measures for national defence which political wisdom and sound economy alike suggest.

It is now about twelve years since a very general opinion prevailed that nations were so fully alive to their own interests, and had become so enlightened, that "war was impossible."

How fatally that delusion has been dispelled is proved by the fact that, within the short period which has intervened between that date and the present, England, France, Russia, Prussia, Austria, Italy, Spain, Turkey, and Denmark have gone to war.

Nor is this all; for in America, that land of promise, we have witnessed the most terrible of all wars, a civil war, and read of battles which, for magnitude and horror, will bear comparison with those of pagan Rome.

Now what is the sad conclusion to which statesmen and philanthropists must at last arrive ? It is simply this—that neither diplomacy, education, the spread of science, the advance of civilisation, commercial enterprise, intercommunication, self-interest, or even the ties of consanguinity, to say nothing of humanity and religion, will prevent the greatest scourge with which the human race is inflicted— *war !*

Wise, therefore, are they in their generation who, admitting this melancholy truth, prepare for a calamity which, judging of the future by the past, appears sooner or later to be inevitable.

In conclusion, allow me to observe that I have confined my remarks to the probability of a war with France alone,

but what would be the condition of this country were
France, at the outbreak of hostilities, in alliance with Russia
or the United States ? *

   *   *   *   *   *

Mr Childers was pleased to regard these observations
favourably, and as they to a certain extent coincided with
his own views as to the state of the navy and the want of
organisation and preparation for war, he embodied some of
the points in his own schemes, and so gave effect to them
It must in justice be said that all Mr. Childers' plans for
organising and augmenting the fleet were carried into effect
in a very modified form to what they would have been had
he had fewer financial and other difficulties to contend with.

Mr. Childers proved to be a very powerful First Lord; he
possessed great administrative ability, displayed untiring
industry, and evinced business-like habits of the very
highest order, in addition to which he was blessed with a
fine temper, clear head, and calm judgment, and was always
courteous and accessable to all; but if he had a fault it was
a disposition to concede too much to the opinion of others,
with a view to temporise and conciliate.

Mr Childers had from the first unprecedented difficulties
to contend with. His Board unquestionably contained
several members of acknowledged talent and experience.
Still, it was far from being a strong one, because divided,
and did not pull together. Great, indeed, is the difference
between theory and practice, and directly I saw its composition, and became acquainted with the distribution of the
business, my knowledge of naval men convinced me at once

---

* It is very curious to observe how identical were the views and
opinions of the Author with those entertained and publicly expressed by
Lord Charles Beresford upon nearly every subject connected with naval
affairs and war organization, yet they never knew each other personally,
neither had they ever been in correspondence.

I

that it would never work satisfactorily. Sir Sydney Dacres was nominated First Sea Lord, and next to him Sir Spencer Robinson, a vice-admiral of the same rank as the First Sea Lord. In addition to being a member of the Board, Sir Spencer was to hold the post of Controller of the Navy. The First Sea Lord has always been regarded for the time being as the naval Commander-in-chief, and up to this date the Controller of the Navy and his department had always been placed under the personal supervision of the First Sea Lord, but if the Controller is an officer of the same rank as the First Sea Lord, and selected on account of his high scientific attainments (as in the case of Sir Spencer Robinson), and is also made a Lord of the Admiralty, it is almost certain that differences of opinion will arise; it being beyond the range of probability that any First Sea Lord can carry out his views without interfering, directly or indirectly, with the departmental arrangements of the Controller. The result turned out as anticipated, and unpleasant dissensions were of frequent occurrence.

Reference has on several occasions been made in these pages to the heavy duties entailed upon the First Sea Lord, and therefore it was most decidedly an error in judgment to hamper Sir Sydney Dacres with the whole *personnel* of the navy, which could only be done by deputy, as ought to have been apparent to Mr. Childers when he distributed the business of the department. The duties ordinarily assigned to the First Sea Lord were excessive, and that too without those more important subjects which have recently been brought to the front by such distinguished and deep-thinking flag-officers as Sir Phipps Hornby, Sir George Tryon, and Admiral Colomb. Whatever errors in judgment Mr. Childers might have made when he first came into office, he ought to have the merit accorded him of acting up to his opinions with firmness and courage, and endeavouring to carry into practical effect what he deemed requisite for the public good. No difficulties daunted him, no labours tired him, and what he undertook he rarely failed to bring to a successful issue. The amalgamation and consolidation of the civil departments was a measure long thought necessary, frequently discussed, and indefinitely postponed Mr. Childers calmly and dispassionately considered how this great object could best be accomplished. The first step he took was to effect a reduction in the Secretary's office, and to abolish the Coastguard Department and distribute its business amongst the various branches at Whitehall. In this he was most ably supported by Mr. Romaine, whose Admiralty experience and sound judgment proved of inestimable value The Controller's Department was then transferred to the Admiralty proper, and the other principal officers, with their staff, were brought from Somerset House and located in Spring Gardens, as a temporary arrangement, until a new Admiralty could be erected which would embrace all the departments under one roof—a proposal then seriously contemplated, but, alas ! a quarter of a century has now elapsed, and yet it is not carried, though its necessity is admitted by all to be urgently needed.*

It would be unreasonable to suppose that a great change, such as the amalgamation of the several departments, could be effected without many objections being raised and considerable friction caused, and especially when we bear in mind how many personal interests were interfered with and the inconvenience occasioned whilst the change was being effected ; but the chief difficulty of all was with the Controller's Department, for when all the troubles of the removal to the Admiralty proper had been got over, that department became an *imperium in imperio*. The business which

* The new Admiralty building does not provide accommodation for all the departments under Admiralty control.—ED.

had been and ought to belong to the First Sea Lord was usurped by the Controller, and the papers rapidly transferred to his office. This, as a matter of course, led to serious personal differences between the First Sea Lord and the Second Sea Lord, as well as to grave departmental inconvenience. So long as Mr. Romaine was Permanent Secretary all went on fairly well, as he managed to uphold the authority of the secretariate, and firmly opposed innovations of a crude and ill-considered type, but after his retirement matters assumed a far less satisfactory aspect *

I have always been a great admirer of Mr. Childers, but I plainly foresaw that his doing away with the meeting of the Board, and transacting the business in his private room, would ultimately lead to personal inconvenience and misunderstandings.

The system adopted by Sir James Graham of having all the business brought before the Board was attended with the greatest possible advantage, for he heard all that could be said on both sides of a question, and no one could complain that he did not know what was being done, or that no opportunity had been afforded him of giving expression to his views. By this course all questions of importance were thoroughly ventilated and well-fought out before the First Lord was called upon to offer an opinion or arrive at a decision. The discussion being public, there could be no mistake as to the opinion expressed by any individual member of the Board, as there were witnesses in abundance to bear testimony to the words employed.

The system pursued by Mr. Childers was the very reverse of this; his wish was to be accessible at all times, and the consequence was that the members of his Board were in and out of his private room all day long. The Controller took

* Vernon Lushington, Esq., Q.C., was appointed Permanent Secretary on 29th June, 1869, in the place of Mr. Romaine, retired.

papers to him with proposed submissions upon them, which the First Lord generally approved, but perhaps a couple of hours afterwards the First Sea Lord called for some of the papers in question, and as they could not be found in the Secretary's office, inquiries were then made of the Chief Constructor, who, however, had not seen them. A messenger was then despatched to the Controller's office, who was told they were with the First Lord. Sir Sydney Dacres then sought his private secretary, and obtained the papers from the First Lord's room. Sir Sydney Dacres then took them back to the First Lord, with the complaint that he has never seen them, and expressed an adverse opinion as to the decision arrived at. This state of things went on from day to day, and naturally led to warm discussions and to much that was unpleasant, which was followed by constant threats of resignation—one day from the Controller, the next day from the Constructor, and not unfrequently from both at once.

At this period Mr. Childers was in a very delicate and distressing state of health, both his physical and mental powers had been greatly overtaxed, and his strength was fast giving way. His official duties began soon after nine o'clock in the morning, and his Parliamentary labours rarely terminated till long past midnight. I heard from his own lips, when on one occasion I was sympathising with his sufferings and expressing my regret at the many difficulties he had to encounter, that he seldom obtained more than three hours' sleep, and the only chance he had of securing that was by diverting his mind from his official and Parliamentary cares by reading the light literature of the day in the hope of falling off to sleep. Enough has been said in reference to the unfortunate dissensions which prevailed between certain numbers of this Board, and it is much to be regretted that the practical sound sense of

Lord John Hay (junior Naval Lord) and the good judgment of Captain Beauchamp Seymour (private secretary to the First Lord, and afterwards Lord Alcester) had not been able to carry greater weight, although it is not difficult to conceive why junior officers are reluctant to express opinions at variance with those who are of higher rank, especially in such a service as the navy.

Notwithstanding that I had always received from Mr. Childers great kindness and consideration, still it certainly was not for me, holding the position I did, to presume to give advice to him, as First Lord.

I was distressed and concerned to observe the pitiable state into which his health had gradually fallen, and the little thought or consideration extended to him by those who should have relieved him. I was daily shocked and annoyed to find that the general topic of conversation amongst the gentlemen of the office was about the "rows" in the First Lord's room, and the resignation of this person and that. It seemed to me, as to others, that it was high time a stop should be put to departmental proceedings of · such unseemly character. ·

"Rows" in a First Lord's room, and threatened resignations openly discussed in the office, were without precedent, and therefore I had no hesitation when in private conversation with Mr. Childers' Private Secretary, Sir Andrew Clark (his particular friend), and with Mr. Stephen Lushington, the Permanent Secretary whom he had appointed to succeed Mr. Romaine, to suggest a line of conduct that would, without fail, in five minutes bring to a termination these dissensions so distressing to witness, so detrimental to the public good, and so disrespectful to the First Lord, in the hope they would repeat it to him.

What I suggested was this, that Mr Childers should send for Sir Spencer Robinson, and, after politely requesting him to be seated upon the sofa, state he had desired his attendance to discuss a little matter in order to avoid, hereafter, unpleasant consequences. What I proposed he should say was that, although he fully appreciated Sir Spencer's ability as a member of the Board and as Controller of the Navy, and would at all times pay due consideration to his recommendations, he nevertheless felt it his duty to remind him that Sir Sydney Dacres was First Sea Lord, and, if after Mr Childers had had the benefit of the opinions of both and should decide in favour of the First Sea Lord, he, Sir Spencer, must accept graciously an adverse decision. In regard to resigning, Mr Childers should merely say that as First Lord he could not be threatened, and should be much concerned if he were deprived of Sir Spencer's valuable services, both in his capacity as a Lord of the Admiralty and as Controller of the Navy, but at the same time the state of the service was such that, if he actually took him at his word, he would find no difficulty in filling the vacancy, there being many officers of high scientific attainments quite equal to the efficient discharge of those duties Sir Spencer so ably performed; and then, to soften this down a little, the First Lord could say, " But, of course, that is a contingency I need not contemplate "—accompanying the words with a cordial shake of the hand. The two secretaries and Sir Andrew Clark thought there was a great deal in what I said, but were all of opinion that, if Mr. Childers acted upon my suggestion, Sir Spencer Robinson would really resign. Upon this point I entirely differed; I had been long enough at the Admiralty to know there was an immense difference between threatening to resign and really doing so. I had heard many threaten to resign, but with the exception of Mr Phinn—whom Lord Halifax unexpectedly and much to his disappointment took at his word—I cannot at this moment bring to my recollection a single other instance having occurred during my protracted connection with the Admiralty.*

In regard to Sir Spencer Robinson I said to them he was undoubtedly a very able naval officer, and was, moreover, a very sensible man; but as he was a very ambitious one, and dearly loved authority and power, he was most unlikely to throw away his high position and lucrative appointment simply because the First Lord happens, from time to time, to decide against him, and in favour of the First Sea Lord, especially when the adverse decision was only upon a question—to borrow the expression so felicitously summarised by Viscount Halifax when on the "Lords Commission to inquire into the state of the navy"—as to the construction of " a big ship or a little one "

To prove how right I was in my estimate of Sir Spencer Robinson's character, and to show how disinclined he was to leave the Admiralty Board-room, it was subsequently found necessary for Mr. Gladstone himself to address a letter to him, to acquaint him that his name would be omitted from the next Admiralty patent.†

No First Lord has ever done more for the good of the navy than Mr. Childers, and that in spite of all difficulties. His scheme of retirement, his re-distribution and composition of the fleet (leading up to the present organisation and mobilisation), his grand works at Portsmouth and Chatham, and the consolidation of the Admiralty departments, are all

---

* There was another instance, although it did not at the moment occur to the Author. In July, 1870, Sir Spencer Robinson, with the concurrence of his Chief Constructor, Mr. (now Sir Edward) Reed, threatened the joint resignation of both in a certain event That event occurred, and Sir Spencer Robinson remained in office, but Sir Edward maintained his resolution and retired.—Ed.

† On the 14th February, 1871, Captain R. Hall, C.B., was appointed Second Naval Lord and Controller of the Navy in succession to Sir Spencer Robinson. On the 13th March, the Rt. Hon. G. J. Goschen was appointed First Lord of the Admiralty.

four most important measures, each bearing lasting testimony to his herculean labours which, together with the differences of opinion amongst the members of his Board, caused his health to fairly break down, and finally compelled him to retire from office and leave to others the carrying into effect of those other important measures he had hoped to have been able himself to achieve—measures calculated to promote the efficiency of the navy and the public good.

Mr. Childers' merits as a statesman stand very high, and have hitherto been very inadequately appreciated Considering what he has done, and the substantial benefits he has conferred upon the two fighting services, the praise awarded to him has been scant indeed. At the time his naval retirement scheme could not fail to be unpopular, as all officers placed upon the retired list naturally felt personally aggrieved, whilst his able and well-thought out measure of territorial regiments was equally distasteful to the officers at the head of the army, because it did away with the old numerical nomenclature to which undue importance was attached by octogenarian generals.

Professional prejudices are so deeply rooted that it takes a couple of generations to thoroughly eradicate them.

Surely the time cannot now be far distant when ample justice will be accorded to so able and judicious a reformer as Mr. Childers proved himself to be.

By this time I had attained to the age of sixty-two, and felt the period had arrived when, if I acted up to my own principles, I ought to retire from the active duties of official life. To this Mr. Childers reluctantly acquiesced, though finally he recommended me to Mr. Gladstone for the honour of knighthood, in consideration of my service, extending over a period of forty-four years—a distinction likewise conferred upon my predecessor, Sir Henry Pennell. I may here mention that my father—who, as Secretary to the Board of Naval Revision, Commissioner of the Victualling, and as Accountant-General of the Navy, completed a period of fifty-four years—also received the honour of knighthood. Thus, between father and son, with the exception of two short years, a whole century was passed in the civil service of the navy.

The chief object I have in mentioning my retirement from the Admiralty is that from henceforth my remarks in reference to the administrations of the distinguished statesmen who filled the office of First Lord of the Admiralty are based upon information acquired from private and public sources, and not upon personal official knowledge as heretofore.

196   *RIGHT HON. G. J. GOSCHEN*

CHAPTER XIX.

THE ADMINISTRATION OF THE RIGHT HON. G. J. GOSCHEN, 13TH MARCH, 1871, TO 6TH MARCH, 1874.

The policy of Mr. Childers pursued—A new office established—Naval volunteers established—Experience in naval affairs acquired.

WHEN illness compelled Mr. Childers to retire from the Admiralty in March, 1871, Mr. G. J. Goschen was appointed to succeed him—a statesman of acknowledged ability and a leading Cabinet Minister of the day. There was no change in the Board, with the exception that G. J. Shaw-Lefevre, Esq., M.P., was appointed Political Secretary instead of Mr. Baxter. A few days of practical experience at the Admiralty sufficed to demonstrate to Mr. Goschen what the daily routine business of the office at Whitehall really was, and induced him to form a very high estimate of the labours undertaken by his predecessor, and further led him to appreciate the soundness of his naval policy, and so he felt he could not do better than adopt the same, and do all he could to carry out the plans Mr. Childers had initiated. This Mr. Goschen did during the time he was at the Admiralty, on this occasion, in the most loyal and successful manner. There had been so many important reforms undertaken by Mr. Childers both as regards the various departments under the Admiralty, and the *personnel* and *matériel* of the navy, that Mr. Goschen had quite enough to do to get things to settle down into proper working order without embarking upon other controversial schemes; and, as a matter of fact, Mr. Goschen appointed another secretary in 1872 to assist in the routine business of the office, who was called the "Naval Secretary." *

It was during this administration that the naval volunteers were first established, and it is to be regretted that the authorities have not been able to turn their zeal and patriotism to account; but, instead, recommend the corps for disembodiment, simply because it does not contain a sufficient naval element. The navy, as is right and proper, is the popular service of the country, and as there is a considerable number of powerful and well-grown young men who are quite ready to wield a cutlass, handle a rifle, or take their places at a gun for the defence of their homes, in the capacity of amateur sailors, but disinclined to do so as soldiers, it does seem a pity not to profit by their zeal and turn their energies to good account, especially when it is remembered what a large proportion of men there are on board our vessels of war who have no pretensions whatever to seamanship, but who nevertheless discharge the duties assigned to them to the satisfaction of their superiors.

The measure which gained for Mr. Goschen, whilst at the Admiralty, the greatest amount of public approbation, was the liberality and fairness he displayed when making an advance in the pay of the men in Her Majesty's dockyards—a most respectable and deserving body of public servants. This act of justice on the part of Mr. Goschen was all the more commendable because it was effected at a period of rigid economy, and he therefore ran the gauntlet of having unjust motives attributed to him, as it invariably happened, that when claims of this description were conceded similar inferences were too frequently deduced and political jealousies and suspicions aroused.

* On the 6th May, 1872, Rear-Admiral J. W. Tarleton, C.B., was appointed Second Naval Lord, and Captain Robert Hall, Naval Secretary (8th May).

But what has led to greater public benefit was, that whilst Mr Goschen fulfilled the duties of First Lord of the Admiralty, he acquired that intimate knowledge of naval affairs and the pressing needs of the service which enabled him, like Mr. W. H. Smith, who subsequently held that office, to render such valuable service to Lord George Hamilton when he brought forward his Naval Defence Bill, in the government of Lord Salisbury. There is no doubt whatever that it was through the hearty support and strong representations of these able and patriotic statesmen that the sanction of the Cabinet was given to the large grant of £21,500,000 for the augmentation of the fleet proposed by Lord George Hamilton, Mr Goschen being at the time Chancellor of the Exchequer, and Mr. W. H. Smith First Lord of the Treasury and leader of the House of Commons.*

* Mr. Goschen has since 1895 (when he was again placed at the head of the Admiralty in this the third administration of the Marquis of Salisbury as Prime Minister) given a still more practical proof of his abilities as a naval administrator; for he has shown to the world that, although he is not to be frightened by pretentious foreign naval programmes, he is nevertheless resolved to place and maintain our naval defences beyond the reach of rivalry in regard to the three great elements of strength—men, ships, and works—as the navy estimates for the year (1897) and the proposed supplementary vote of half-a-million bear ample testimony.

The Author of this volume had been looking forward for months to this year's navy estimates, as he was impressed with the conviction that it would be a very important year to those taking an interest in naval and military affairs. But, alas! after a protracted illness he suddenly became weaker, and died on the very day the navy estimates were brought forward. Although he had arrived at the advanced age of eighty-nine, he, to the last day of his life, took the keenest interest in all that appertained to the navy; and on the day of his death I read to him the "Naval and Military Intelligence" out of the *Times.*—ED.

CHAPTER XX.

THE ADMINISTRATION OF THE RIGHT HON. G. WARD HUNT,
6TH MARCH, 1874, TO 15TH AUGUST, 1877.

A popular country member—An enquiry into the actual state of the navy
—A request for a vote to increase the navy highly distasteful to
Lord Beaconsfield—Obliged to back out of his statement—Paper
ships and phantom fleets—Dockyards filled with ships in various
stages of completion—The needs of the service subservient to
party politics on both sides of the House—Naval debate emptied
the House of its members—The result of a failure in a banking
firm upon the finances of the country—English people slow to adopt
reforms.

WHEN Lord Beaconsfield formed his ministry in 1874,
Mr. Ward Hunt was appointed First Lord of the Admiralty
in succession to Mr. Goschen. He had previously held the
high office of Chancellor of the Exchequer, when he showed
himself to be a man of marked ability; he was a North-
amptonshire country gentleman, and was unusually popular amongst the country members whilst at the Treasury,
and, though a Conservative in politics, he entertained liberal
and advanced views on all public questions. Upon first
taking his seat at the head of the Board of Admiralty, he
naturally wished to make himself thoroughly acquainted
with the actual condition of the fleet Being a statesman
free from the bias of party politics, he instituted an immediate
and most impartial enquiry into the existing state of the
several naval departments, and desired to arrive at the exact
truth. He found in his naval advisers those who did not

hesitate to express their opinions in a frank and outspoken. manner.   The members of his Board were—

Admiral Sir Alexander Milne, G.C B. ;
Vice-Admiral Sir J. W. Tarleton, K.C.B. ;
Captain Lord Gilford, R.N. ;
Sir L. Massey Lopes, Bart., M.P. ;
The Hon. Algernon Fulke Egerton, M.P., Political
     Secretary ;
  . Vernon Lushington, Esq., Q.C., Permanent Secretary ;
Rear-Admiral Robert Hall, C.B., Naval Secretary.

In addition he had a most discreet counsellor in his dear friend and connection, Sir Charles Eden, whose long Admiralty experience enabled him to offer valuable suggestions to Mr. Ward Hunt during his tenure of office, which were generally in perfect harmony with those of the naval lords of his Board, all officers of distinction and entertaining advanced and enlightened views.

So impressed was Mr Ward Hunt by the representations made to him, and with the result of his own personal enquiries as to the condition of the navy that, very shortly after his accession to office, he made a most unwelcome statement on the subject in the House of Commons, setting forth the imperative necessity of an increase to the navy estimates.   There never was a more just or more inopportune demand preferred.   Lord Beaconsfield had a short time before been dilating upon bloated armaments, and advocating economy, therefore for his incoming ministry, at first starting, to come down to the House with a demand for money was highly inconsistent and the reverse of agreeable.   Mr. Ward Hunt was consequently compelled to back out as adroitly as he could, and make the best of a very insignificant addition as compared with the amount really required   He was forced to explain that perhaps he had been somewhat precipitate in forming this opinion; for, upon further enquiries, he was gratified to find that several ships upon the stocks were in a more advanced state than he had been led to believe, and that many of the ships which had returned from foreign service were found with defects far less extensive than the dockyard officers had at first anticipated, and might be repaired at a moderate expense, and within a reasonable period. He was further obliged to add that he had every reason to believe that the money now placed at his disposal, if judiciously applied (as he was sure it would be), would effect considerable addition to the fighting strength of the navy, and was sufficient to meet its immediate requirements Mr. Ward Hunt soon found, like many other statesmen imbued with good intentions, that patriotism weighed but lightly in the balance compared with party and political convenience.

It was about this period that the public again heard something more about paper ships and phantom fleets; nor was the criticism far wrong, for the majority of our most powerful battleships and cruisers were in various stages upon the stocks, whilst the ships which had returned from foreign service with rotten boilers, broken-down machinery, obsolete armament, and shipwrights' defects to be made good, were blocking up our harbours, waiting for repairs (which were indefinitely postponed for economical and party purposes), the annual amount voted being altogether inadequate to the completion of the ships building and the requirements of those standing in need of repairs. It was only upon the pages of the Navy List that the fleet presented an imposing appearance; but that was quite sufficient to satisfy the members of the House of Commons and the British public. The real state of the navy was perfectly well known, however, at all foreign courts, through the zealously acquired information of their several naval attachés.

It requires no great mental effort to perceive that until men-of-war are able to discharge efficiently the duties required of them, they represent so much capital giving no return for the money expended upon them. No system ever was so expensive as cramming the dockyards with a great number of ships in various stages of construction, the more so as they were permitted to remain so long upon the slips, that, in order to meet modern requirements, they were in numerous instances half taken to pieces and rebuilt, with a view to the reception of augmented armaments, and the necessary internal fittings consequent upon the change   In order to give some idea of the amount of public money lying idle in our several dockyards, Mr. Forwood, the able Political Secretary to the Admiralty under Lord George Hamilton, stated that he calculated that eight millions and a half of money was locked up at one time in Her Majesty's dockyards giving no return. It is but natural that the country, the service, and the Press should find fault with a department when matters go wrong, but it too often happens that blame is imputed to the Admiralty when it is chiefly due to the Cabinet.

Mr. Ward Hunt's health had been failing for some time, and, in consequence, he visited Homburg in the hope of deriving benefit from the waters   Whilst there, I had the pleasure of several long and interesting interviews with him, which, as might be expected, frequently turned upon naval affairs. I was forcibly struck with the clear conception he entertained of the real needs of the navy. He distinctly foresaw the many advantages that, in future, would accrue from Mr. Childers' scheme of naval retirement, and fully recognised the desirability of employing younger officers in positions of high command. In the course of conversation it became very evident to me that he felt the heavy responsibilities of his high office, and it would have made him only too happy if he could have secured by any means a substantial addition to the fleet, but he added in a desponding tone, " You know, Sir John, this cannot be done without money." Little did I think that, within ten days from the date of the last conversation, he would have passed away ; so sudden was his demise, and much did I regret his loss.   He was a distant connection, with whom I had always been on friendly terms.

As First Lord of the Admiralty, Mr. Ward Hunt was unquestionably the right man in the right place, and his death was a great blow to the navy as well as to the department over which he presided.

The public are too apt to forget that First Lords are seldom free agents; there are so many influences at work, both political and departmental, that, unless some serious danger is apprehended, there is an indisposition on the part of the other members of the Cabinet to listen to complicated details in reference to ships, guns, and machinery, about the technical explanation of which they know little and care less. I will adduce two instances in point where two First Lords, of opposite politics, made ineffectual efforts to induce their respective Cabinets to vote the necessary money to augment the fleet; Mr. Childers, a Liberal, on one side, and Mr. Ward Hunt, a Conservative, on the other.   Both these statesmen were equally desirous of placing the naval defences of the Empire on a more efficient footing.   But, as usual, the moment was regarded as very inopportune, and consequently the patriotic intentions of these two able administrators, as in the case of others, were made subservient to the political exigencies of the hour.   Nevertheless their failure cannot be considered as very surprising, when we remember that the great Duke of Wellington himself was unable to persuade his contemporaries to take measures to avert a tragedy which he prayed the Almighty would spare him from witnessing.*

* *Vide* the Duke of Wellington's letter to Sir John Burgoyne, p. 278.

It is impossible to entertain the thought for a single moment that the distinguished noblemen and statesmen who have held the high office of First Lord of the Admiralty, belonging to both of the great political parties in the State, were wanting in patriotism and zeal, or were indifferent to the honour and safety of their country; but, in almost every case, their best and most earnest endeavours have been frustrated by that extreme party spirit which, for so many years, has proved the bane and misfortune of our political system.

In order to illustrate that, it is not this party or that party which is to blame, but successive governments, which, for so many years, have vied with each other in reducing the navy estimates to the lowest possible ebb, with a view to meet the popular clamour for economy and retrenchment; and, as each successive government passed out of office, there was a visible sign of depletion in one branch or another of the naval establishments: sometimes in the materials, sometimes in the number of artificers and workmen, sometimes by postponing the repairs of storehouses and other buildings, and putting off indefinitely new works of pressing importance. Ships which were intended to be launched in one year were delayed until another, and the shipbuilding programme of the year was rarely completed   Sometimes the depletion appeared in naval ordnance, gun-carriages, or in ammunition, and, not unfrequently, reduction was apparent in the number of seamen, marines and boys.   All these and other depletions, which might be adduced *ad infinitum*, were made to meet the demands of the Treasury, which, as far as the resources of the country were concerned, had no sense or reason.

No public service was ever regarded with more pride and favour by any people, of any nation, than the Royal Navy of England until the peace of 1815, and richly did it deserve its high renown for the many glorious exploits it achieved; but alas! from that date to the year 1885, the national interest it excited was either languid or spasmodic. The country had been living upon the prestige of bygone generations, without taking those precautionary measures to ensure the same successes in future times which had in the past given it the undisputed supremacy of the sea.

It was happy in the comfortable belief that Britannia ruled the waves, utterly regardless of the change in naval warfare, the altered relative position of foreign navies with our own, and, last but not least, the immense increase of responsibility thrown upon the navy by the gigantic extension of our commerce and dependencies. The debates in the House of Commons upon the navy estimates had had for years the effect of emptying the benches of its members, because it was anticipated that the evening would be spent in an unprofitable wrangle between naval members as to the respective merits of rival naval architects; knowing that the views expressed upon one side would be flatly contradicted upon the other, which left those present in difficulty as to the better course to pursue.

It is only since the controversy consequent upon the unfortunate speech of Lord Northbrook, in the House of Lords in July, 1884, that the public mind has been directed once again to the national interests of this great commercial country as identified by the power and efficiency of the navy.

What the result would have been to the financial interests of this kingdom if the great House of Baring had collapsed is most conclusively set forth in the Address presented by Mr. Rokeby Price, Chairman of the Stock Exchange, on behalf of the members of that body, to Mr. Lidderdale, Governor of the Bank of England,* expressing their high appreciation of the "admirable and effective manner in which the recent monetary crisis was met . . . which threatened

* Governor of the Bank of England, 1889; made Privy Councillor, 1891.

to disorganise, if not overwhelm, the vast financial and commercial interests of this and other countries." If the failure of one single leading city firm leads to consequences so disastrous as those averted by the timely aid of the Bank of England to Messrs. Baring Brothers, what would be the loss of national credit if, at the first outbreak of war, the navy proved unequal to the demands made upon it?

Lord Overstone—one of the ablest financiers the country has ever known—represented to the House of Lords some years ago, in carefully thought-out detail, the financial loss that would inevitably accrue to the commercial and mercantile prosperity by any naval discomfiture.

In no country does public opinion operate so slowly as in England. There is a natural indisposition to take the initiative; but, once roused to action, no people are more energetic or determined to accomplish their object thoroughly and completely. We were slow to substitute gas for the dim oil lighting of our streets, and the general adoption of electricity progresses at a snail's pace. For years we entrusted, during the dark hours of the night, our lives and property to the custody of the paupers of the parish, attired in so grotesque a costume as to render locomotion all but impossible; though now they are replaced by a body of police, the admiration of all foreigners. We allowed our beautiful river, the Thames, to be converted into the main sewer of the metropolis; and it was not until typhoid fever attacked the members of the Legislature, in some cases fatally, that any effectual remedy was applied to the crying evil, which ultimately led to the construction of the Thames Embankment, one of the finest works in Europe.

London, the wealthiest and most populous capital in the world, for the want of a little combined energy, allows itself to be periodically "enveloped in a dense fog and canopy of gloom during the winter months."

It is most regrettable that the same amount of zeal is not displayed by those who combine for purposes of good as is exhibited by those who are confederate for the accomplishment of evil. If we are indisposed to relieve ourselves from an inconvenience which all admit, and from which we suffer daily annoyance, it is not surprising that we neglect to provide against dangers which seem so far removed from the range of probability as war. It is, naturally, disagreeable to provide funds for a contingency it is more congenial to dismiss from our mind; nevertheless, it is a contingency which cannot be too frequently brought before the public by the members of the Legislature and by the Press; for it is astonishing, even in the higher grades of society, whose pecuniary interests are so deeply involved in the efficiency of the navy and the defence of the country, how indifferent and ill-informed they were and, in a less degree still are, upon all matters relating to naval and military affairs.

CHAPTER XXI.

The Administration of the Right Hon. W. H. Smith,
15th August, 1877, to 13th May, 1880.

Observations on Mr. Smith's political career—The office of Permanent
Secretary abolished—Experience acquired in naval affairs.

Upon the melancholy demise of Mr. Ward Hunt, Mr.
W. H. Smith was appointed to succeed him on the
15th August, 1877, the members of the Board retaining
their seats as before. Mr. Smith, from his first entry into
parliamentary life, had always been a most popular member
in the lower house, and, as Secretary to the Treasury, had
by his tact, temper, and courteous manners gained golden
opinions from all parties. His advancement to the Cabinet,
as First Lord of the Admiralty, afforded universal satisfaction,
the more so as he was known to be an excellent man of
business, and to possess many other qualifications which
peculiarly fitted him for that office; though why, and under
what circumstances, he was induced to abolish the office of
Permanent Secretary, almost immediately after his appointment to the Admiralty, has never been clearly explained.
The office of Permanent Secretary, or Second Secretary, was
first established in 1694, but only intermittently occupied
until 1756. Since that date it has been continuously filled
(with but one break, 1763 to 1765) by gentlemen of ability,
who have, without exception, discharged the grave responsibilities of the office with marked efficiency. From the
year 1756 only ten officials have held the post. The length
of the services of seven I will give, in order that it may
bear testimony to the zeal and constancy with which they
responded to the demands made upon their energies and

powers of endurance, and at the same time in no uncertain manner to the high estimation in which they were held by the various Cabinet ministers and political superiors who, from time to time, held office at the Admiralty:—Mr. George Jackson was there sixteen years, from 1766 to 1782; Mr. John Ibbetson, twelve years, from 1783 to 1795; Mr. William Marsden, nine years, from 1795 to 1804; Sir John Barrow, forty-one years, from 1804 to 1845; Captain Baillie Hamilton, ten years, from 1845 to 1855; Mr. W. G. Romaine, twelve years, from 1857 to 1869; Mr. Vernon Lushington, eight years, from 1869 to 1877, when Mr. W. H. Smith abolished the office, substituting another Political Secretary and retaining the Naval Secretary which Mr. Goschen had appointed.

The naval policy adopted by Mr. Smith was in strict accordance with that of his predecessor, whose views he endeavoured to carry out to the best of his ability with the means at his disposal. From Mr. Smith's personal acquaintance with all that passed at the Treasury, and with the example of Mr. Ward Hunt's recent failure before him, he did not attempt to get any substantial increase to the navy estimates, for he knew how futile it would be for him to do so. But the knowledge and experience he acquired whilst at the Admiralty enabled him, like Mr. Goschen, to form a sound and conclusive opinion as to the absolute necessity of adding to the numerical and fighting strength of the navy, which he turned to good account in 1889, during the administration of Lord George Hamilton; and most fortunate it was for the navy that the financial affairs of the country were, at this critical juncture, under the able management of Mr. W. H. Smith as First Lord of the Treasury, and Mr. G. J. Goschen as Chancellor of the Exchequer—two ex-First Lords of the Admiralty, both recognising the urgent needs of the navy, the necessity of placing it in an efficient condition, and having at heart the best interests of the service.

P

CHAPTER XXII.

THE ADMINISTRATION OF THE EARL OF NORTHBROOK, 13TH MAY, 1880, TO 2ND JULY, 1885.

Long experience in a department sometimes tends to contract the mind, not applicable to Lord Northbrook—A strong Board of Admiralty—A strong party man—The wealth of the country as exemplified by the income-tax—Lord Salisbury's visit to Plymouth—A casual remark and a speech in the House of Lords—Tonnage no test of the efficiency of a warship—No hostile force has landed on our shores for centuries—Summary, by "One Who Knows the Facts," from the *Pall Mall Gazette* —The defence of our coaling-stations—The Russian war scare—Lord Northbrook declares he would not know what to do with three millions, and spends five-and-a-half before the end of the year—A comparison between a First Lord that does not want to spend money and has to, and another, who is anxious to improve the navy and has to back out of his statements, and can obtain none—How the deficiences in the navy were demonstrated—The celebrated controversy—The names of some who took part in it—The leaders in the *Times* by Mr. Delaine, and the effect they produced in the Admiralty Board-room.

IN 1880 a change of ministry placed Mr Gladstone again at the head of the Government,* and appointed Lord Northbrook to be First Lord of the Admiralty. His lordship had had unusual experience in that department, for, as far back as 1849, he was private secretary to his father, Sir Francis Baring, who, at that date, was First Lord of the Admiralty, and subsequently filled the offices of Civil Lord and Political Secretary. It not unfrequently happens that they who have been brought up in a department become imbued with all

* Mr. Gladstone was Prime Minister in 1868, when Mr. Childers was First Lord of the Admiralty.

the prejudices and antiquated ideas of a bygone generation; departmental education, like purely professional, too often tends to contract rather than expand the mind, and in such cases proves the reverse of beneficial.

Lord Northbrook had held several important appointments under Government, at the War Office, at the India Office, and had been Viceroy and Governor-General of India, and certainly we have no right to assume that he entertained upon Indian affairs less grand and comprehensive views than the many distinguished Governor-Generals who had preceded him in that office; therefore these remarks cannot be regarded as applicable to Lord Northbrook, so we must endeavour to trace the motives which guided his naval policy whilst First Lord of the Admiralty to some other cause. His lordship's Board was an unusually strong one; every member, naval and civil, had made his mark either in the naval service or in the political arena. They were—

> Admiral Sir A. Cooper Key, K C.B.;
> Vice-Admiral Lord John Hay, C.B.;
> Rear-Admiral A. H Hoskins, C.B.,
> Thomas Brassey, M.P. (afterwards Lord Brassey);
> G. J. Shaw-Lefevre, Esq., M P., Political Secretary;
> G. O. Trevelyan, Esq., M.P., Political Secretary;
> Vice-Admiral Robert Hall, C.B, Naval Secretary.

In 1882 Lord Northbrook abolished the office of Naval Secretary, and re-established that of the Permanent Secretary, and the secretariate was once more restored to its ancient and proper status, in which it is to be hoped it will long continue.

Lord Northbrook had during his administration, in addition to the distinguished naval officers and civilian experts mentioned, the advice of Lord Alcester, an admiral of proved gallantry, of liberal and advanced ideas, combined with good, sound judgment and practical experience, and of Admiral Brandreth, Sir Frederick Richards, and Vice-Admiral Sir William Hewett, officers held in the highest esteem. Sir Cooper Key was not only one of the most popular, but was considered one of the most scientific and capable flag-officers of the day. Lord Brassey had already gained a high reputation for his knowledge of naval affairs and for the keen interest he had always taken in them, and as for Sir George Trevelyan * he had already proved himself a valuable member in the Board of Mr. Childers.

Lord Northbrook therefore entered upon the duties of this public office under the most favourable and promising auspices, and sanguine expectations were formed by the navy and the public as to the substantial benefits likely to accrue from such an administration. But Lord Northbrook was a politician, and, what is more, a very strong party man. From the date of his entering into public life he imbibed the extreme views advocated by his party in regard to economy and retrenchment; he was at all times disinclined to incur any expense which he thought might be inconvenient or embarrassing to the Ministry, and was consequently far more solicitous to keep down the estimates than to add to the efficiency of the navy.

The decrees of fate are inscrutable and past finding out, for Lord Northbrook was himself destined to carry out, in his own person, that augmentation of the fleet which he declared to be unnecessary, and forced to incur the very expenditure which he had so imprudently denounced

The state of the navy had for some years past excited well-grounded apprehensions amongst those who had access to the information that could be depended upon; and a general consensus of opinions prevailed that it had fallen far below the standard of safety. It was perfectly notorious

* Succeeded his father as second baronet, 1886.

that France, Italy, Germany, and Russia had been directing greatly increased attention to the state and augmentation of their respective navies, and consequently our relative position as a naval power, compared with bygone days, had materially altered and greatly diminished in strength. Our annual navy estimates remained practically stationary, whilst those of foreign powers had been greatly increased from year to year.

Hitherto it had suited the political convenience of our rulers to ignore the numerous representations made to them by their naval and military advisers as to the imperative necessity of adding to the strength of the navy, and improving our military defences at home and abroad, so that the growing duties of both services might, even during a period of peace, be more efficiently discharged. It must be admitted by the most economical optimist that the expansion of our territorial possessions, our commerce and shipping -- which comprises that of half the world—and the necessity for importing corn and other food supplies, for the daily sustenance of the ever-increasing population of these islands, combined with our greatly augmented national wealth, as exemplified by the receipts received from the income tax, afforded ample justification for the representations which have been made so continually to the Government by the naval members of various Boards of Admiralty on behalf of the navy, and to which a liberal response should have been extended. As its efficiency is the best of all assurances for the security of property and the stability of this colossal empire, surely it is not unreasonable to expect that our naval and military establishments should proceed *pari passu* with our wealth, commerce and possessions. For years the public mind had been so completely absorbed in domestic affairs that it was futile to attempt to divert it into imperial channels. But the sound and practical opinions, so forcibly expressed by the advanced school of naval thought, had commenced to exercise a powerful and salutary influence. Several events occurred which rendered it evident that the question of such national importance as the actual state of the navy would soon have to be brought prominently before the public, and be thoroughly entered into. And this was effected most unexpectedly, and by the merest accident.

Lord Salisbury had paid a visit to Plymouth, and was somewhat disconcerted at the opinions he heard freely expressed, in naval circles, as to the very unsatisfactory condition of the navy. Shortly after his return he made a casual remark in his place in the House of Lords, expressing the views entertained by the leading members of the naval profession at that important naval station. This induced Lord Northbrook, a few days afterwards, to deliver in the House of Lords an exposition, confidentially prepared, in defence of the Government and of his own naval administration. He set forth, in glowing and exaggerated language, the very efficient state of the navy, and its decided superiority, so far as ironclads were concerned, over that of France, and his lordship so allowed his zeal in supporting his party, and in the cause of economy, to outstrip the limits of prudence as to declare that, if three millions of money were thrust into his hand he would really be at a loss to know how to spend it. Lord Northbrook unfortunately based his argument upon a most unstable foundation, namely, tonnage; the consequence was that his elaborate superstructure upon investigation fell to the ground like a house of cards. Now every tyro in naval affairs is perfectly aware that a more worthless test than tonnage could not, by any possibility, have been selected, or one more calculated to misrepresent and mislead. It is easily shown that two vessels, each of 10,000 tons, might possess very different qualifications for warlike purposes; for instance, one might steam nine knots an hour, the other sixteen or eighteen knots. One might have $4\frac{1}{2}$ inches of iron protection, the other 16 or 18 inches of steel; one might be armed with old smooth-bored muzzle-loaders, the other with improved breech-loaders of the heaviest calibre, together with 3 and 6-pounder quick-firing guns; the one a vessel seventeen or twenty years old, the other perfectly new, fitted up with all that modern improvements can suggest. Thus it is seen that nothing could be more illusory or deceptive than to take tonnage alone as a test of superiority, the more so when it appeared that, in order to swell the amount of tonnage, Lord Northbrook included in his list ironclads known to be obsolete and utterly unfit for active service.

When this speech became public, the heads of the naval profession and experts were thoroughly astonished and taken aback; and a famous controversy was the immediate result, which led to the publication of a series of articles in the *Pall Mall Gazette*, remarkable for the masterly and exhaustive manner in which the whole subject of our naval defences was handled, under the signature of "One Who Knows the Facts." In this controversy the most distinguished admirals and naval experts soon took a part, and, in their numerous contributions to the Press, gave ample proof of the great ability and skill with which they were able to defend their cause, and uphold the vital interests of their country. There are no people so difficult to arouse to a sense of danger as the English nation. For centuries no hostile force has landed on our own shores, and the horrors of war are therefore almost unknown to the great mass of the population—the question of national defence does not consequently excite that interest which it does on the Continent, where recent experience has taught a practical lesson.

The following summary, by " One Who Knows the Facts," extracted from the *Pall Mall Gazette* of 8th September, 1884, is so replete with sound sense and valuable statistics, setting forth the actual state of the navy and its shortcomings at that date, that I feel I cannot pay a greater compliment to its author, or mark the high opinion I entertain of its merits better, than by embodying it in this volume for the benefit of my readers.

" 1. *Increased Risks.*—Our risks from war have enormously increased since 1868-9. The naval expenditure of other powers has increased 40 per cent. Our population has increased 16 per cent., our trade 40 per cent., our wealth 40 per cent., our shipping 30 per cent., and our possessions have been enormously extended. Yet, in face of all these increased responsibilities and increased danger, our naval expenditure has been slightly diminished. To bring it up to the relative position of 1868-9, it ought at least to be increased four millions a year, and even then the increased premium would not be equivalent to the increased risks.

" 2. *Ironclads Afloat.*—So far from being able to demonstrate our 'irresistible superiority' in armour, guns, and speed to any probable combination of fleets, we are just a little ahead of France in ships, behind her in guns and in the age of our ships, and about equal in armour and speed. France has outbuilt us by 10,000 tons of ironclads in the last ten years. To restore the proportion between the shipbuilding votes of the two countries that existed before 1879, our shipbuilding vote should be increased by at least one million per annum.

" 3. *Ironclads Building.*—Instead of making up lost ground we are losing it, and two years hence France will be ahead of us in second-class ironclads, and our superiority in the first-class will have been slightly diminished.

" 4. *Repairs.*—Repairs have to some extent been sacrificed to building, with the result that more than half our third-class ironclads can hardly be regarded as fit to go into battle.

" 5. *Guns.*—Our guns actually fitted are inferior both in weight and in power to those of France and Italy. We have not one ironclad afloat armed with the new breechloader, of which five hundred have been made since 1880.

" 6. *Our Foreign Stations.*—In case of sudden war, the French have better fighting ships on the China station than England; the Chilian ironclads are stronger than our Pacific cruisers; the new ironclad of Brazil would sweep our South American squadron off the sea. On the other stations we have ships better than the best that could be sent against them.

"7. *The Protection of our Marine.*—Our fast ocean cruisers available for policing our maritime highways against the *Alabamas* of the future are insufficient to allot three to each station. We have nineteen thousand merchantmen scattered all over the world to protect, and only twenty-four unarmoured ships of a speed exceeding 14 knots for their protection.

"8. *Coaling and Telegraph Stations.*—A hostile cruiser could, with almost entire impunity, destroy to-morrow the coaling stations of Hong-Kong, Singapore, Bombay, the Cape, Ascension, St. Helena, Mauritius, St. George's Sound, Fiji, and Vancouver's Island, which are virtually unprotected, although Hong-Kong has four torpedo-boats, and there are slight fortifications at one or two of the other ports.

"9. *Docks.*—We have eight foreign stations and four docks. There is no dock in all India in which an ironclad could refit; and although a dock is building at Hong-Kong, if the *Audacious* were injured, she would have to go to Sydney or come back to Malta to refit.

"10. *The Defence of Home Ports.*—There are not more than two harbours in the United Kingdom adequately protected, and some of the most important commercial ports absolutely lack a single torpedo-boat.

"11. *The Personnel of the Navy*—We have not sufficient trained men to man our fleet when war is declared without drawing eight thousand from the Reserve, and that Reserve is not half as numerous as that of France.

"12. *The Mosquito Fleet.*—In the cheapest and deadliest mode of defence our naval supremacy, instead of being absolutely irresistible, is absolutely non-existent. To bring us into line with our rivals one hundred torpedo-boats should be laid down at once."

I prefer facts simply stated to figures, and have therefore refrained from introducing the various lists prepared respectively by Lord Northbrook, Sir Thomas Brassey, and "One Who Knows the Facts" to prove the accuracy of their several returns. But as the differences between the three mainly depended upon whether these vessels or those vessels should be included in this class or that class, under this head or that head, the grand result is much the same; and for the same reason I have not gone into the shipbuilding programmes of various Boards. For years nothing could be more unsatisfactory than the relations which existed between the Admiralty, the War Office, and the Colonial Office, in respect to the defences of the Colonies and the coaling stations, and the duties to be assigned to the navy in reference to their protection. Had it not been for the energetic persistence of the late Earl of Carnarvon, the forcible representations of " One Who Knows the Facts," and the numerous spirited articles in the *Times* upon the subject, no definite result for good even yet would have accrued, as the desire to procrastinate and put off the evil day was so intense. The first question which arose was, which were the coaling stations which ought to be fortified, and then came the order in which they should be taken. This was followed by a consideration of the nature and extent of the works absolutely necessary, which led to endless correspondence and various plans and estimates being submitted to the Treasury. These again were constantly revised, and reductions suggested in the estimates, and as a matter of course differences of opinion were rife as to the plans. Whilst these estimates were under consideration H.R H the Duke of Cambridge, the Commander-in-Chief, most opportunely reminded her Majesty's Government that coaling stations, even when fortified and armed, would be of little value unless provided with garrisons, and that troops would also require barracks—two important facts quite forgotten, both involving expenditure. Subsequently another interesting controversy arose as to whether the ships of the navy were or were not to be held responsible for the protection of these same coaling stations instead of the troops, who it was generally supposed had been despatched to their several destinations for that particular purpose; and it is very doubtful whether a final decision upon this important question has, even to this day, been satisfactorily adjusted.* All

---

* The Marquess of Lansdowne's Military Bill, which was read a second time April 6, 1897, will go far to settle this question. It may be considered as one of the most important measures for national defence of the century.—ED.

these serious revelations, coming as they did from such high authority, shook public confidence in Admiralty representations as to our naval efficiency, which was greatly increased when the panic arose as to the probability of a war with Russia; and when Lord Northbrook, who, in July, declared that he would be at a loss to know how to spend three millions of money upon the navy, did actually dispose of more than that amount before the close of the year, out of the five and a half millions—the naval portion of the Supplementary Vote of eleven millions—obtained by Mr. Gladstone upon a representation made by him to the House of Commons. As to our relations with Russia, and the necessity of adding to our military defences, Lord Northbrook, when dilating upon the satisfactory state of the navy and expressing his opinion that no increase of expenditure was needed to add to its efficiency, only did that, as a strong party man, which many ministers on both sides of the House had often done before, and it forms a somewhat amusing contrast to the position in which Mr. Ward Hunt found himself, after his vain endeavour to extract an additional vote to augment the navy from the ministry of Lord Beaconsfield.

Thus we find Lord Northbrook involved in serious trouble by concealing the real deficiencies of the navy, and Mr. Ward Hunt in an awkward position before the public by inconveniently exposing its shortcomings. As I observed almost at the beginning of this chapter, the decrees of fate are inscrutable and past finding out—Lord Northbrook, who was anxious to keep down expenditure, was compelled, from the force of circumstances, to spend five and a half millions in excess of his estimate; whilst Mr. Ward Hunt, on the other hand, in his patriotic endeavour to augment the strength of the navy, was obliged to content himself with a very insignificant sum and eat up his own words. Such, at

times, is the painful position in which statesmen of the
highest character and probity are unavoidably placed.
Representations such as those made by Lord Northbrook
may be regarded by some who are struggling for place and
honours as strictly within the limits of party politics. It
has nevertheless become a grave question whether a minister
is, under any circumstances, justified in setting forth before
the public exaggerations so great, and misrepresentations so
palpable, as those made by his lordship in his unfortunate
speech of July, 1884, even though he could plead precedents in his favour. But this is not by any means so
culpable as for an official holding high office to make confidential communications which he knows to be incorrect
and misleading, to a prime minister anxious to ascertain the
real truth at a critical crisis. In the first case, the statements
being public are capable of easy refutation, and the minister
who makes them must run the risk of paying the penalty by
the loss of his political reputation; but, in the other instance,
the statements being strictly confidential and implicitly believed may be attended with more serious consequences, and
might lead, in case of war, to the gravest national disaster,
as must inevitably have occurred upon the two occasions to
which reference has been made in a preceding chapter, had
war been declared, as, at the moment when the misleading
representations were made, appeared most imminent.

Party zeal and precedent may in a measure condone for
Lord Northbrook's unfortunate speech; but it is far less easy
to find excuse for his refusal of the patriotic and generous
offer urged upon him by Mr Childers, when Chancellor of the
Exchequer, and which, under less favourable circumstances,
he might, from political considerations, have been compelled
to withhold, as greater difficulty might be experienced in
obtaining the approval of the Cabinet. The inadequacy of
the navy was placed beyond the range of further disputation

by Lord Northbrook himself when he accepted the supplementary grant of five and a half millions; and the necessity that existed for largely increasing the strength of our fleet could not by any possibility be better demonstrated than by a succeeding Government demanding a vote of £21,500,000 for that specific purpose, an amount which, even at the time, was doubted whether it would be sufficient to bring up the navy to its proper position* It has since been shown that the sum, large as it was, was inadequate to make good the deficiencies of every kind in the *personnel* and *matériel* of the navy which the parsimony of successive Governments had accumulated.

The grand result of £21,500,000 to augment the fleet, and the public interest aroused in naval affairs, must have been most gratifying to all those distinguished naval officers, experts, and civilians who took part in this celebrated controversy or contributed in any way to this end; but particularly so to the talented author of the able and exhaustive articles which appeared in the *Pall Mall Gazette* under the signature of " One Who Knows the Facts." It is most fortunate for the country that there are admirals and captains of such ability upon the active and retired lists as Sir Thomas Symonds, Sir Phipps Hornby,† Lord John Hay, Sir Edward Fanshawe, Sir George Elliot, Sir Houston Stewart, Admiral Colomb, Lord Charles Beresford and Captain Penrose Fitzgerald, possessing the professional knowledge and literary ability which enable them to place before the public, through the instrumentality of the press, the requirements and shortcomings of the naval service. The *Times*—the most powerful

---

* Since Lord Northbrook accepted the grant of five and a half millions, over sixty millions, including that sum, have been spent upon the navy for material over and above the estimates for its repair and maintenance.

† Sir Thomas Symonds and Sir Phipps Hornby have both died since the above was written.

organ of public opinion in this or any other country—has ever been to the front in lending its columns to set forth the needs of the service; and it is a pleasing duty to me to bear personal testimony to the great benefits it has conferred upon the navy by the powerful and trenchant leaders of the late Mr. Delaine, which for years excited so much interest in naval circles, and from time to time occasioned an amusing flutter in the Admiralty Board-room amongst the anti-reforming admirals of the old school, whose vociferous denunciations against it afforded no slight entertainment to the non-professional First Lords and Political Secretaries.

CHAPTER XXIII.

THE ADMINISTRATION OF THE RT. HON. LORD GEORGE HAMILTON, 6TH AUGUST, 1886, TO 23RD AUGUST, 1892.

Short administration of Lord G. Hamilton followed by another, of the Marquis of Ripon—Second administration of Lord George Hamilton — Marks a grand era in naval history — The preparations for the Crimean War form no precedent for any future war — A mistaken belief in our naval superiority — Speed reduced to a mathematical certainty—The ministry should explain the grounds upon which they withhold their sanction in reference to the recommendations of the naval advisers of the country—The state of the navy upon Lord George's accession, 1886—Confidential memorandum by Lord Charles Beresford — Credit to Lord George Hamilton and his Board for carrying out the provisions contained in the memorandum—The good fortune of Lord Charles Beresford—Differences of opinion in regard to the Intelligence Department—The duties of a First Sea Lord; for the time being the Commander-in-Chief of the Navy—An anecdote to show the result of divided authority—The officer at the head of the Intelligence Department to be second to the First Sea Lord—The Naval Defence Act and the grant of £21,500,000—Lord Charles Beresford, an enthusiastic seaman given to exaggeration—The prompt construction of fast cruisers—The policy of France, Russia and the United States in regard to large ships—The position of the admiral in battle and the opinion of Prince Henry of Prussia—The blots which the naval manœuvres have brought to light—The dockyard accounts placed upon an intelligible basis—An economical method of adding ships to the fleet—Harbours blocked up—Ships nine years on the stocks—Ships not proceeding to sea because their guns and ammunition had not been delivered—Lord George a successful minister—A list of measures he successfully carried.

ON the 24th June, 1885, the Marquis of Salisbury became Prime Minister, and appointed Lord George Hamilton First Lord of the Admiralty, which office he held only from

2nd July, 1885, to 16th February, 1886, but to which he returned on the 6th August, of the same year, upon another change in the ministry, and therefore I will reserve my remarks for his second administration.

During the few months Mr. Gladstone was in power in 1886, the Marquis of Ripon was at the head of naval affairs. The noble marquis obtained much public approbation for strenuously resisting a reduction in the naval expenditure which the Cabinet had endeavoured to force upon him. His lordship's tenure of office was so brief that he had scarcely time to make himself acquainted with the daily routine business of the department, much less make changes and introduce reforms.

The second naval administration of Lord George Hamilton will most deservedly occupy a very conspicuous page, and mark a grand era in the naval history in this country. It has been my earnest endeavour throughout this volume to represent, in as forcible language as I could venture to use, the perils and dangers that must have befallen this country had it been suddenly involved in war, from the utter inadequacy of the fleet as regards ships, organisation, and due preparation. The success which attended the Crimean War forms no precedent, as there was ample time to make arrangements of every description. During this war our shores were exposed to no danger, and all our mercantile and commercial operations were carried on with the same security and facility as they were in a period of profound peace; but had our differences with France or with the United States ended in a war, the result must have occasioned great national disquietude, and led to serious consequences. During my Admiralty experience of forty-four years, I may safely affirm that no measures were devised, nor no practical arrangements thought out, to meet the numerous duties which devolve upon the Admiralty, and which at once present themselves at the very beginning of a war with a first-class naval Power; on the contrary, there had been unqualified apprehension on the mere rumour of war, especially amongst the naval members, arising from their consciousness of the inadequacy of the fleet to meet the various duties it would be required to discharge in such an eventuality. How such a state of things could exist for so many years in a country possessing boundless wealth, and amongst a people renowned for superior intelligence and practical common-sense, and reputed to possess a remarkably keen eye to their own interest, is utterly incomprehensible; but such is the indisputable fact

To what must we ascribe the principal causes for this extraordinary neglect of the navy?

1st, the rivalry between the two great political parties in the state.

2ndly, a mistaken view of economy.

3rdly, because the professional opinions of the naval lords of the Admiralty carry no weight, as no publicity was given to their representations

Lastly, public indifference, consequent upon a mistaken belief as to our naval superiority.

It is most unsatisfactory to look back upon the political controversies of past years; for they only too plainly demonstrate how completely the real interests of the country have been sacrificed to the fleeting exigencies of the hour, and how subservient the requirements of the navy have been made to the convenience of party. The struggle for place and honours has been so fierce that the plainest obligations of national duty have been entirely ignored, and risks and perils encountered which have been averted rather by the interposition of Providence than by any foresight or patriotism on the part of those in power. It is marvellous that one Cabinet after another should be so blind and indifferent to a

Q

subject of such vital importance, nay, one upon which our very existence as a nation depends, namely, the maintenance of our naval supremacy   Both parties in the state have encouraged the political cry of economy and retrenchment, which has, on more than one occasion, led to panics fatal to the prestige and dignity of a great empire.   In order to meet an immediate requirement, hasty and ill-considered demands are made upon the Treasury, as in 1885, when large sums are expended which can render little or no assistance at the time, but only prove advantageous at a more distant date.

Differences of opinion there are, and always will be, in regard to the vessels that ought to compose a fleet with such varied duties to discharge as those which devolve upon the British navy.   Expenditure must always form an important item, and there is consequently a greater desire to add to the numbers rather than to the powerful ships, which last, in time of war, will prove the real fighting strength of the fleet. Ships combining power and speed cannot, in these days, be constructed, except at considerable cost; but, if the real efficiency of the navy is calmly and dispassionately considered, it soon becomes evident that such expenditure is alike judicious and prudent, and must be incurred.   Just experience has shown that the smaller vessels must necessarily become a prey to the larger, especially as speed (upon which everything depends) can be calculated to almost a mathematical certainty.   It would not be at all impossible for a single powerful ship, possessing high speed, to dispose of all smaller vessels, upon a given station, in detail.   Arguments have been advanced as to a simultaneous attack being made upon such a vessel, but how can this be done if the large vessel possesses the superior speed which enables her to choose her own time in seeking or evading an action ?

The responsibilities of the Admiralty are so grave and

various in time of war, that it is only the naval lords who are able to form a just and accurate estimate as to what is absolutely necessary to meet the duties the navy will be called upon to discharge; and yet their voices are never heard, nor their representations laid before the Cabinet in a manner to produce that effect which, had their professional opinions been placed on record, and brought forward with the navy estimates before the Prime Minister and the other members of the Cabinet, could not have failed to secure that serious attention to which they, as coming from the naval advisers of the country, are entitled. If this course were pursued, and the representations of the naval lords made known to the House of Commons and the public, the ministry would be obliged to explain the grounds upon which they thought fit to withhold their sanction, and then the respon- sibility would rest with them in the event of the Admiralty being unable to respond, as it ought to, to the pressing requirements of any sudden demand. The fact that the representations of the naval lords have received so little attention, and carried so little weight, has been a source of constant, and, it must be admitted, well-founded complaint on the part of the distinguished admirals who have held office under successive First Lords, who, for the last sixty-five years, have been civilians, with the exception of H.R.H. the Duke of Clarence (William IV.) and the Duke of Northumberland.

The languid interest and public indifference exhibited for so many years in naval affairs is mainly attributable to the firm conviction in the minds of the masses of the population that nobody would venture to dispute our naval superiority, and this lulled the nation into a state of false security, which the long-continued peace greatly tended to foster. Little credence has been placed by the general public in the statements made in regard to the increase of foreign navies,

and a misconception is entertained as to the influence exercised by the changes in modern warfare, which are, unfortunately, but imperfectly appreciated by the educated
classes, or even amongst those who, from their position
in the world, ought to be much better informed on the
subject.

When Lord George Hamilton returned to the Admiralty
in August, 1886, his Board consisted of the following
distinguished naval officers :—

> Admiral Sir Arthur Hood, K.C.B.;
> Vice-Admiral Sir Anthony Hoskins, K.C.B.;
> Vice-Admiral W. Graham, C.B, Controller of the Navy;
> Captain Lord Charles W. D. Beresford, C.B., M.P.;
> E. Ashmead-Bartlett, Esq , M.P.;
> A. B. Forwood, Esq., Parliamentary and Financial
> Secretary, M P.;
> Evan MacGregor, Esq., C.B., Permanent Secretary.

In order to do ample justice to Lord George Hamilton, and
to fairly represent the great benefits he has conferred upon
the navy, it is necessary to bring under consideration its
actual state and condition at the time of his accession to
office, and, to a certain extent, this has been done in the
preceding chapter, by which it will appear the strength of
the fleet was proved to be utterly inadequate, the organisation and preparation such as ought not to exist in a country
like this. But the deficiencies of the navy, and the shortcomings of the Admiralty, have been so ably and exhaustively
embodied in a confidential memorandum drawn up by Lord
Charles Beresford—a member of the Board—and which was
made public through the instrumentality of a dishonest
messenger at the Admiralty, that I feel I cannot do better
than present it to my readers in substance for their perusal,
extracted from the *Pall Mall Gazette*, 13th October, 1886.

"War Organisation.

"*Introduction and General Remarks.*—The perilous absence of any plan or preparation for war, and the gravity and imminence of the danger which may result to this country from such a state of affairs, has induced me to write this paper for the prompt consideration of the present Board of Admiralty

"I propose, first, to point out definitely the dangers that exist, and then to submit proposals for a scheme of organisation, in order that the question may be dealt with *immediately.*

"The scare of 1885 showed, approximately, what we should actually require in officers, men, merchant shipping, armament, ammunition, coal, medical and commissariat stores, in a war with a second-rate maritime power, *over and above* what is now at our disposal

"*It is quite incredible that, with the knowledge we possess as to what will actually be required at the moment of a declaration of war, no steps have been taken to organise or prepare any method or plan for showing how or where these absolutely necessary requirements are to be obtained.*

"*Foreign Headquarters' Plans.*—We know that France, Germany, Russia, Austria, and Italy have a regular headquarters' staff at their Admiralties, whose duties consist solely in organising plans of the most elaborate description for war preparations. These plans are kept to hand in the office, and corrected in detail every three months, so that in the event of war being declared the fleet can be mobilised, reserve ships filled with men, ammunition, coals and provisions, and the commanders of squadrons given immediate and decisive instructions as to the line of attack they are to pursue. In fact, so complete is the organisation in the offices of these countries, that the War Minister may ring his bell, order a telegram to be sent to the admirals and heads of departments, 'War with England' (Russia, or any other country, as the case may be), and then, like Moltke, he can lie on his sofa and continue the latest novel with the knowledge that every officer and man of the *personnel* will be in his place, and every article of material exactly where it is wanted.

"In England no similar plan or system exists, although it is far more necessary to this country in consequence of the larger extent and scattered position of her possessions, which, from their weak and isolated condition, would invite, and be certain of receiving, an enemy's attack.

"*If you read between the lines of the Report on the Mobilisation of Ships in Reserve, dated the 31st of January, in 1885, in anticipation of an outbreak of war in the spring of that year, it will be seen that this report—by stating in black and white the personnel and matériel considered necessary in case of war—is an absolutely conclusive proof of the imperative necessity for immediate organisation in the direction I shall endeavour to point out, and clearly exhibits what a dangerous state of affairs exists through our utter ignorance as to how or where we should get what we know is required in the event of war being declared.*

"*Proclamation of War.*—In these days of electricity and speed the first point scored may not only save the country which gains this advantage millions, but may have the effect of ultimately winning the campaign This is peculiarly applicable to our foreign stations. Through neglect of organisation and systematic instruction, as well as from *the total want of ordinary foresight*, the Admiralty render it not only possible, but probable, that an active and enterprising enemy like Russia or France would most certainly score the first advantage, because a delay of two days must elapse, owing to the antiquated formalities of the present system, before the Admiralty could communicate the proclamation of war to the commanders-in-chief on different stations, there being at this moment no precise wording for the proclamation declaring war.

"Under present conditions, the enemy would undoubtedly receive the official news of intended hostilities first, which would be an enormous advantage.

"It should be immediately arranged that the British commanders-in-chief on foreign stations shall be in a position to receive news of a Declaration of War, if not before certainly as soon as the enemy. The delay which must occur under the present system may be fatal on such stations as China or Australia, where there is floating wealth to the value of millions, as the enemy, during the interval referred to, would certainly cut the telegraph cables, and the first intimation of war to the English Fleet would be the sinking of the valuable English merchant vessels, or even of English men-of-war.

"I know for a fact, from a conversation with Captain ——, of the Russian ship ——, that is one of the chief provisions of the Russian scheme of preparations for war that the enemy's telegraph wires should be picked up and cut at certain indicated places. Captain —— inferred that no matter what country Russia went to war with, the English ocean wires would in any case be cut, as through them passes the news of the world. There is good reason to believe that this was contemplated by Russia in 1885, as it is an actual fact that Russian men-of-war were stationed at all the most important cable centres

"So far these remarks have been general. I will now proceed to particulars, dealing first with the *personnel*, and then with the *matériel*.

'PERSONNEL.

" *Captains and Commanders.*—From the report, already referred to, on 'Mobilisation of Reserve,' it would appear that there is a sufficient number of captains and commanders for the vessels which could be got ready for commission within three months, *but quite irrespective of war.*

"*Lieutenants.*—In regard to the present numbers of the lieutenant rank, we are at least three hundred deficient, considering that the services of this most useful class of officers are needed for torpedo-boats, coast defence, armed merchantmen, colliers, and ammunition ships. Although we know we are at least that number short, there is at present no plan or suggestion as to how we are to fill up this deficiency in numbers required for mobilisation in case of war. In my opinion, with a scheme of organisation such as *ought to exist*, the actual names and addresses should be kept in the headquarters' office of those people who would be required for positions we know will have to be filled up if war is declared; this list to be corrected every three months.

" *Sub-Lieutenants.*—The *sub-lieutenants'* list is lamentably small, and would be reduced to a ridiculously inefficient number if these officers were taken to occupy posts for which there are no lieutenants available, the only course possible.

",*Warrant Officers.*—The *warrant officers'* lists, also, are too small for what we should require. Their places, indeed, could on an emergency be supplied by petty officers, but there is no plan or suggestion as to what particular men should be taken to fill up these vacancies. With perfect organisation, as exists in Germany, lists would be kept showing the men's names, ratings, and ships. We should then at any time be able to place them, without delay, in the positions we know would have to be filled up in certain contingencies.

" *Petty Officers, Seamen, and Marines.*—The *personnel* of petty officers, seamen, and marines of the fleet afloat is excellent in point of physique and discipline, although their numbers would have to be enormously increased in time of war by the Reserves, as well as by large entries from the mercantile navy; but the method of securing and disposing of these men is left to conjecture, and there are no lists accurately laid down on paper of their names and addresses ready for mobilisation, as is the case in France and Germany.

" *Engineers, Assistant Engineers, and Engine-room Artificers.*—With regard to the Engineer and Assistant Engineer officers, and the engine-room Artificers, the position as to members is most unsatisfactory, as the duties they would have to perform must be carried out by men well skilled and accustomed to the use of engines, proficiency in which is only begotten by time and experience. We should have to obtain a large extra number of these officials from outside sources directly war was declared, but here, again, there is no detailed list of who are available, or where they are to come from, though we know we shall want them.

" *Stokers.*—The complement of stokers to the navy would also have to be very largely increased. Although it would be possible to procure them, still there is no system now which will enable us to do so quickly, and the time lost by this want of foresight would cost the country millions. Similar conditions exist with regard to the medical department, though not to the same extent.

"*No Increase of Estimate proposed.*—It must not be imagined, because I am calling attention to the deficiencies in the numbers of the *personnel* of the fleet *in time of war*, that I wish to increase the estimates by an extensive permanent addition to the complement of the fleet. My object is to point out that, for the purposes of mobilisation, the *personnel* would have to be enlarged in the direction mentioned; therefore, it is imperative for efficiency and safety that this necessary increase *in time of war* shall be prepared for by economical organisation *in time of peace*.

"MATÉRIEL.

"*Medical Department.*—In regard to the medical department a similar want of forethought is discernible, though there are more reserve stores actually ready in this than in any other department in the navy. At the Cape of Good Hope, Hong-Kong, and Esquimault provision is made for 2000, 5000, and 1000 men respectively. The quantities would have to be augmented immensely, but there is no arrangement for such augmentation.

"At Deptford, and at the Haslar, Plymouth, and Chatham hospitals there are stores at this moment for over 20,000 men, but no detailed plan for their distribution, so that they may be quickly sent away when wanted. This would add to the countless difficulties to be faced in the event of war.

"*Merchant Shipping, etc.*—Knowing as we do the *necessity for the increase* in officers, men, merchant shipping, armament, ammunition, coal, medical and commissariat stores, still there is *not an atom of system or organisation* or plan of the simplest description to suggest how we are to procure these absolute necessaries in war time, or where they should be forwarded when they are procured.

"*Transport Department.*—The transport department appears to be in a thoroughly well-regulated condition, looking at what occurred in the Suakin campaign, where, in a very short time, this department was enabled to place as many as 116 vessels of various tonnage at the disposal of the Government."

"I must repeat again that it is well known what would be our additional requirements in case of war being declared. Why, then, *in the name of common sense*, do we not organise for these requirements in time of peace, by having detailed lists arranged of officers and men (with their stores, ammunition, etc.) that we can instruct by telegraph to proceed at once to their destinations, instead of meeting the usual panic, confusion, and disorganisation certain to occur on a Declaration of War, through the omission to work out this simple question beforehand,

---

'* The transport service has always been able to discharge its duties efficiently. *Vide* pages 22 and 121.—ED.

and courting disaster by not having the necessary supplies ready till after war has been declared? It will probably be argued that there is a system proposed, to be found in 'The Report of Committee on Naval Matters in 1883.' That Report does contain much useful matter, but it is as a whole entirely theoretical, and is, moreover, in itself a splendid proof of the immediate necessity for tabulating together all that the Report points out *would be* necessary for the fleet in time of war. The provision for these necessities is at present left to Providence, as it appears to be *nobody's duty to undertake the organisation.*

"Always bearing in mind the fact I have pointed out of the necessity for this country being first in the field, it is *disgraceful*—I will go so far as to say *positively criminal*—that no organisation exists in the following all-important matters :—

> "*No Organisation.*—(*a.*) For rapidly commissioning the vessels in the first reserve ;
>
> "(*b.*) For the rapid completing to full complement of the crews of the coastguard ships ;
>
> "(*c.*) For obtaining, fitting, manning, and commissioning, either at home or abroad, mercantile cruisers ;
>
> "(*d.*) As to how or where we should obtain coal, ammunition, torpedo, depôt, telegraph, and store-ships ;
>
> "(*e.*) Detailed lists of coal and ammunition required for actual use and spare, as well as the names of individuals and places where each is to be supplied from ;
>
> "(*f.*) For framing a plan of naval campaign suitable for each station in the event of war with different countries.

"Here again, although *we know* we shall require all that has been mentioned in these paragraphs, we recklessly allow the chances of a disaster by not planning and thinking all this out *in peace time;* and we actually invite a panic (which means paying the highest price for the worst article) by not thinking of getting these things ready till after war is declared.

"*Mobilisation of Reserve* —With reference to paragraph (*a.*), I find in the 'Confidential Report on Mobilisation of Ships in the Reserve' that it is stated as an *actual fact* that, while the whole of the French ships of the First Reserve can be ready for action within forty-eight hours of the receipt of orders to commission, the best that can be said of the English vessels of the First Reserve (consisting of twenty sea-going ships always supposed to be ready for commission) is that *three* might be ready for sea (not necessarily for action) in five to seven days! and even this is only a *supposition.* Now, why does this *wicked* state of affairs exist? Simply because there is no efficient staff employed at the Admiralty in organising our fleets for war, and no attempt is made at practising this most necessary evolution. The Germans, Russians, Italians, and Austrians commission and mobilise at least a portion, and sometimes all their reserve ships for summer manœuvres every year.

"The same remarks will apply to paragraph (b.).

"*Merchant Vessels, etc.*—Referring to paragraph (c.), I find that in the panic of 1885 there were obtained altogether fifty merchant vessels of different tonnage, made up of—

For use as armed transports	16
As coal ships to accompany cruisers . . .	9
Hired troopships engaged in *anticipation* . . ,	12
Tugs bought	5*
„ hired	8*

The total sum paid for these ships being £783,171 15s. 11d., which was vastly out of proportion to what it ought to have been, putting the country to much needless expense Although we have gone through the experience of this waste of money, caused by not having detailed arrangements to hand as to fitting and manning these cruisers which were really wanted, though it is known that similar ships will be wanted again if war is announced, still nothing has been done in the direction of preliminary arrangements, so that at the next scare we shall go again through precisely the same amount of panic, demoralisation, and unnecessary expense.

"*Coal-ships, etc.*—With respect to paragraph (d.), I must point out the immense danger that would exist from our not having worked out how the supply of fuel is to be increased on foreign stations. It is needless to state that coal is the life and breath of the fleet, and yet, on the outbreak of war, we should want at least 60,000 tons sent out to the coaling stations abroad, independently of the coal carried in the steam-colliers which must be attached to every fleet. These 60,000 tons are a very small proportion of the extra coal which would be required, considering that 350,000 tons were purchased for Her Majesty's ships in 1885 (and although it must be admitted that this was an exceptional year on account of the scare, still it is the best year for the purpose of comparison), but here again there is nothing tabulated or detailed at the Admiralty with respect to this important question, and this would add one more to the list of panics which would ensue if war was declared.

¦ "The Reserve Squadron the other day was put to great inconvenience on account of the non-arrival of coal at Vigo. Delay such as this in wartime would be fraught with the gravest consequences.

"*Ammunition.*—The question of 'ammunition' is even more serious, for the coal supply exists, whereas the supply of ammunition does not exist at all.

"A Headquarters' Staff modelled on the basis suggested in this paper,

---

* To supply dangerous deficiency in our small craft and gunboats.

by representing such deficiencies every three months, would be continually calling attention to the vast danger of allowing the question to slumber trustfully as it does at present, it being nobody's business to take notice of it.

"In the confidential paper already alluded to, it is estimated that the shells required, which constitute the most important factor in the gun armament, could not be filled under six weeks! *Is it to be believed that nothing* has been done to remedy such a state of affairs, and this when we know that the organisation of reserve ships in France and Germany is so complete that a single telegraphic dispatch to the ports is sufficient to start the whole scheme of mobilisation, and that all the First Reserve ships can be actually at sea within forty-eight hours from receipt of such order?

"With regard to paragraph (*f.*), when we consider that *other nations* not only have a plan of campaign clearly defined at headquarters, which is varied according to the nations with which they may find themselves engaged, but that this plan is also communicated to the admirals commanding fleets and squadrons, the disadvantage England rests under, though possessing *no outline even* of a plan of campaign, is a matter for very grave anxiety to anybody who studies the question.

"*Plan of Campaign necessary.*—With a staff such as I am proposing, a plan of campaign would certainly be made out embracing the different contingencies which would occur in fighting different nations, and the Commanders-in-chief on stations would not be left in the hopeless and helpless state they are at present from want of knowledge with regard to the responsibilities they may be *expected* to undertake, and for which responsibilities they are justified in expecting some sort of guidance in the way of previous information from the recognised headquarters.

"There are plans of campaigns for service on shore, the preparation of which is considered necessary; but it appears to be quite forgotten that steam and machinery will enable a plan of campaign to be carried out with actually more precision afloat than ashore, for it is perfectly possible to name the day and hour you can land men in the north of China after starting from Plymouth, but it is next to impossible to say when they could reach a point one hundred miles inland.

"Having, to the best of my ability, pointed out the *indispensable necessity for immediately recognising the gravity of the present state of affairs*, I will now submit a proposal for placing matters in that state of efficiency which every one must acknowledge to be positively essential. I am not egotistical enough to imagine I have made some novel discovery, as I know perfectly well from conversations I have had that every seaman who has sat on the Board of Admiralty of late years has felt and recognised the importance of the subjects embodied in this paper. The question naturally arises, 'Why, then, has not this subject been prominently brought forward before?' The answer to this is simple (as I have already remarked), '*It has been nobody's business to do so.*' *This is*

*proved by studying the table of 'Distribution of Business' among the
members of the Board, in which table there is not a single reference to
'preparation for war' and 'mobilisation of the fleet,' subjects which in
the French and German Admiralties are considered among the first and
most important items of business.*

"It would be impossible, owing to the large amount of work for which
the Sea Lords are at present responsible, to add to their duties anything
of so extensive a character as would be involved in carrying out any such
proposals as these. This is notably the case with the First Naval Lord,
who, in my humble opinion, has always had too much to do, but as the
work has been done by so many seamen before, the loyalty of a naval
officer prevents his complaining of the work hitherto undertaken by his
predecessors. I believe the present able First Naval Lord has privately a
plan of preparation; but if this is so, it only emphasizes the necessity for
such a scheme being considered by the Board, and is an indication of his
patriotism in adding to his already overcrowded duties by devoting his
spare time to so important a matter. To meet the difficulty of the extra
duties entailed, I submit the following proposal:—

"*Proposal.*—I would extend the present *Foreign Intelligence Committee*, doing away with that nomenclature, and call it the Intelligence
Department, dividing it into sections 1 and 2. The head of this department should be an admiral, with a staff of junior captains, two lieutenants
or commanders, two marine officers, one higher division clerk, three lower
division clerks, and two writers.

"The admiral should eventually be a permanent appointment, and he
and the captains would receive, in addition to their *half-pay*, the salaries
shown in the accompanying list. The captains could be readily procured, as they are generally on compulsory half-pay for three to four
years after their promotion. The lieutenants (or commanders) should
receive their *full pay* in addition to salaries named, because, owing to
our being so short of these officers, they would be actually on *full pay* if
not employed in the way indicated.

"The Marines are always on full pay, the extra lower division clerk
and writer proposed above the number already employed in the present
Foreign Intelligence Committee would probably be obtained from some
other department of the Admiralty.

"Proposal for an Intelligence Department.

"*Head of Department.*

Admiral   .   .   .   . £1200 a year and half-pay.

"Section 1.

"To gather all information relative to foreign navies, inventions, trials,
and foreign maritime matters in general.

" *Staff.*

	£	s	
1 Captain . . .	500	0	and half-pay.
1 Lieutenant or Commander . .	270	0	and full pay.
2 Marine Officers. . . .	540	0	and full pay. '
1 Clerk (higher division) . .	387	10	
1 „ (lower division) .	190	0	
1 „ „ „ .	95	0	
1 Writer „ „ .	91	0	

£2073 10

" Section 2.

" To organise war preparations, including naval mobilisation and the making out of plans for naval campaigns to meet all the contingencies considered probable in a war with different countries, corrected frequently and periodically.

" *Staff.*

	£	
1 Captain	500	and half-pay.
1 Lieutenant or Commander .	270	and full pay.
1 Clerk (lower division) . .	190	
1 Writer „ „ . .	91	

£1051

" *Summary.*

	£	s.
Admiral	1200	0
Section 1	2073	10
Section 2	1051	0

£4324 10

" I wish to particularly point out that in this scheme the entire staff in section 1 already exists, the expenses of which are £2073 10s. To this I wish to add the staff of section 2, with an admiral as head of department over both sections. The increased expense, therefore, would only be—

	£
Salary for Admiral	1200
„ „ Staff, section 2	1051
Making a Total of	£2251

" But (assuming this will be allowed) it is only an increase of £251 on

Vote 3 of Navy Estimates for 1885-86, as there was at one time an extra
Civil Lord (Mr. Rendel), who received a salary of £2000, which position
has not been filled up since, though the money may have been utilised.

"If the organisation I propose is carried into effect, then, for the small
sum of £250, we should be, at least, better prepared for war. We know
that our fleet is very short of cruisers, torpedo-boats, gun-vessels, and
gunboats, and, speaking generally, is *not in the state of strength* it should
be. It appears *wicked and criminal* to me to delay a moment in
organising what we have got, and formulating a plan for calling, at any
moment, on our vast resources. The scheme which £250 gives us will
not only save millions in the prevention of scares and panics, but prevent
most probably an actual disaster on the first commencement of hostilities
The gloomy and threatening appearances in the East make it a matter
of Imperial necessity that a plan of preparation for war *should be taken in
hand at once.*

"I would most earnestly entreat the present Board, with all the fervour
at my command, not to neglect this question for another moment; we
have some of the most able naval officers of great experience, judgment,
and practical knowledge, who could instantly take the position suggested
as head of the Intelligence Department. The keen anxiety I feel upon
this question will be sufficient excuse for my mentioning names in this
paper. We have an officer on the present Board eminently suited for the
position (which for many apparent reasons ought to be held by an admiral)
—I refer to Sir Anthony Hoskins, while outside the Board there is Sir
William Dowell and Vice-Admiral Nowell Salmon.

"I do not say that my plan is the best or only plan for grappling with
the immediate danger. Perhaps it is not, but that is easily remedied by
debate and consideration.

"But I do most *distinctly and emphatically*, with all the power at my
command, that the very gravest state of affairs would occur to this
country if war was declared with a first-rate maritime Power, simply
through want of organisation, forethought, and ordinary common sense,
which would be simply ludicrous if not so perilous.

"I am confident that the country as well as the service would be
simply aghast, and filled with justifiable anger, if they fully understood
the *utter absence of any plan or preparation for war*, and the immense
loss which would instantly accrue to this colossal Empire through the
neglect of such preparation if war were suddenly declared.

"In conclusion, the questions I would ask the Board are these—

"1. Can it be denied that the gravest and most certain danger exists to
the country if the facts stated in this paper are true?

"2. Can it be denied that these facts *are* true?

"3. If so, should not *immediate* steps be taken to minimise the
danger?"

To the general accuracy and truthfulness of the statements contained in Lord Charles Beresford's confidential Memorandum I feel compelled, by a sense of justice to his lordship and to the public, to bear the testimony of my official experience. I regret to be obliged to do so, but as I have so repeatedly deplored the perils to which this country has been exposed and have dilated, even *ad nauseam*, in office and out of office, as to the utter inadequacy of the fleet to meet the difficulties and responsibilities devolving upon the Admiralty in the event of war, that I have no alternative left, and the country cannot feel too grateful to Lord Charles Beresford for his Memorandum, and to Lord George Hamilton and the members of his Board for so energetically and judiciously carrying out the suggestions contained therein.

This, however, was not done until after Lord Charles Beresford's resignation; the Defence Act and the whole of the re-awakened interest in the fleet dates from the resignation of Lord Charles, who sacrificed himself in his endeavour to benefit the service of which he is so distinguished a member.

Captain Lord Charles Beresford entered Parliament at a very early period of life, and by several speeches in the House of Commons displayed so much ability, tact, and knowledge of his profession as to at once obtain the ear and attention of the House, which marked him as an officer of great promise. Fortune favoured him, for when in command of the *Condor* at the bombardment of Alexandria, by his nautical skill and gallantry, he secured a high reputation, and where he subsequently rendered most valuable and important services on shore. His lordship was again brought to the front by the Nile Expedition. Whilst in command of the *Safie*, he, with chief engineer Benbow, repaired the boiler, which had been pierced by a shot, the repairs being effected under fire, during which time he was exposed to the greatest personal danger, and under the most trying circumstances exhibited a coolness and courage which excited general admiration amongst his brother officers and country-men at home.

There can be no second opinion that the Intelligence Department of the Admiralty had for years been in a very unsatisfactory state. As a matter of fact there had been no Intelligence Department. There was a department called "a Foreign Intelligence Committee," founded by Sir George Tryon, but it had nothing to do with war organisation; its sole duty was to inform the Admiralty what foreign govern-ments were doing, but had nothing whatever to do with the many important and vital points in Lord Charles's paper. Abroad the Admiralty and War Office are in the Intelligence Department, and everything else is subservient to it.

It having been decided at last that there should be an Intelligence Department, and that it should be placed upon a proper and permanent footing, it was much to be regretted that differences of opinion should have arisen between the First Sea Lord and Lord Charles Beresford. The importance the latter attached to this new department was so great that, in consequence of a reduction in the proposed staff of which he disapproved, it was generally supposed that he tendered his resignation, though in reality it was only one question out of many on the great subject of the strength of the fleet and war organisation.

The retirement of Lord Charles Beresford was at the time universally deplored by the service and by the country; though perhaps he has conferred more substantial benefits upon both by the frank and outspoken expression of his opinions, to which he could not have given utterance had he been hampered by the proprieties of official restraint.

The fact that all his proposals have been taken up and, to a certain extent, carried through during the last few years, added to the immense sums of money that have been spent on the fleet, show how right Lord Charles's calculations were, and it is to him, in no small degree, that the country owes its approximate safe position.

In the formation of a new establishment, such as the Naval Intelligence Department, it is but natural that a variety of opinion should be entertained as to its extent and composition: by the Treasury from a financial point of view, by the Admiralty as affecting the status and duties of the First Sea Lord.

I have shown elsewhere that the departmental duties entailed upon the First Sea Lord were so arduous and multifarious that it was with difficulty he could get through the daily routine of office work, much less find time for the careful consideration of those grave and important questions of national defence and commercial protection which rightly devolve upon the Admiral filling that responsible office, and which would have been impossible, under any circumstances, without the professional aid of the staff of an Intelligence Department. To what extent it will be necessary to augment this important department will in all probability be for some time a moot point, as the duties of the First Sea Lord are year by year becoming more arduous and embarrassing. He is entrusted with the composition of the fleet, its organisation and mobilisation, and its most judicious distribution, so as to effectually protect our shores, commercial ports, homeward-bound trade, and many other pressing duties which must be anticipated and provided against. Plans must be devised and well considered as to the best means to be employed for shutting up the ports of the enemy, or, by acting from a given base, to prevent depredations being made upon our commerce. Arrangements must be made for protecting the four principal trade routes as pointed out by Sir Phipps Hornby, and for the despatch of cruisers so as to maintain

R

a complete line of inter-communication; the cable stations must also be protected, so as to prevent the mother country from being cut off from her Colonies. Also the defence or destruction of the Suez Canal is a subject that requires to be seriously dealt with. In case of troubles in the North, it would be necessary to be provided with a North Sea and Baltic Fleet, so as to be able to meet at once any unlooked-for eventualities in that quarter; and, lastly, to ensure the daily supply of food and raw materials for our yearly-increasing populations, by convoy or other means—a duty never yet entailed upon the Admiralty.

This is but a brief and imperfect summary of the duties which will devolve upon the First Sea Lord in the future on the first outbreak of war, and which cannot be too soon thought out and elaborated under various heads by an efficient and experienced staff of the Intelligence Department, placed under the First Sea Lord. It is only by such means that we can hope to be first in the field in the day of trial, upon which success depends, and to obliterate the national reproach of being " England the Unready."

Although I am strongly of opinion that no method could be devised that would be better than that adopted by Sir James Graham in the general management of the Board, still I am firmly convinced that in all matters of purely naval operations, the First Sea Lord should be held solely responsible, the same as the Commander-in-chief of the army, and that the former should have the same rank and position as the latter. The advantages of a Board meeting at stated times are undeniably great for eliciting and imparting general information; but when it becomes a question of conducting naval operations, and deciding upon the naval defences of the Empire, the responsibility for the advice should rest upon the First Sea Lord, and not upon the Board as such, as it possesses no individuality. It is just as impossible for a Board of half-a-dozen gentlemen to arrange for a naval campaign as it is for the same number of sailors to sit at the helm of a vessel to direct its course.

As a matter of fact, a certain First Lord, accompanied by his naval advisers, were proceeding from Milford Haven to Queenstown, on their visitation in the Admiralty yacht, when a difference of opinion arose between the naval officers on board in regard to certain lights and headlands, and in consequence they undertook to steer the vessel themselves instead of the officer in charge of the helm. What was the result? They nearly made shipwreck of their vessel off the Welsh coast. Whence once their lordships were on *terra firma* this little episode was a subject of playful banter, each imputing the blame to the other, and declaring that his own particular plan would have answered perfectly had it not been interfered with But, at the time, it was an agonising moment in the lives of the First Lord and the civilians on board the *Osborne*.

I am most decidedly of opinion that the Naval Intelligence Department, considering the important and complex problems to be worked out, should be largely augmented by officers of acknowledged skill and ability, and presided over by a flag-officer of high reputation and distinction, working in harmony with the First Sea Lord, and only second to him; I say second, because experience has proved to me that, unless the line is clearly defined, difficulties will arise. The head of the staff should collect and prepare all the information which the First Sea Lord may require, and it is for the latter to turn it to the most useful and profitable account. I entirely concur in opinion with Sir G. Phipps Hornby that, if the Naval Intelligence Department of the Admiralty is placed on a thoroughly efficient and permanent footing, it "will thereby conduce more to the strength of Her Majesty's navy than even the reinforcement of ships" Lord Salisbury's Government had ensured to it.

Lord George Hamilton will always be celebrated in the naval annals of this country as the minister who introduced and carried to a successful issue the provisions of the Naval Defence Act of 1889, when he obtained a grant of £21,500,000 for the construction of seventy vessels of war of various classes to be added to the strength of Her Majesty's navy; although on the 13th of December, 1888, when Lord Charles Beresford propounded the identical same scheme—copied by the Admiralty within three months—Lord Charles was described in the House of Commons as an enthusiastic "seaman given to exaggeration." The Naval Defence Act was a patriotic measure, of which Lord Salisbury, his Cabinet and all his supporters in the House of Commons and outside, may feel justly proud. Especial merit is due to Lord George Hamilton and the members of his Board for the prompt, steady and earnest manner they prosecuted the construction of the vessels sanctioned by the vote; the great deficiency being that of swift and powerful cruisers, therefore the Board acted most sensibly in first pushing forward the ships of that particular type. The *Marathon* class had proved upon trial not to have come up to expectations in some respects; the First Lord consequently, in accordance with the recommendations of his naval advisers, determined not to order any more of that class, but to construct second-class cruisers of 3400 tons, which were in other ships gradually increased, and finally brought up to 4360 tons, upon finding that an even greater addition of tonnage would render them more efficient, and better fitted to perform the especial duties for which they were designed, and at the same time give greater speed, increase the coal capacity, and afford better accommodation for the ships' company, and improve the ventilation of the vessels.* It is unquestionably of the utmost importance that fast cruisers should be added to the fleet, and that as quickly as possible; and all steps taken for the attainment of this object are deserving of all praise. At the same time the suggestions of Lord Brassey, that there should be an augmentation to the *Blake* and *Blenheim* type for service on the Australian, Pacific, and far-distant stations, is one that ought to commend itself to the favourable consideration of the Board of Admiralty in the near future, and it is the more deserving of attention when we learn that Mr. Tracey, the Secretary of the Navy for the United States,† attaches so much importance to size and speed, that in a proposal to his Government to construct twenty-nine cruisers, no less than twenty-two are to be of 5400 tons and upwards. It must be admitted that Lord Brassey's suggestion gains momentum when we bear in mind that Russia has recently laid down the keel of a vessel to be named the *Rurick*. She is to be 426 feet long, 67 feet broad, with a draught of water of 27 feet, and a displacement of 11,000 tons. She will have a side armour of 10 inches, and a deck armour of 2½ inches. Her speed is to be 18 knots, without any arrangement for forced draught, and a coal capacity for 20,000 miles at 10 knots. It is impossible to over-estimate the mischief that such a vessel would be capable of inflicting upon the Australian, China, or Pacific stations from her power, speed, armour defence, and coal endurance; and there is every reason to believe that this is the class of vessel which Russia and the United States contemplate building, to prey upon our commerce in the event of war—a precedent only too

---

* The second-class cruisers, since the above was written, have gone on steadily increasing in tonnage.—ED.

† Mr. Tracey was Secretary of the Navy for the United States at the time the above was written.—ED.

likely to be followed by other naval powers.* The proper course for England to pursue is to take and keep the lead in this as in everything else appertaining to naval affairs. It is perfectly true that vessels of the *Blake* and *Blenheim* type are very expensive, but it is only such vessels that can effectually protect our extensive commerce on distant stations ; and be it remembered by those who begrudge the money that it is the most economical mode of insurance and the most certain method of diminishing risk. The people of this country do not realise that the money spent in the augmentation of the navy will be repaid ten times over to the nation by the protection it affords to life and property in time of war, to say nothing of the millions saved by *not* going to war, for the stronger our navy the less probability there is of war.

At the conclusion of the naval manœuvres of 1887 the two squadrons, under the respective commands of Sir William Hewitt and Admiral Fremantle, anchored in the Downs, thus forming a fleet of ten sail-of-the-line. The deficiency in speed and coal capacity was painfully exhibited during these manœuvres, the average speed of the squadrons being only from nine to ten knots an hour, the coal capacity inadequate in every instance, though varying in extent in every ship. Much about the same time that distinguished admiral, Lord Alcester, directed public attention to the speed and superior qualifications of a new French cruiser named the *Tage*, which was reputed to have attained to the speed of eighteen knots an hour. It may therefore be reasonably asked what protection could a fleet of ten sail-of-the-line, steaming only from nine to ten knots an hour, afford to the

* Since the above was written the *Rurick* has been completed and put into commission ; and another vessel, still more powerful, has been constructed by the same Power, named the *Russia*. The *Powerful* and *Terrible* were built as a reply to the *Rurick* and *Russia*.—ED.

wealthy towns upon the south coast, or to the commerce in the Channel, against the probable exploits of such a cruiser as the *Tage*, steaming eighteen knots, issuing from Cherbourg or Brest, unless England could despatch cruisers of equal power and speed to put a stop to her depredations? Since that time a great change for the better has been effected, and it is indeed most cheering and encouraging to observe the vast improvement that has taken place in the composition and augmentation of the Channel Squadron and Mediterranean Fleet, as well as in the vessels employed as district ships, and those in the first-class reserve at the several ports. The improved condition of Her Majesty's navy reflects the highest credit upon Lord George Hamilton and the members of his Board, and clearly shows how much can be accomplished by well thought-out arrangements in, comparatively speaking, so brief a period. There are two or three other questions awaiting solution, namely, whether the transatlantic steamers, and others under Admiralty contract, will be able efficiently to discharge the duty of scouting (a duty in which our captains cannot be too frequently exercised), or whether a special class of vessels possessing the highest possible speed (all other considerations being regarded as secondary) should not be constructed to perform a duty of such vital importance? Another question is the employment of the ram, which latterly has not been discussed with the frequency and thoughtfulness so important a subject undoubtedly demands. When we see the terrible results which have followed recent collisions at sea, the ram cannot fail to be regarded as an instrument of warfare likely to exercise an immense influence in any future naval action, if judiciously handled and brought boldly into play at the right moment. There is a third question which as yet has never been brought to the front in this country, though, strange to say, that young and promising naval power, Germany, has already been seriously discussing it, and in which Prince

Henry of Prussia has taken a prominent and distinguished part. The question is the duty and personal position of a naval Commander-in-chief in a general action? Whether, under the altered conditions of naval warfare, it is his duty to lead into action, as in the days of Nelson and Collingwood, or whether with a choice selection of a few vessels in reserve it would not be more advantageous that he should watch the progress of the encounter at a given distance, and at the right moment bring the reserve to bear with telling force upon the weak part of the enemy, and thereby bring the battle to a final and decisive issue? It is a very delicate matter for naval officers themselves to deal with, but it ought to be clearly defined during a period of profound peace. No Englishman doubts for a moment the personal courage of our naval commanders; but this is a subject in which there is a strong professional feeling, and in which personal gallantry may reasonably be expected to outweigh tactical prudence. It is therefore to be hoped that our German neighbours will, by the discussion raised by Prince Henry of Prussia, clear the way for the settlement of a question so gravely affecting the real interests of the navy and the delicate susceptibilities of the gallant and distinguished naval officers of whom England has for centuries been, and is to-day, so justly proud.

It would be impossible to estimate too highly the great and numerous advantages which have accrued from the naval manœuvres of the last four years. Everybody admits that great benefits have resulted from the annual training, practical tactics, and gunnery exercises of our squadrons. During these manœuvres errors have been discovered in the construction of our ships which will, when remedied, tend materially to improve them, and in all future vessels these errors can be provided against. Through the naval manœuvres deficiencies have been rendered apparent in the *personnel*, especially in the complements of lieutenants, sub-lieutenants, and midshipmen , likewise in the staff of engineers, artificers, trained stokers, coal-trimmers, signalmen, and others whose services it is indispensably necessary to hold in reserve for rapid mobilisation. These, with one or two exceptions, are matters of mere detail, but all most necessary, though varying in importance. It is fortunate that Lord George Hamilton takes in such good part the numerous representations made to him in regard to the blots which, from time to time, are brought under his notice, and which, instead of producing a feeling of irritation, as was often the case in days gone by, they, on the contrary, have been received by him in a kindly spirit, and, what is of more importance, a remedy applied as promptly as circumstances would admit. A stronger proof than this could not be adduced to demonstrate his lordship's personal desire to remedy the shortcomings of the service. To have effected thus much good would alone confer no slight boon upon the naval service, but these naval manœuvres have, at last, led to the consideration of those far more important subjects which First Sea Lords, and other naval officers of ability and experience, found so much difficulty in bringing under the serious attention of the Cabinet through the medium of First Lords, namely, the duties devolving upon the Admiralty and the First Sea Lord at the first outbreak of war, which I have already touched upon when dealing with the desirability of extending the Naval Intelligence Department.

Lord George Hamilton has done much towards providing a magnificent material, and our fleet is month by month increasing in numerical strength; and, what is of greater consequence than mere numbers, we now have vessels possessing power, speed, and coal endurance, which qualities are well calculated to enable the vessels to efficiently perform the duties which in time of war they will be called upon to discharge; but this is not all, for Lord George

Hamilton has pointed out that ships are of little value unless adequately armed, efficiently officered, and properly manned. Ships hastily equipped with crews new to their duties are not those which ought to be permitted to take part n a first engagement, upon the success of which our prestige and naval supremacy mainly depends. Assuming that our fleet is all that could be desired, the one great question still to be thought out and decided upon is its judicious distribution, so that it can at once take the initiative, defend our shores and protect our commerce, and let us take care that we enter upon the fight with all the odds in our favour.

To Lord George Hamilton, and to the several members of his Board, must be accorded the unusual merit of anticipating and providing against those very national dangers which preceding governments have been only too ready, for party purposes, to postpone indefinitely, and in some cases to utterly ignore.

Amongst the many valuable reforms carried into effect by the administration of Lord George Hamilton, perhaps the most conspicuous and important are the two introduced into Her Majesty's dockyards—the one which relates to the more rapid construction of ships, the other to the improved system of keeping the accounts. The course pursued, during the past sixty years, in the building of our men-of-war was misleading, dilatory, and very expensive It nevertheless possessed many departmental advantages which were capable of being cleverly turned to profitable account for party purposes whenever convenient opportunities presented themselves Ships building make a great show in the Navy List, and those in office were always able to point to the great activity prevailing in the dockyards by referring to the large number of vessels in course of construction. If any doubt was expressed on the subject (as neither the House of Commons nor the general public knew anything of the degree

of forwardness these ships were in), it was very easy to add
to their numbers by ordering the keels of more vessels to be
laid down, and the names of the new ships at once put in
the Navy List. Thus official ingenuity is at times equal to
a great emergency! The line-of-battleships on a certain
occasion being several short of the number the navy was
supposed to possess, the difficulty was promptly and most
economically remedied. A new heading was forthwith opened,
entitled "Ships ordered to be built," and under this head were
placed the names of line-of-battleships sufficient to meet the
required number, and in connection with this clever stroke of
the pen the well-known phrase of paper ships and phantom
fleets in all probability originated.

To show the extent to which the several dockyards were
filled with unfinished ships by many preceding Boards of
Admiralty, I need only draw attention to a statement made
at Blackpool by Mr. Forwood, the able Political Secretary to
this Board of Admiralty, and, in confirmation of what I have
advanced above, I will quote his words: " When in 1886 the
present Board came into office, the amount of capital expended in incomplete ships—and therefore lying dormant so
far as their effective worth was concerned—was £8,500,000."
A system so faulty could only lead to a wasteful expenditure.
Even at the risk of repetition I feel I cannot too forcibly
bring the evil of the course pursued before the attention of
the public, so great was the delay and so ruinous was the
extravagance in the completion of our ships. In some cases
vessels positively remained nine years on the stocks, and
were frequently, when near completion, half taken to pieces
to make alterations consequent upon the change of armaments
and to introduce improvements which the progress in naval
architecture and in the machinery had, during those nine
years, rendered necessary; so that when the ships were
actually launched, they bore little or no resemblance to their

original design. In some way or other, I have on almost every page of this volume set forth the utter inadequacy of the fleet to perform the duties that would devolve upon it in time of war. Our reserve force for years consisted, for the most part, of ships upon the stocks, some with their keels only just laid down, and of vessels which had returned from foreign service standing in need of extensive repairs, which latter, for want of funds, could not be taken in hand, and were therefore blocking up our harbours. Yet these were the vessels which were to uphold our naval supremacy!

Nothing could be more judicious than the course adopted by this Board of Admiralty, in first completing the vessels they found upon the stocks before commencing the ships sanctioned by the Naval Defence Act. The rapid and the successful progress made in the last named contrasts most favourably with the dilatory and wasteful system now happily exploded

In addition to the many advantages that will accrue to the country from the vessels constructed under the Defence Act, it is most encouraging to observe that a powerful augmentation is being made to our fleet, by placing new engines and modern armaments into ironclads of an older type, which will enable them to render valuable service in time of war * In fine, the whole arrangements as now carried on in regard to our shipbuilding is deserving of the highest commendation, and must inevitably lead to the still more beneficial results as greater experience is gained.

For the last sixty years, to my certain knowledge, the tinkering of the dockyard accounts has been an amusing and favourite pastime with First Lords and Political Secre-

---

* At the meeting of the Naval Architects this year Lord Charles Beresford read a Paper recommending seventeen old but useful vessels for re-armament, and was cordially supported by Sir Edward Reed.

George Hamilton

taries, and it is indeed fortunate for the country that at last they have been taken in hand by a gentleman of such acknowledged ability as Mr Forwood,* who has grasped and mastered the difficulties of this complicated question, and has reduced them to a practical and intelligible form. To Mr. Forwood we are likewise. indebted for one of the most important reforms the navy has stood in need of for many years, namely, the transfer of the Naval Ordnance from the War Office to the Admiralty—a measure which numerous committees have hitherto failed to bring to so desirable a result. Many were the complaints made by Commanders-in-chief at the several ports that ships under sailing orders could not proceed to sea because their guns or gun-carriages had not been delivered, or that the ammunition had been unexpectedly delayed. Inconveniences of this description must constantly arise, to the great detriment of the public service, when one department is dependent upon another, but this, the transfer of the Naval Ordnance to the Admiralty, will in future effectually remove, so far as the navy is concerned.

The minister who is brilliant in debate and ready in reply is apt to obtain for himself an amount of praise, from both the country and from his party, which is not so willingly accorded to the successful financier, the sound and practical reformer, or to the able administrator who, with patience and labour, masters complicated details and brings to a successful issue measures which confer permanent and substantial benefits upon the country; and, amongst the latter, Lord George Hamilton and Mr Childers occupy prominent places, and their names will appear in history in the front rank of the leading statesmen of their day

Lord George Hamilton has been a great, successful, and most fortunate naval administrator. Great, because he has taken a grand and comprehensive view of the duties devolving

* Now the Right Hon. Sir Arthur Forwood, Bart.—ED.

upon his high office ; successful, because he has accomplished
so much for the good of the navy during his tenure of office ;
and fortunate, because he carried public opinion with him,
and had the support of Mr. W. H. Smith and Mr Goschen,
two ex-First Lords, as members of the Cabinet presided over
by the Marquess of Salisbury, a Prime Minister who had the
courage to boldly encounter the many difficulties and heavy
liabilities bequeathed to him by his predecessors, and apply
an effectual remedy

I have dilated, at considerable length, upon the great
services rendered by Mr Childers to the navy some twenty
years ago, and it is from that date that a very marked change
is discernable in the opinions expressed by the leading
members of that distinguished profession, in reference to
the requirements and reforms so indispensably necessary
towards placing the navy in the high state of efficiency to
which it is fast approaching.   Mr. Childers' scheme of naval
retirement, unappreciated as it was by some, is nevertheless
the pivot upon which everything turned, and from that
period the powerful influence which was opposed to all
change is now happily thrown into the contrary balance ;
and distinguished officers are as anxious to urge on salutary
reforms as they were in days gone by to obstinately obstruct
them.   This change in naval opinion has greatly facilitated
the carrying out of the measures proposed by Lord George
Hamilton and his naval colleagues.   Some of the most
important I will briefly recapitulate, to enable my readers
more fully to appreciate the success which has attended the
unceasing labours of this Board.

1. First in importance is, unquestionably, the Naval
Defence Bill, the provisions of which have been carried
out in a steady and most satisfactory manner.

2. The establishment of the Naval Intelligence Department can be regarded only as a measure that is second

to that of the Naval Defence Act, for upon its efficiency everything depends.

3. The Mediterranean Fleet has been augmented up to ten sail-of-the-line and four powerful cruisers and a flotilla of smaller craft.

4. The Channel Squadron has been reorganized, and now consists of four powerful ironclads of the *Admiral* class, to which have been added two first-class cruisers.

5. The district ships have been gradually superseded by those possessing greater speed and improved armaments.

6. All the vessels in the first-class reserve have been placed under the direct command and supervision of the Commanders-in-chief at the several ports, and a certain number of experienced hands are told off for each ship, so as to form a valuable nucleus for the ships' companies, should they be suddenly commissioned.

7. The institution of the naval manœuvres, which have led to many beneficial results, and the deficiencies they have brought to light both in ships and *personnel*, have either been remedied or are in course of amelioration.

8. All telegraph stations along the coast have been placed in direct communication with the Admiralty, an arrangement which has greatly facilitated the despatch of instructions to cruisers on the whole of our sea-board.

9. The composition of our squadrons upon several distant stations exhibits a marked improvement.

10. The erection of naval barracks is a measure which will tend materially to the rapid mobilisation of the fleet, as well as add to the health and comfort of our brave sailors, who have hitherto been located in old hulks and receiving-ships.

11. The transfer of the Naval Ordnance from the War Office to the Admiralty.

12. Important reforms in the dockyards, and the more rapid construction of our men-of-war.

13. Dockyards' accounts placed upon a vastly improved and more intelligible footing.

The foregoing briefly summarises, though imperfectly, the great amount of good work that has been effected by the administration of Lord George Hamilton; but, great as it is, there still remains much more to be accomplished, as it must be borne in mind that the great battle for naval supremacy has yet to be fought. Eighty-seven years have elapsed since the glorious victory off Cape Trafalgar was achieved. Mighty changes have been wrought since then in everything appertaining to naval warfare; therefore it is of paramount importance that the first action should be entered upon with ships of the most powerful type, guns of the most approved description, crews trained to the highest point of efficiency, and, what is even of greater moment, the command of the fleet, and the officers entrusted with the command of ships, should be selected from those recognised by the service as being the most able and distinguished upon the list, so that not a single chance of success is thrown away. The destinies of the country depend, as it were, upon the cast of the die.

The people of this country are so accustomed to regard our fleet as invincible, and to view with indifference the great armies of the Continent, that they are but little aware of the amount of money, time, talent and labour which has been so lavishly expended in order to bring them up to their present high state of perfection. Let us be wise in time, and take care that we in future bestow the same unremitting care and attention upon our navy which the great military powers upon the Continent do upon their armies, and not allow a mistaken idea of economy to curtail that expenditure which those entrusted to give professional advice to those in power consider as indispensably necessary for the efficiency of the fleet to ensure victory and success.

CHAPTER XXIV.

Remarks upon the Naval Programme of 1894-5.

The necessity of leaving to the pen of a younger man the duty of record-
ing the administration of the Rt. Hon. Earl Spencer—Merits accord for
refusing to yield to party pressure for retrenchment—The advantages
of large ships.

It is a source of sincere regret to me that old age and
infirmities preclude me from following, as closely as I could
wish, the naval policy of Lord Spencer, who succeeded Lord
George Hamilton as First Lord of the Admiralty in 1892,*
when Mr. Gladstone became Prime Minister for the fourth
time. In the nature of things these infirmities must increase,
as I am now in my eighty-seventh year, and, however much
I may deplore it, I am compelled to forego the gratification
of including in this volume Lord Spencer's naval administration, and must leave to the pen of a younger and abler man
to bear testimony to the patriotic zeal and comprehensive
views entertained by his lordship and the members of his
Board, in regard to the naval requirements of the country,
who were—

Admiral Sir A. H. Hoskins, K.C B.;
Vice-Admiral Sir F. W. Richards, K.C.B.;
Rear-Admiral Lord Walter Kerr;
Rear-Admiral J. A. Fisher, C.B., Controller of the Navy;

* The Author did not originally intend to refer at all to the naval
administration of Lord Spencer for the reasons stated, and because he was
abroad, but Sir John was so pleased with his lordship's explanation of
his naval policy that he could not forego the desire to express, in a few
words, the gratification he experienced.—Ed.

s

Edmund Robertson, Esq., M P.;

Sir Ughtred J. Kay-Shuttleworth, Bart., M.P., Parliamentary and Financial Secretary;

Sir Evan MacGregor, K.C.B., Permanent Secretary.

Especial merit should be accorded to this Board for reso-
lutely refusing to yield to party pressure to abstain from
bringing forward that enlarged scheme of ship-building,
works, etc., which certain members of Parliament clamoured
for, but which Lord Spencer and his naval advisers deemed
requisite to our national defences, and not to sanction by
silence any misrepresentation of their professional opinions
made in the House of Commons.

Although I am ˙ precluded from performing a duty so
congenial to my predilections, I nevertheless cannot refrain
from expressing the pleasure I derived from the perusal of
Lord Spencer's naval programme for 1894–5, in which
he proposes to initiate the grand works at Gibraltar and
Keyham, which are so urgently needed, and to take in hand
the other necessary works at the several arsenals at home.
But it was in comparing the vessels which were first built
when the Naval Defence Bill first came into operation, with
those of a later date, and especially the new ones ordered to
be built by Lord Spencer and his Board, that I experienced
so much personal gratification.

There can be little doubt that the *Magnificent* and *Majestic*
will be in advance of all line-of-battleships hitherto constructed, but it is still more in the cruisers that I observed
the most marked improvements. I noticed the first-class
have been gradually increased in tonnage from 7700 tons
with 10,000 horse-power—the *Royal Arthur*; to 14,200 tons
with 25,000 horse-power—the *Terrible*: whilst the second-
class in the same way has been increased in tonnage from
3400 tons with 7000 horse-power—the *Andromache*; to
5600 tons with 8000 horse-power—the *Minerva*. This

augmentation of tonnage to the cruisers is of the utmost importance, for an increase to the size of the vessel indicates at once that she possesses higher speed, heavier armaments, and great coal capacity, which latter qualification enables her to keep the sea for a longer period. Numbers and small vessels have always been in favour with economists, because they are cheap and make a greater show. The policy pursued at the Admiralty under Lord George Hamilton and continued by Lord Spencer is identical with that of Sir Thomas Hardy in the administration of Sir James Graham in 1830. Sir Thomas advocated, even in the days of sailing-ships, the paramount importance of three-deckers, 90-gun ships, and powerful 50-gun frigates.

Why I attach so much importance to Sir Thomas Hardy's opinion is because he took an active and prominent part in all the principal actions of the great war, and therefore the policy he urged was the result of practical and personal experience. He used to say "that the powerful battle-ships carried everything in a general action, and it was the large frigates which disposed of the smaller craft." Now, if that was the case with sailing-vessels, how much more certain is it to be so in these days of steam, when the speed of every vessel can be reduced to a certainty.

Sir Thomas Hardy was perhaps the ablest naval officer who ever held the appointment of First Sea Lord, and in confirmation of his superior qualities, I have the words of England's greatest admiral, Lord Nelson, who said, "I never knew Hardy wrong upon any professional subject; he seems imbued with an intuitive right judgment."

Sir Thomas Hardy was thirty years in advance of the service, and he alone, of all the great admirals of his day, foresaw the mighty changes steam and science would effect throughout every branch of the naval service, and his prophetic words are being verified year by year.

CHAPTER XXV.

THE *PERSONNEL* OF THE NAVY.

Chronic complaints in regard to promotion—Port-admirals reporting upon screw line-of-battleships—The crowded state of the lists—Officers advanced in age unfit for high commands—Opinions of distinguished admirals in regard to young officers—How an admiral was cured of complaining—Beyond the power of man to form plans to meet the needs of the service and the wishes of the officers—The case of the lieutenants—A proposal in regard to the nomenclature of naval officers —Merit rewarded—The crushing effects of responsibility on advancing years—The service is maintained for the good of the country—Selection from the captains' list for promotion—The difficulty of doing what is right—The status of engineer officers—The annual entry of boys into the navy—The present system of enrolment of the Naval Volunteer Committee—Lord George Hamilton's knowledge of managing the navy.

THE *personnel* of the navy is one of the most important and perplexing subjects connected with naval administration that any First Lord can be called upon to deal with. The question had never been fairly met until Mr. Childers took it in hand in the year 1870, which did away so successfully with all those complaints and chronic discontent in regard to captains not being able to obtain the command of ships, and of undue favouritism displayed in the selection of those officers who did, are now seldom if ever heard in the service. The task undertaken by Mr. Childers was a very difficult· one, whether viewed financially or professionally.

The great war caused the various lists to be swollen to a most inconvenient extent; the result was general dissatisfaction at the want of employment and promotion Nor was this all, for the officers at the head of the profession in active service were, in many instances, upwards of eighty years of age, and from their bodily infirmities were utterly unequal to the responsibilities devolving upon them; and under these circumstances the important duties which they as commanders-in-chief ought, personally, to have discharged were invariably deputed to the flag-captain and the admiral's secretary. It was positively ridiculous to require port-admirals to report upon the efficiency of screw line-of-battleships and men-of-war steamers, they being entirely ignorant of everything connected with steam. Many admirals were appointed to commands who had been on half-pay for fifteen or twenty years, and who naturally enough regarded with little satisfaction the many innovations which the advance of science had gradually introduced into every branch of the naval service during the time they had been unemployed. I can recollect an instance in which a captain paid off a frigate in 1826, who never served a day afloat until he was appointed Vice-Admiral and Commander-in-chief at the Nore in the year 1854, having been the whole of this time on half-pay. The officers, previous to the administration of Mr. Childers, were admirals of great distinction, and had in their day performed many brilliant services; it was therefore difficult to place them upon a retired list, a step Mr. Childers took with reluctance, and for which neither the service nor the country in previous years would have been at all prepared, however advantageous such a measure might have been regarded for both. It was not only the admirals' list that was over-crowded, but that of the captains' to a still greater degree. Sometimes upwards of thirty years elapsed before they could attain to flag-rank; for instance, Admiral the Hon. Sir Richard Dundas (Lord Melville's son) was promoted to be captain at the age of twenty-two, and did not obtain his promotion to rear-admiral's rank until he had reached his fifty-fourth year, being at the time a Lord of the

Admiralty. These were his words upon my congratulating him upon his promotion: "You are very kind, Mr. Briggs, but it has come too late; had I been made an admiral ten years ago there was nothing I. then felt I could not do,' but now I have had forty years' service taken out of me. Officers of my standing have usually served in every part of the globe; they have had to encounter the heat of Jamaica and Hong-Kong, they have been frozen off Halifax and New-foundland, to say nothing of the gales which prevail in the Channel, North Sea, and Baltic; and when you consider that they are night after night drenched to the skin, that their eyes suffer by looking through night glasses, and the drums of their ears are cracked from gunnery practice, it is not very surprising if they suffer in some way or other as they advance in years, more especially when you bear in mind the fevers and illnesses they are liable to in the course of their protracted service in unhealthy climates. Few officers are really good for much after fifty or fifty-five years of age." It is a singular fact that the most distinguished officers of the profession one and all seemed to be impressed with the necessity of employing young officers. Sir George Cockburn was of opinion that if a captain was not fit to command a line-of-battleships at thirty he never would be. Sir Thomas Hardy thought the younger the officers were the better, provided they knew their duty. The following Admiralty lords and admirals—Sir William Gage, Sir William Parker, Sir Charles Napier, Lord Fitzhardinge, Sir Fanshawe Martin, Sir Richard Dundas, Captain Lord Charles Beresford, and many others—have expressed themselves strongly upon the subject and all have advocated the employment of young officers in responsible commands; but perhaps the strongest argument I can advance is the fact that admirals when appointed to commands almost invariably select as their flag-captain a young officer at the bottom of the list in preference to an old one at the top of it.

Some of the most brilliant actions during the great war were fought by captains who in these days would be regarded as of extreme youth, which statement can be confirmed by reference to 'James's Naval History.' Neither need we go so far back as the great war, for the names of Sir William Peel, Captain Burgoyne, Sir William Hewitt, and the Victoria Cross lieutenants who served in the Black Sea, and during the Crimean War and Indian Mutiny, are well known throughout the service, and still more recently—the lieutenants of the Egyptian campaign. But if ever there was a time when officers in the prime of life and well-strung nerves were required, it is now; for the command of a modern ironclad of 14,000 tons, and of 13,000 horse-power, armed with 110 or 67-ton guns, and steaming at a speed varying from 18 to 21 knots an hour, is enough to test the capabilities of our best and ablest officers. If so much is required in a captain, it is not difficult to imagine the grave responsibility devolving upon an admiral in actual command of a fleet of some fifteen or twenty ironclads, each representing a money value of from £500,000 to something little short of a million. He ought indeed to bear comparison to the Great Charles of Sweden, as described in the fine lines of Dr. Johnson:

> "A frame of adamant, a soul of fire,
> No dangers fright him, and no labours tire."

It was plainly evident that, until some comprehensive scheme of naval retirement was devised, it would be impossible to remove the chronic discontent which for so many years had existed in the naval service, in consequence of officers not being able to obtain either employment or promotion, attributable to the crowded state of the several lists. Nor was their discontent to be wondered at when I state that there were 800 captains upon the list, and only between 60 and 70 employed. When a captain applied for employment, he was generally told that he stood too high on the list for a small frigate, and not high enough for a large one; and again, too high for a frigate, and not high enough for a line-of-battleship; added to which, under the most favourable ،circumstances, after having obtained the command of a line-of-battleship, thirty years elapsed between promotion to the captains' list and obtaining flag-rank · for example, Sir Richard Dundas, to whom I have already referred, was made a captain in 1824, standing 806 upon the list, and was not made a rear-admiral until 1856, having remained no less than thirty-two years upon the captains' list   Under these circumstances it must be admitted that captains had excellent grounds for complaint, of which they liberally availed themselves; the Admiralty, the First Lord, and the members of the Board coming in for a fair share of blame.   During the administration of Lord Minto, Sir Charles Adam frequently complained to me that a certain captain, who took a prominent lead at the Senior United, was always abusing Lord Minto, his brother-in-law, and the Board for not giving him the command of a line-of-battleship, and that his denunciations had become intolerable.   I replied: " The remedy is in your own hands, sir!   You can easily silence him if you like—appoint him to a ship.   It is the last thing he really wants, and he will be down here in half-an-hour to entreat you to get him off "   Sir Charles then inquired, "Do you really think so ? "   I replied, " Certainly."   Sir Charles upon the moment addressed him a note, to inform him that the First Lord had asked him to suggest the name of a captain for a fine 80-gun ship intended for the Mediterranean, and, knowing his extreme anxiety for employment, he had much pleasure in acquainting him that he had proposed his name.   The letter was forthwith despatched, and, before an hour had elapsed, the captain was at the Admiralty soliciting an interview with Sir Charles Adam.   He appeared in a state of extreme agitation, and said to Sir Charles nothing could be more unfortunate, for he was involved in an important law suit in which his interests were deeply concerned, and which compelled him to remain in England He was trustee for a nephew who occasioned him much anxiety, and he might further mention, in confidence, that his health was impaired, and altogether he felt he was not the man he had been; he therefore begged and entreated that Sir Charles would as a great favour get his nomination cancelled. This the First Sea Lord promised to do, which elicited from the captain his warm and grateful thanks. But just before he went away he said, "Don't let it be known, sir, at the 'Senior' that I have declined a ship, will you?" Sir Charles, remembering all that he had said at the club, thought this was asking a little too much, and replied, "No, no; I cannot go quite so far as to promise that, my dear captain." Whereupon the captain started by the mail that night for Scotland, and was not seen at the "Senior" for upwards of a year.

There was another very just and well-founded complaint throughout the service. In former days officers received neither half-pay nor retiring allowance for length of service afloat, that is to say, if one commander was made a captain at twenty-three and another at forty or forty-five, they both received the same amount of half-pay as captains, and the same amount of pay on retirement, though one officer might have served nine years afloat and the other twenty-five years, and several of those years as first lieutenant and second captain in most responsible positions. Thus it will be seen that time served afloat brought neither increased half-pay nor augmented retiring allowance. This complaint was happily removed, as well as many others, by Mr Childers' scheme of naval retirement; and from that date the service has presented an aspect of contentment very different from that of my early reminiscences.

It is beyond the powers of man to frame regulations that would completely comprise the wants of the service and at the same time meet the wishes and expectation of the profession.

Looking calmly and dispassionately at the well-considered regulations drawn up by Mr. Childers,* and the admirable manner in which, as a whole, they have worked during the last twenty years, he had every reason to feel gratified at the result. There have been, as there always must be, particular cases in which bad luck rather than hardship is apparent, for rules once laid down must of necessity be rigidly adhered to. The case of the lieutenants, in spite of all that has been done to improve the condition of the *personnel* of the navy, is one that calls loudly for remedial measures. It is truly distressing to see gentlemen of high scientific attainments, with excellent service and strong claims for promotion, attaining to years which virtually disqualify them for further employment in the ranks in which they have served with honour and efficiency, still encumbering the lieutenants' list and deprived of all hopes of professional advancement. It is no wonder, knowing the life, pay, and prospects of the executive officers, if men of independent means retire before they have been many years in the service. When we consider the varied and responsible duties which the officers of this class are now called upon to discharge, and the severe examination they are required to pass, it must be admitted that their pay is inadequate, and the rank assigned to them far too subordinate for their years and position in the service. I think it would in some degree mitigate the extreme severity of their disappointment if an addition was made to the commanders' list, and, to ensure employment, if commanders were appointed instead of first lieutenants to all vessels of upwards of two thousand tons, which would enable them in due course, if not advanced to the rank of captain on the fatal score of

* Died, 1896.

age, to be ultimately placed on the list of retired captains
Lieutenants labour under another great disadvantage, which
they feel very acutely as they advance in years. Officers of
this rank, after eight years' service, rank with majors in the
army, but except those in the profession and a few at the
naval ports, it is not in the least understood; and consequently, in private society, they never have assigned to them
the position to which their services entitle them.

I have always considered the nomenclature of the navy
most misleading from the rank of captain downwards. If
captains were designated commodores, a good naval rank,
commanders retaining their present title, lieutenants were
designated captains, as in the army (as their duties may
be regarded to a considerable extent as corresponding with
that of captain in the sister service), and sub-lieutenants of
three years' standing were made lieutenants, and midshipmen, when passed, had the rank of sub-lieutenant, this
change would, to a certain extent, relieve their case, and
tend to reconcile them to their lot, especially if it carried an
increase of pay. This proposal has been several times under
consideration and very nearly adopted; but professional prejudice, in days gone by, was opposed to every change, which
was regarded by the heads of the profession in the light of a
dangerous innovation, and that without any substantial reason
being assigned.

To dilate upon the *personnel* of the navy is indeed a most
delicate and unpromising subject. It is impossible to reconcile the real requirements of the country with the personal
interests and professional feelings of the naval service, so as
to carry into practical effect what is so urgently needed
without an appearance of injustice and hardship, and without
those in power being most unfairly charged with partiality
and favouritism.

The days of nepotism and favouritism have long passed

away; and whatever may be said to the contrary, there never was a time in the history of the navy when real merits, superior intelligence, and good service were so certain to receive their due reward as now. So anxious are those in power to acknowledge long and faithful service, that captains seldom, if ever, attain to that rank nowadays until they are from thirty-seven to forty-five years of age, the precise period of life at which they would be advanced to flag-rank, if only the good of the country and the real efficiency of the navy were considered. It is impossible to deny that, with advancing years, responsibility has a crushing and overwhelming influence, and that over-caution and the fear of running risks induce those in supreme command to underrate their own power and strength, and thereby lose good opportunities; and it is upon such occasions, particularly in these days when so much will depend upon decision and prompt action; therefore it is most necessary that the commander-in-chief should have his nerves braced by the support of younger men around him, ready to encourage him and share his responsibilities.

It is most desirable that there should be upon the rear-admiral list some officers from thirty-five to forty years of age, in the very prime of life and energy. At the present time captains do not attain to flag-rank until they are fifty-three or fifty-four, and in most cases do not obtain commands for two or three years afterwards.

I am reiterating the strongly expressed opinions of the distinguished admirals with whom I have had the honour of serving as to the imperative necessity of having younger officers upon the flag-list. There are few subjects upon which naval officers agree, but upon this particular subject I never heard a second opinion. My position at the Admiralty enabled me to know the professional and private convictions of the most distinguished officers who had taken an active and, in some cases, a conspicuous part in the operations in the Black Sea and Baltic, and the general consensus of opinion was, that the responsibility of command virtually crushed and overpowered both the Commanders-in-chief. It is natural enough for those advanced in years to imagine that they are equal to high command, and it is impossible not to admire the spirit which engenders this belief; but it is mistaken kindness on the part of those in power to place officers of advanced years in positions in which they are likely to forfeit the high reputation they acquired, by their gallantry and skill, in the earlier days of their professional career.

It must be borne in mind that the service is maintained for the good of the country, and, with every desire to consult the feeling of the naval officers, there are occasions when they must submit to regulations distasteful to them.

One or two measures must be had recourse to ere long Either there must be a selection from the captains' list to flag-rank, as in the army, a measure which, from my knowledge of naval officers, would, I am sure, be extremely unpopular; or, every year, some three or four officers of superior intelligence and professional ability must be promoted to the captains' list at about thirty-three years of age ; and even under these circumstances they could not attain to flag-rank until they were forty-five or forty-eight, as it takes fifteen years to pass through the grade of captain, and it is from that age that every year begins to tell. For the general good of the service the latter course would be the more desirable, although it could not fail to produce some heartburnings on the part of meritorious commanders who are passed over.

At the present time there is not upon the admirals' list a flag-officer who is not senior in age (forty-seven) to that at which Lord Nelson and the Duke of Wellington had attained when they finished their glorious careers.

It would never do in these days of rams, ironclads, swift cruisers and torpedo squadrons, to entrust everything to none but elderly and middle-aged gentlemen. Naval opinion, long experience and naval history, unmistakably demonstrate that it was the spirit, dash, and ambition of youth which raised the navy to the present high standard, in which all Englishmen delight to regard this favourite service.

Age, responsibility and matrimony exercise a very turning influence. Old age and experience are able to tender sage advice, but there is the greatest difference between expressing sound opinions and possessing the nerve to carry them into practical effect in our own person. Responsibility weighs heavily at all times, and especially upon those advancing in years. And matrimony, for reasons upon which I need not dilate, is more detrimental to naval efficiency than even age or responsibility.

Promotion always has been, and always must be, a very delicate and difficult question. To make a selection from among a very large number of gallant and experienced officers cannot fail to be a painful and invidious task. The fortunate recipient of Admiralty favour regards his promotion as a tardy recognition of long-neglected merit, whilst numbers of his brother officers consider they possess far superior claims, and denounce his advancement as an Admiralty "job." I will relate an amusing instance to show the impossibility of doing what is right. It had been known at the clubs for some days that there was a difference of opinion at the Admiralty as to promotion of a very deserving and meritorious officer of long standing in the service, and the advancement of a young and very gallant commander who had recently distinguished himself in action, and had been severely wounded. On the one side, long, steady, and good service; but the officer had attained to years which precluded him from ever obtaining flag-rank. On the other hand, the opportunities of promoting young and efficient officers were of rare occurrence, and could only be done upon very special occasions; therefore it was thought the Board might fairly promote this gallant young officer, who might hereafter prove a valuable addition to the list of flag-officers. As I was passing through the Admiralty courtyard I was accosted by Captain ——, an old friend of mine, who immediately inquired which of the two had got the promotion. Without thinking, I replied, "The old commander." Captain —— exclaimed, "What an infernal shame it is to clog the list with a parcel of old men after this fashion!" I then said, "I beg your pardon, I made a mistake; it is the young commander they have promoted." At this he said, "Is it not abominable that such a mere boy should be put over the head of such an old and deserving officer as the one so cruelly passed over?" I could not help laughing at seeing how rapidly he had wheeled round, and reminded him of what he had said in reference to the old commander, that if promoted, he would only clog the list. Then, with great laughter at his own inconsistency, he replied, "So I did; the fact is the Board should have promoted both." This was very fine talk, but the captain did not explain how two officers could fill one vacancy.

I am quite ready to admit that naval officers have had good grounds for complaint; for the number who really deserve promotion for good service and ability are so many, and the opportunities for promoting are so few, comparatively speaking, that there must always be disappointment on the part of those who find themselves passed over. The promotions, however, of the present day contrast most favourably with those of my earlier years.

I have already dilated at considerable length upon the strong claims of the lieutenants of the Royal Navy for favourable consideration, both as regards rank and pay; and the only other class of officer whose position appears to me calls for amelioration is that of the engineers. The question, however, is beset with grave difficulties, and it seems as if the time had arrived when the status of the engineer officers should now be considered from two points of view, and a line should be drawn between the educated and scientific officer who directs and controls the machinery, and the intelligent and skilled artificer who performs the mechanical duties of the engine-room. The service contains navigating lieu-tenants, gunnery lieutenants, and torpedo lieutenants. Why not engineer lieutenants? Surely, among the junior officers of this rank, there must be in these days many young and scientific officers who, with very little instruction, would be found equal to the duties· of the higher grades of this branch of the naval service, and who might hereafter prove a valuable addition to the *personnel*.

The large augmentation made to the fleet under the Naval Defence Act of 1889, and since, necessitates, as a matter of course, a corresponding increase to the *personnel*, not only in the commissioned ranks, but equally so in the more subordin-ate branches of the service where long training and practical experience are indispensably necessary. Artificers, seamen, gunners and torpedomen, signalmen, coal-trimmers and . others, cannot be extemporised, and, as they will be required in considerable numbers in time of war, no measure could be more sound, sensible and judicious, than the one proposed by Lord George Hamilton and the members of his Board, by which they provide for the new and growing requirements of the naval service. The annual entry of boys of good character will, in due course, if steadily persevered in, secure for the service the class of artificers and petty officers so much required at the present time. No expenditure of public money gives . a better return than that spent upon the training of boys for the fleet, who, as years go on, and as past experience proves, grow attached to the secrvie, take a pride in it, and become year by year most valuable servants of the Crown. A depôt of such men will, in times to come, form an excellent nucleus for the ships in first-class reserve. Another measure proposed by their lordships to increase the fighting reserve of the fleet, is the taking from the troopships and surveying vessels the well-trained and efficient petty officers and seamen, so as to increase the number of men in the naval barracks and depôts.

In the event of a naval war it would be unreasonable to expect the Admiralty could provide a sufficient number of men from the regular establishments to meet such an emergency, and therefore it is most desirable in a time of peace to ascertain, with unmistakable accuracy, the amount of assistance which can be depended upon from the reserves and naval volunteers;* and with a view to a thorough investigation of this important subject, Lord George Hamilton appointed a committee, presided over by Vice-Admiral Sir George Tryon, "to inquire into, and report on, the present system for the enrolment and maintenance of the naval volunteer forces, raised under 22 & 23 Vict., and under 36 & 37 Vict. . . . also to inquire and report on the numerical strength of the force, with a view to a possible increase, both in numbers and efficiency, of a reserve closely and intimately connected with the regular naval force of the country, with authority to call witnesses and report, and to inquire at ports when necessary, personally, or by sub-committee."

By the regular adoption of some such course valuable and important results cannot fail to accrue. Lord George Hamilton, during his tenure of office, has certainly displayed an unusual amount of departmental knowledge, energy and ability, and has shown himself so perfectly master of naval affairs, that the *personnel* of the navy and the future manning of the fleet might with safety be left in his hands.

* The naval volunteers have been disbanded.—ED.

T

CHAPTER XXVI.

The Defence of the Empire.

The indifference displayed for sixty years by successive Governments—
Facts and scares to demonstrate our undefended condition—The
Duke of Wellington's celebrated letter—The south coast still in the
same defenceless state—What the great Duke failed to accomplish
for the army Lord Charles Beresford has effected for the navy—
National defence never seriously taken up—The interpretations put
upon the law of nations—Nineteenth-century civilisation—War
carried on at the dictates of the *vox populi*—Augmentation of the
Mediterranean fleet—Annual manœuvres—Blockading *versus* acting
from a base—Assurances of peace accompanied by increased preparation for war—"We are not going to war"—The importance of
speed and coal capacity—The supply of food convoyed by men-of-
war—Protection of trade—The predictions of Sir Thomas Hardy
verified—The heads of the profession all advocating advanced views—
Much done in the right direction, but much still left to do—The
advice of Count von Moltke—The result of experience—Let a good
example be followed—The good fortune of having two ex-First
Lords in the Cabinet—Our annual increment of wealth—The mistaken economy of the miser—No plan for the defence of the Empire
—Postponing a national duty—No steps taken to carry out the
recommendation of the Royal Commission—Mr. Stanhope "waiting
for the expression of public opinion"—Sir John Pope Hennessy on
submarine mines—Lord Carnarvon on the defence of our colonies
and coaling-stations—Elaborate fortification deprecated, but moderate
land defences recommended for the south coast—The utility of
torpedo-boats—A calculation to reduce Brighton to ashes—The
United States developing naval resources—Concession carried to
extremes—A paper read at the Institute of Naval Architects—The
policy of the United States—The state of the vessels in the first-
class reserve—A grave omission on the part of Lord G. Hamilton
—Credit to Lord George Hamilton for his comprehensive view of
naval requirements—The support of the commercial communities—
First Lords who have taken special interest in the navy—The

interest excited by the Naval Exhibition—References to *brochures* and standard works—The importance of fast cruisers, colliers, rams, and vedettes—The navy outside party politics—Participation in the world's commerce—How First Lords can ascertain the opinion of the various members of his Board—A naval officer should not retire if he cannot carry his point—Two naval lords that did—Many problems still to be solved.

I AM now in my eighty-fourth year, and for the last sixty years I have observed with surprise and pain, during that long period, the utter indifference displayed by successive Governments, the highly educated and intelligent classes, and, indeed, by the whole nation, to the defenceless condition of the country and its dependencies. In order to clearly set forth the extent to which the naval and military services have been neglected and the perils the country has escaped, rather by the kind dispensation of Providence than by any wisdom or patriotism on the part of our rulers, I will adduce the following instances which came under my personal observation during my tenure of office.

To show the unprotected state of the Thames and the defenceless condition of Sheerness, as regards men-of-war and fortifications, the following occurrence might be received with incredulity had it not been notorious at the time and frequently referred to by the *Times*:—Whilst the Admiral-Superintendent at the Nore was dressing, he heard his flag saluted from under the windows of the Admiralty House, and, to his surprise, observed three French frigates at anchor, one bearing the flag of an admiral He was immediately waited upon by the commanding officers of engineers and artillery, who represented that, as the works were under repair and the guns dismounted, they were unable to return the salute. These officers were quickly followed by the flag-captain, who came to explain that the guns of his ship were landed, as the vessel was being painted, and therefore it was impossible for him to return the salute. At this critical juncture the flag-lieutenant reminded the admiral that there was a small piece of ordnance on board the receiving-ship which fired the morning and evening gun, and it was just possible it might return the salute without bursting !

A communication was consequently made to the admiral, the Prince de Joinville, to the effect that his salute would be duly returned, but was accompanied with an explanation that if the salute was not returned in consecutive order it would be solely attributable to the necessity of sponging out the gun, as it was unfortunately the only available piece of ordnance at the port, as the fortifications were under repair, the battery guns dismounted, and those of the flagship on shore whilst the ship was being painted !

Some years after this event occurred I happened to be discussing the subject of national defence with the officers of the 34th Regiment at Shorncliffe and related the above anecdote, who regarded it as an amusing *canard* far too good to be true and invented for the benefit of the mess. Curiously enough on the following morning, to their surprise no less than to my own, there appeared in the leading article of the *Times* a detailed account of the whole incident.

The differences which had existed between Ibrahim Pasha and the Sublime Porte had for some time assumed a threatening aspect, and had been the cause of much anxiety to the great European powers, at last broke out into open hostilities The Egyptian troops defeated the Turks in several pitched battles, and were advancing triumphantly upon Constantinople when four of the great powers deemed it necessary to interpose their authority. In July, 1840, England, Austria, Prussia and Russia concluded a treaty by which they bound themselves to compel the Egyptian Viceroy to accept the terms of his suzerain—a treaty which proved highly distasteful to France.

Sir Robert Stopford, the Commander-in-chief in the Mediterranean, had an interview with Mehemet Ali, the Viceroy of Egypt, at Alexandria; and as he gave a formal refusal to the demands of the allied powers the admiral left two line-of-battleships and a corvette to prevent the Pasha's fleet from leaving Alexandria, Sir Robert himself proceeding to Beyrout, where hostile operations were immediately commenced upon the coast of Syria and conducted with great energy and ability by Commodore Sir Charles Napier, and shortly afterwards St. Jean d'Acre was successfully bombarded by Sir Robert Stopford.

The relations of England with France at this time became extremely critical, our ambassador at Paris having represented to our Government that the language of M. Thiers, who was then Minister for Foreign Affairs under Louis Philippe, was of a threatening and alarming character; and grave apprehensions were entertained that war with France would be the result.

My official position enabled me to know only too well the great anxiety that was felt at the Admiralty on the subject. There were no less than fourteen sail-of-the-line together with frigates, corvettes, steam-vessels, and smaller craft, upon the coast of Syria; but, incomprehensible as it may appear, the shores of England were left utterly unprotected, as the ordinary guardships at the ports had been despatched to the Mediterranean to augment the fleet upon the coast of Syria; and so critical were our relations regarded by the Admiralty, and so defenceless was the condition of the Solent, that the Board deemed it necessary to detain the *Collingwood*, an 80-gun ship bearing the flag of Rear-Admiral Sir George Seymour, who had just been appointed Commander-in-chief on the Pacific Station, to defend the anchorage at Spithead. Although on this occasion we escaped a war with France, the Government were in much the same predicament a little later; for the imprisonment of Mr. Pritchard involved us again in angry negotiations which nearly ended in hostilities.

A few years afterwards, referring to these incidents, Captain Henry Eden, who was at the time in command of the *Collingwood*, told me that at the time of her detention she had upwards of 200 merchantmen on board that had never been put to a great gun. I may further mention that at this period we had no militia, no volunteers, and no reserve of any kind; not even 20,000 men could have been got together for the defence of London. In so serious a light did the Duke of Wellington regard the defencelessness of the country and its military requirements, that he indited his celebrated letter to Sir John Burgoyne in 1847; but so infatuated were the ministry of that day with economy and retrenchment, that even the representations of the great Duke himself availed but little, for he concluded his letter with these touching words, "I am bordering upon seventy-seven years of age passed in honour. I hope that the Almighty may protect me from being the witness of the tragedy which I cannot persuade my contemporaries to take measures to avert." As few of my readers have not probably done more than heard of this celebrated letter, and fewer still have read it with the care and attention it deserves, I feel I cannot do better than transcribe it *in extenso* for their especial benefit.

STRATHFIELDSAYE, *9th January*, 1847.

To MAJOR-GENERAL SIR JOHN F. BURGOYNE, K.C.B, etc., etc.

MY DEAR GENERAL,—

Some days have elapsed, indeed a fortnight has, since I received your note, with a copy of your observations on the possible results of a war with France, under our present system of military preparation.

You are aware that I have for years been sensible of the alteration produced in maritime warfare and operations by the application of steam to the propelling of ships at sea.

This discovery immediately exposed all parts of the coasts of these islands which a vessel could approach at all, to be approached at al times of tide, and in all seasons, by vessels so propelled from all quarters. We are, in fact, assailable, and at least liable to insult, and to have contributions levied upon us on all parts of our coast; that is, the coast of these, including the Channel, islands which to this time from the date of the Norman Conquest have never been successfully invaded.

I have, in vain, endeavoured to awaken the attention of different administrations to this state of things, as well known to our neighbours (rivals in power, at least former adversaries and enemies) as to ourselves.

I hope your paper may be attended with more success than my representations have been.

I have above, in few words, represented our danger. We have no defence, or hope of defence, excepting in our fleet.

We hear a great deal about the spirit of the people of England, for which no man entertains a higher respect than I do. But, unorganised, undisciplined, without systematic subordination established and well understood, this spirit, opposed to the fire of musketry and cannon, and to sabres and bayonets of disciplined troops, would only expose those animated by such spirit to confusion and destruction. Let any man only make the attempt to turn to some use this spirit in case of partial local disturbance, the want of previous systematic organisation and subordination will prevent him even from communicating with more than his own menial servants and dependants, and while mobs are in movement through the country, the most powerful will find that he can scarcely move from his own door.

It is perfectly true that, as we stand at present with our naval arsenals and dockyards not half garrisoned, five thousand men of all arms could not be put under arms if required, for any service whatever, without leaving standing, without relief, all employed on any duty, not excepting even the guards over the palaces and the person of the Sovereign.

I calculate that a declaration of war should probably find our home garrisons of the strength as follows, particularly considering that one of the common accusations against this country is that the practice has been to commence reprisals at sea simultaneous with a declaration of war, the order for the first of which must have been issued before the last could have been published.

We ought to be with garrisons as follows at the moment war is declared:—

	Men
Channel Islands (besides the militia of each, well organised, trained, and disciplined) . . .	10,000
Plymouth	10,000
Milford Haven	5,000
Cork	10,000
Portsmouth	10,000
Dover	10,000
Sheerness, Chatham, and the Thames . .	10,000

I suppose that one-half of the forces of the country would be stationed in Ireland, which half would give the garrison for Cork. The remainder must be supplied from the half of the whole force at home stationed in Great Britain.

The whole force employed at home, in Great Britain and Ireland, would not afford a sufficient number of men for the mere defence and occupation, on the outbreaking of war, of the works constructed for the defence of the dockyards and naval arsenals without leaving a single man disposable.

The measure upon which I have earnestly entreated different administrations to decide, which is constitutional, and has been invariably adopted in time of peace for the last eighty years, is to raise, embody, organise and discipline the militia of the same numbers for each of the three kingdoms, united as during the late war. This would give a mass of organised force amounting to about 150,000 men, which we might immediately set to work to discipline. This alone would establish the strength of our army. This, with an augmentation of the force of the regular army, which would not cost £400,000, would put the country on its legs in respect to personal force, and I would engage for its defence, old as I am.

But as we stand now, and if it be true that the exertions of the fleet alone are not sufficient to provide for our defence, we are not safe for a week after the declaration of war.

I am accustomed to the consideration of these questions, and have examined and reconnoitred, over and over again, the whole coast from the North Foreland, by Dover, Folkestone, Beachy Head, Brighton, Arundel to Selsea Bill, near Portsmouth, and I say that, excepting immediately under the fire of Dover Castle, there is not a spot on the coast on which infantry might not be thrown on shore at any time of the tide, with any wind, and in any weather, and from which such body of infantry so thrown on shore would not find, within the distance of five miles, a road into the interior of the country through the cliffs practicable for the march of a body of troops.

That in that space of coast (that is, between the North Foreland) there are not less than seven small harbours or mouths of rivers, each without defence, of which an enemy, having landed his infantry on the coast, might take possession, and therein land his cavalry and artillery of all calibre, and establish himself and his communication with France.

The nearest point of the coast to the Metropolis is undoubtedly the coast of Sussex, from the east and west side of Beachy Head to Selsea Bill. There are not less than twelve great roads leading from Brighton upon London, and the French army must be much altered indeed, since the time at which I was better acquainted with it, if there are not now belonging to it forty *chefs d'état Major-General* capable of sitting down and ordering the march to the coast of 40,000 men, their embarkation with their horses and artillery, at the several French ports on the coast; their disembarkation at named points on the English coast, and the artillery and cavalry in named ports or mouths of rivers, and the assembly at named points of the several columns, and the march of each of these from stage to stage to London.

Let any man examine our maps and road-books, consider the matter, and judge for himself.

I know of no mode of resistance, much less of protection, from this danger, excepting by an army in the field capable of meeting and contending with its formidable enemy, aided by all the means of fortification which experience in war and science can suggest.

I shall be deemed foolhardy in engaging for the defence of the Empire with an army composed of such a force of militia. I may be so, I confess it. I should infinitely prefer, and should feel more confidence in, an army of regular troops. But *I know* that I shall not have these. I may have the others; and if an addition is made to the existing regular army allotted for home defence, of a force which will cost £400,000 a year, there would be a sufficiently disciplined force in the field to enable him who should command to defend the country.

This is my view of our danger and our resources. I was aware that our magazines and arsenals were very inadequately supplied with ordnance, and carriages, arms, stores of all denominations, and ammunition.*

The deficiency has been occasioned in part by the sale of arms, and of various descriptions of ordnance stores, since the termination of the late war, in order to diminish the demand of supply to carry on peace service of the ordnance, in part by the conflagration of the arsenal which occurred in the Tower some years ago, and by the difficulty under which all governments in this country labour in prevailing upon Parliament, in time of peace, to take into consideration measures necessary for the safety of the country in time of war.

The state of the ordnance, arms, ammunition, etc., in magazines is, in part, the question of expense, and perhaps, in some degree, one of time.

I would recommend to have an alphabetical list of the stores examined by a committee, and made out in form—as upon the endorsed half-sheet of paper—by ascertaining what there was in 1804, and what there is in store now of each article, and the difference between the two accounts.

I have taken the year 1804 as the standard, as that was the year in which the invasion was threatened. It was previous to the employment of the armies in the Peninsula or North America. In short, as nearly as possible similar to the political circumstances in which we stand at this moment, excepting that we are now at peace with France—we were then at war.

A fourth column would be the estimate of the expense of bringing the magazines to the state in which they were in 1804.

---

* Compare this with Lord Charles Beresford's confidential memorandum, page 234.—ED.

With this information before him, the Master-General could give the Government accurate information of the wants of the ordnance, arms, ammunition, and stores in the magazines of the country.

You will see from what I have written that I have contemplated the danger to which you have referred. I have done so for many years. I have drawn to it the attention of different administrations at different times.

You will observe, likewise, that I have considered of the measures of prospective security, and of the mode and cost of the attainment.

*   *   *   *   *   *   *

I have done more; I have looked at and considered these localities in great detail, and have made up my mind upon the details of their defence

These are questions to which my mind has not been unaccustomed. I have considered and provided for the defence—the successful defence—of the frontiers of many countries.

You are the confidential head of the principal defensive part of the country. I will, if you and the Master-General of the Ordnance choose, converse, or otherwise communicate (confidentially) with you upon all the details of this subject; will inform you of all I know, have seen, and think upon it, and what my notions are of the details of the defensive system to be adopted and eventually carried into execution.

I quite concur in all your views of the danger of our position, and of the magnitude of the stake at issue. I am especially sensible of the certainty of failure if we do not at an early moment attend to the measures necessary to be taken for our defence, and of the disgrace—the indelible disgrace, of such failure.

Putting out of view all the other unfortunate consequences, such as the loss of the political and social position of this country among the nations of Europe, of all its allies, in concert with and in aid of whom it has, in our times, contended successfully in arms for its own honour and safety, and the independence and freedom of the world.

When did any man hear of allies of a country unable to defend itself?

Views of economy of some, and I admit that the high views of national finance of others, induce them to postpone those measures absolutely necessary for mere defence and safety under existing circumstances, forgetting altogether the common practice of successful armies, in modern times, imposing upon the conquered enormous pecuniary contributions, as well as other valuable and ornamental property.

Look at the course pursued by France in Italy and Russia! At Vienna, repeatedly, at Berlin, at Moscow the contributions levied, besides the subsistence, maintenance, and equipment of the army which made the conquest! Look at the conduct of the allied army which invaded France, and had possession of Paris in 1815! Look at the account of the pecuniary sacrifices made upon that occasion, under the different heads of contributions, payments for subsistence, and maintenance of the invading armies, including clothing and other equipments, payments of old repudiated

State debts, payments of debts due to individuals in war in the different countries of Europe, repayment for contributions levied, and movable and immovable property sold in the course of the revolutionary war.

But such an account cannot be made out against this country. No; but I believe that the means of some demands would not be wanting. Are there no claims for a fleet at Toulon in 1793? None for debts left unpaid by British subjects in France, who escaped from confinement under cover of the invasion in 1814 by the allied armies? Can any man pretend to limit the amount of the demands on account of the *contributions de guerre?*

Then look at the conditions of the treaties of Paris, 1814, 1815.

France, having been in possession of nearly every capital in Europe, and having levied contributions in each, and having had in its possession or under its influence the whole of Italy, Germany, and Poland, is reduced to its territorial limits as they stood in 1792.

Do we suppose that we should be allowed to keep—could we advance a pretension to keep—more than the islands composing the United Kingdom, ceding disgracefully the Channel Islands, on which an invader had never established himself since the period of the Norman Conquest?

I am bordering upon seventy-seven years of age passed in honour.

I hope that the Almighty may protect me from being the witness of the tragedy which I cannot persuade my contemporaries to take measures to avert.*

Believe me,
Ever yours sincerely,
WELLINGTON.

It might have been supposed that such a letter from so illustrious and great an authority as the Duke of Wellington would have opened the eyes of the country, if not those of the Government, to the perils incidental to the introduction of steam into naval warfare; but, alas! it was all in vain. In it his Grace points out in forcible language the unprotected condition of the south coast from Dover Castle to Selsea Bill,

---

* The Marquis of Lansdowne, by his Military Bill, which was read a second time in the House of Lords on the 5th of April, covers, to a certain extent, the deficiencies set forth in this celebrated letter, in which he was (as far as the coaling-stations were concerned) well supported by Lord Spencer. When the War Office administrations come to be written, Lord Lansdowne ought to occupy a prominent page for carrying to a successful issue those measures of national defence and coast protection for which the great Duke of Wellington so pathetically pleaded in vain just fifty years ago.—ED.

yet that coast remains to-day practically in the same defence-less condition as it was in 1847; and be it remembered that at that date ironclads were not heard of, and steam-vessels had not attained to a speed of twenty-one knots an hour. Torpedoes were not invented, and modern artillery had not attained to a range of twelve miles, nor had a gun been constructed which could discharge a shot of 1200 pounds filled with the most inflammable material; whilst the changes in the army have been even as great as those in the navy.

It is a curious fact that what this great and distinguished field-marshal failed to accomplish for the defence of his country in 1847, a young captain* in the navy was practi-cally able, by his spirited representations, to achieve ; which representations, backed by others of the same patriotic type, led, in 1889, to the magnificent vote of twenty-one millions for the augmentation of the fleet.

In 1860 so violent was the feeling of France against this country, and so thoroughly impressed were the military authorities with our defenceless state, that nothing was talked of but the invasion of England. So serious did affairs appear in the eyes of Lord Malmesbury, then our ambassador at Paris (an old and intimate friend of the Emperor Napoleon III.), that he confidentially inquired of him what it all meant, and whether there were any real grounds for apprehension.

His Majesty replied, " I am the victim of circumstances. Nobody knows better than I do the power of England; yet my advice is comprised in one word—arm."

This interesting fact was related to me by Mr. Corry when First Lord of the Admiralty, a personal friend of Lord Malmesbury.

It would be well for the people of this country if they could

---

* Lord Charles Beresford was forty years old when he accepted office in the Conservative Ministry of 1886 as Junior Naval Lord of the Admiralty, and had then been a captain in the navy four years.—Ed.

be prevailed upon to bear in grateful recollection the wise and friendly advice tendered by Louis Napoleon, embodied in a monosyllable, speaking volumes, which was preceded by that sad phrase which foreshadowed only too faithfully the melancholy end of the Emperor's once brilliant career.

In the following year the captain of the *Sun*, belonging to the United States navy, forcibly abducted four passengers from Her Majesty's s.s. *Trent*, a West Indian mail-packet, notwithstanding an energetic protest from her commander and Her Majesty's mail agent on board. This proceeding threatened at the time to be attended with the most serious consequences, but fortunately the representations made by Lord John Russell through Lord Lyons, our minister at Washington, were received by the United States in a very conciliatory spirit. Immediate orders were given for the release of the prisoners, and the conduct of Captain Wilkes was repudiated and disapproved. It invariably happened that, when any misunderstanding took place with a foreign power which might lead to serious results, undue anxiety was evinced by the Government and public from the consciousness of our weakness and inability to meet any sudden emergency; other instances of panic and undignified apprehension, unbecoming a great country like England, might be adduced, but it will serve my purpose to refer to one of recent date. In 1884 the ministry made a peremptory demand that the Russian troops should recede from Sarakhs, to which a flat refusal was given, and a further advance to the south was made. So threatening was the aspect of affairs, that Mr. Gladstone went down to the House of Commons and solicited a vote for no less than eleven millions, a somewhat substantial proof of the deficiencies in our naval and military establishment.

Why is it that this country, more exposed than any other upon the littoral, should form a solitary exception, and entirely disregard those precautionary measures of coast defence which prudence and common sense alike dictate? The coast of Italy, the shores and harbours of France, are all well defended; and in an interesting letter in the *Times* of December 6th, 1889, will be found an elaborate account of the fortifications in the Baltic and North Seas constructed for the defence of the towns and harbours of Germany. Nor is this all; for, even on the other side of the Atlantic, the United States are so impressed with the necessity of home defence, that they are fortifying the weak points upon the littoral and have ordered twenty ironclads to be constructed for the special purpose of coast defence.

It is deeply to be deplored that the great question of national defence has never yet been seriously taken up by any government and treated as a national question of grave and primary importance. I fully sympathise with the benevolent exertions of those philanthropists who advocate arbitration with a view to avert the horrors of war. I likewise fully appreciate the praiseworthy motives which have induced Professor Holland and others to interpret the law of nations in the most favourable and humane light, so as to mitigate the severities of war; but one thing is perfectly certain, that when war does break out, which in the course of years it must, the stronger power will interpret international law according to its own interest and convenience.

We have heard a great deal about nineteenth-century civilization, but facts are stubborn things, and very decidedly controvert opinions which amiability and perhaps self-interest are apt to suggest.

Let any calm, sober-minded individual look back upon the present century and point out the occasions upon which this boasted civilization has been exhibited.

Was it apparent under the *régime* of Napoleon and his marshals?

Was it exhibited upon the barricades of Paris during the revolution of 1830 ?

Was it displayed in the significant announcement " that order reigned in Warsaw " ?

Was it exhibited when Louis Philippe was driven from his throne in 1848, and when the whole of Europe was on the verge of a revolution ?

Was it displayed at Paris when General Cavaignac and two hundred deputies and others were dragged out of their beds and conveyed to prison in 1851, or when the *canaille* of Paris was swept down by artillery and Louis Napoleon proclaimed Emperor ?

I could adduce numerous other instances bearing testimony to the fallacy of believing in nineteenth-century civilization, but perhaps the strongest that could be advanced are the events which took place in 1870, when Paris was half burnt down ; the archbishop, the rector of the Madeleine, and some Dominican priests, with three general officers, were shot in cold blood, and a protracted conflict was carried on between the commune and the Government, and every crime that could disgrace humanity and civilization was openly and daily perpetrated in the streets of the capital, and positively more damage done to Paris by the Parisians themselves than by the Germans during the Franco-German War.

Since the establishment of the Republic, scarcely a ministry has lasted beyond six months, so brief has been their tenure of office, and so unsettled the state of the nation. It is impossible to repose confidence in a people whose policy varies with every change of ministry; for who can venture to predict how soon some successful adventurer may not be at the head of the Government, as was so nearly the case with General Boulanger ?

Let it be borne in mind by the people of England that in these democratic days war will be carried on in all probability, not under the direction of sober-minded and responsible Statesmen, but under the violent and excited passions of an infuriated mob, who will dictate to their rulers the course to pursue, and the latter will find themselves, like Louis Napoleon, the "victims of circumstances."

> " Just experience shows in every soil
>   That those who think must govern those who toil;
>   Reverse the rule and let the suffrage sink,
>   Till those who toil shall govern those who think;
>   Then law, order, liberty give way,
>   And ancient chaos reassumes its sway."—*Pope.*

The great danger to this country will not come from monarchs or statesmen, but from the *vox populi*, which is unfortunately only too often the impassioned voice of ignorance ; dangerous because it is not amenable to reason. We see it in our own country, we see it in Ireland, and we have seen it recently even in staid and sober Scotland. We see it in France, we see it in the United States, and a short time ago we had a miserable exhibition of it in Lisbon and in Oporto. A great country like England can afford to act with dignity and magnanimity towards a smaller power, but the same passions which influenced the Portuguese may, at any moment, be suddenly aroused amongst the population of France or the United States, and then this country, however unwilling, would be compelled to hold her own, and the stronger she is, both at home and abroad, the less will be the probability of so fearful an alternative as war being forced upon her. It is impossible to deny that the navy presents a far more imposing appearance than when Lord George Hamilton assumed office. The Mediterranean fleet has been augmented up to ten sail-of-the-line and four powerful cruisers. The Channel Squadron, instead of consisting of slow and obsolete vessels of various types, is now composed of four magnificent line-of-battleships of improved speed and are all of the exact same class, armed with modern breachloaders, to which are attached two first-class cruisers. His lordship has carried into practical effect many other valuable measures which will add very materially to the fighting efficiency of the fleet; but what is of the greatest importance, is that he has the courage of his opinions, and has spoken out in a manner which gave the House of Commons and the country to distinctly understand that it is necessary for the defence of the Empire, and the protection of its immense commerce, to keep in commission a larger proportion of powerful iron-clads than heretofore; as vessels fitted out in haste, with inexperienced and untrained ships' companies, would tend rather to diminish than increase the efficiency of a well-organised fleet, and he has plainly shown that, as there is a large increase to the number of our ships, there must also be a corresponding increase in the *personnel*, both as regards officers and men.

The annual manœuvres which have taken place during the last few years are universally admitted by the most distinguished officers and experts to have been productive of most important and valuable results. They have been instrumental in putting to a practical test the steaming and fighting properties of various classes of warships, as well as the arrangements made for rapid mobilisation and the tactical skill of officers and men. In addition to these great naval problems, upon which the greatest diversity of opinion prevailed in the profession, two others have been practically solved, namely, the feasibility of blockading the enemy's ports and the system of watching the enemy's ports from a given base, each proposal being surrounded with its own special difficulties; the former impracticable, because the blockading squadron cannot maintain full speed but for a limited period, whilst the blockaded squadron can get up steam whenever the enemy may decide to make a dash out of port

U

to carry out their designs. How, on the other hand, acting from a base, it may be possible to catch vessels which have emerged from the enemy's ports is a matter which can only be satisfactorily proved by actual experience ; but one fact is demonstrated—that it could only be successfully accomplished by a very large increase to the number of our fast cruisers These are very great and grave questions , and looking at our immense commerce, our undefended commercial ports, and our defenceless towns upon the south coast, they cannot be too carefully or promptly considered by the Admiralty, the War Office and the Government.

The defence of the empire, and more particularly our own shores and coaling-stations, becomes a question of more importance and urgency year by year; and it is to be most fervently hoped that the ministry, which has already done so much, will be able to effect and make good those shortcomings which the royal commission has described as pregnant with danger. Our national defences call for calm and mature consideration, and can be far better discussed during a period of profound peace than under the excitement of a sudden and unexpected outburst of hostilities. It is a subject which has been too long postponed, or only taken up by fits and starts under pressure, and never dealt with in a grand and comprehensive manner Although it is true that nothing is heard of but assurances of peace from all the great powers of Europe, it is nevertheless to be observed that they are universally accompanied by earnest representations as to the imperative necessity of increased preparations for war, and supplemented by a demand for additional expenditure for men and works.

Nobody doubts but that Germany desires peace, yet it has been deemed necessary to add seventy batteries of field artillery and 18,000 infantry to her peace establishment, and more recently a still larger addition has been made to her peace establishment.* Russia desires peace ; but notwith-standing, great uneasiness is occasioned from time to time by the arrival of troops from the Caucasus, the reorganisation of the Cossacks, and by the movement of masses of cavalry upon the Austrian frontiers.

. Italy and Austria desire peace, and no two countries more than Holland and Belgium; yet the Hague is to be fortified and Antwerp is to be still further strengthened, and other fresh works are to be undertaken for the defence of Belgium, almost regardless of expense.

France, our nearest neighbour, also says she desires peace, but no indication of disarmament is discernible ; on the contrary, there is an increase to the army and immense additions to the navy. And what is more especially deserving of attention are the great works in course of construction at Dunkirk, Calais, Boulogne, Havre-de-Grace and other ports in the English Channel, but those at Boulogne, which are on a grand and imposing scale and rapidly progressing towards completion, are particularly conspicuous. It is all very well for us to talk about enjoying the blessings of peace, but has the history of the world ever yet exhibited such a gathering of armed millions during a period of peace ? Such an appalling state of affairs may well justify apprehension and alarm, and entail a frightful responsibility upon those to whom the safety and interests of the Empire are entrusted.

For years I represented to those in power the dangers to which this country was exposed in the event of sudden war, but I was invariably told the country was not going to war, that the Government regarded the moment as very ·in-

* On March the 5th of this year the Secretary of State for the German Navy announced a new shipbuilding programme, involving a total expenditure of 328,000,000 marks for the years 1897–1901, for new construction. Considering the Emperor's predilection for the navy, His Imperial Majesty is very unlikely to acquiesce in even a partial reduction of the vote demanded —ED.

opportune for any increase to the naval and military establishments, and the Chancellor of the Exchequer could not
provide the necessary funds I have dilated, throughout the
whole of this volume, upon the inadequacy of the fleet, the
indisposition of those in power to provide the money needful
to make and keep it efficient. It has always appeared to
me utterly incomprehensible how distinguished statesmen
(with few exceptions) holding the high office of First Sea
Lord of the Admiralty, should have been so little impressed with the grave responsibilities with which they
were entrusted. There have been many occasions, during
my long official career, when, if war had suddenly burst
upon us, discomfiture and disgrace must have been the
inevitable consequences. The serious questions connected
with commercial defence were virtually ignored, and ministry
after ministry left everything to the chapter of accidents
and a more convenient season. Fortunately a decided
change for the better has at last set in; the Government
of the day, the great capitalists, the commercial bodies,
and the public at large have been roused by the able and
earnest representations of the heads of the profession to a
real appreciation of the dangers we have escaped, and seem
prepared to provide for future contingencies. But, notwithstanding the recent interest taken in naval affairs, and after
all that has been done and promised, the result comes simply
to this: the country does not as yet possess a fleet equal to
the blockade of the ports of France, or a sufficient number
of swift and powerful cruisers to adopt the plan of acting from
a given base We therefore stand in this position, that our
commerce and our towns are at the mercy of any vessels
which may be let loose from the ports of France. When we
remember that we had to pay three millions sterling for the
raiding performances of a single vessel, the *Alabama*, an
approximate estimate may easily be arrived at as to the loss

and destruction likely to be inflicted upon British commerce by a number of fast cruisers sent to sea for that especial purpose. I have been at a total loss to understand how, looking to the importance of speed and coal capacity, the value of these qualities has been so imperfectly appreciated during the past, and even up to the present time too many cruisers inferior in size and speed have been constructed, such as the *Medea* and *Medusa;* but most praiseworthy efforts have been made by Lord George Hamilton and his Board to remedy this mistake, and the second-class cruisers have been gradually increased from 3400 to 4360 tons, which increase in tonnage it is expected will render them more efficient vessels to perform the duties for which they are especially designed.

In support of the views I have so long entertained, it affords me sincere gratification to observe that Sir Thomas Symonds,* one of the ablest authorities in the naval service, has represented in several admirable articles the imperative necessity of augmenting the number of our cruisers, and has set forth, in strong language, the great importance of size, speed, and coal capacity. It has been suggested by Lord Clarence Paget * and Sir George Tryon * that, in time of war, a squadron of commercial steamers should be specially organised for the supply of food, to be convoyed by men-of-war. This proposal seems deserving of consideration, and if acted upon, something very superior to *Medeas* and *Medusas* must be assigned for so important a duty. The supply of food for the nation in time of war is a duty which has never yet devolved upon the Admiralty, and entails upon that department a responsibility of unprecedented gravity; for upon the successful protection of the homeward-bound trade the life of the nation depends, as the population of these

* Admiral of the Fleet Sir Thomas Symonds, Admiral Lord Clarence Paget, Admiral Lord Alcester, and Vice-Admiral Sir George Tryon have all died since the above was written.—ED.

islands live by the daily importation of food, and if that were cut off, the nation stands face to face with starvation; and without the importation of raw material the poor would have no wages to purchase their daily bread. What Sir Thomas Symonds advocated and urged upon the naval administration is precisely an embodiment of the predictions of Sir Thomas Hardy just fifty years ago It is a great satisfaction to me to have lived to see the opinions expressed by that great admiral come to pass, and the high estimate I have formed of his foresight and sound judgment verified to the very letter. I have ever looked up to him as my kind professional preceptor, and I have every reason to feel grateful to him for the good advice he gave, when young in office, against broaching any advanced opinions in the Admiralty Board-room, assuring me that neither the naval lords nor the service were prepared for those changes which I should, in all probability, live to see carried into effect at a later period of my official career. About a week before he died, he sent for me to Greenwich Hospital, and there I had a long and interesting conversation with him upon naval affairs. One of the burning questions in naval circles at that date was the hogging of ships, on account of their length, vessels of 250 feet being regarded as dangerous. Sir Thomas thought this great nonsense, and said, " I will venture to predict that you will see vessels 500 feet and upwards, and even they will not hog " He further added, " You will see great changes in naval architecture Some people laugh at science, but science will alter the whole character of the navy; depend upon it steam and gunnery are in their infancy." This conversation I have never forgotten, and his death, which followed so quickly after- wards, grieved me sorely; for he had always treated me with the greatest kindness and confidence, and upon all professional subjects he seemed to me to be imbued with the intuitive right judgment which Lord Nelson so early discovered, for his words were always those of wisdom.

Nothing can be more satisfactory or encouraging than to observe the opinions entertained upon naval affairs by such distinguished flag-officers as Sir Phipps Hornby,* Sir Thomas Symonds,* Lord John Hay, Lord Alcester,* Sir E. Fanshawe, Admiral de Horsey, Admiral Colomb, and many others, as compared with those entertained by admirals of high rank and position in days gone by, so far from bringing their professional and practical experience to bear upon the real requirements of the navy and the duties that would devolve upon it in time of war, it was with the greatest difficulty they could be prevailed upon to entertain the subject at all, much less regard it from its various aspects and have it thoroughly thought out, as is now happily the case. The country cannot feel too grateful, and especially the commercial interests and mercantile marine, to the distinguished officers above mentioned for the valuable time, labour, and deep thought they have bestowed upon the various able articles which have been contributed from time to time to the *Times*, the *Morning Post*, and other leading journals of the day; for they have gone far to educate the public upon a subject which they had hitherto been ignorant of, or at most ill-informed, and which formerly excited but scant interest.

The Government and Lord George Hamilton have undoubtedly done much in the right direction; but notwithstanding, there is painful evidence that, at the present moment, we are unprepared to enter upon any great naval war, and that there are still many grave questions to be thought out and settled before the country at large can feel that confidence in the management of our naval and military affairs which every German seems to possess in the system

* *See* page 293.

and organisation inaugurated by Count von Moltke and the officers of the German staff

Sir Phipps Hornby * is an admiral of the fleet on the active list, and is recognised by the profession as an officer of mark and distinction, and as a first-rate authority on all naval matters. That Sir Phipps is not altogether satisfied with the existing state of affairs is plainly indicated by the following question, which he has asked in an admirable article contributed by him to the *United Service Magazine* of April, 1890, under the title of " Our next Naval Need." Does any man in England feel confident "that, if war were declared to-morrow, we should see our fleets and squadrons, great and small, all moving to the many, and in some cases distant, points that it is of vital importance to us to occupy instantly to protect our widespread commerce ? "

This question he answers in the negative, and in doing so, I am convinced he fairly expresses the opinions of his brother officers, and all those who have in past years had any acquaintance with Admiralty management at any critical juncture.

Let us hope we have seen the last of discreditable panics, and that those who rule, and those who are called upon to contribute towards the national defence of, the Empire will avail themselves of the sage advice offered by that great statesman and distinguished marshal, Count von Moltke, to the German nation in his famous speech in the Reichstag on the 14th of May, 1890, upon the bill for the increase of the Prussian Army, when he reminds his countrymen of what they suffered during the six years that Prussia was under the dominion of Napoleon, who boasted that he had squeezed a milliard out of the small and poverty-strickened nation, and supplemented it by a reference to the French marshal, in taking leave of Hamburg in 1813, then a French city, who

* Admiral of the Fleet Sir Phipps Hornby, G.C.B., died 1895.

took away with him a Hamburg bank as a parting souvenir! This speech of Count von Moltke states facts, and imparts a lesson which cannot be too strongly impressed upon the minds of all classes of society in this country, from the highest to the lowest. We do not know what war really means; but if unfortunately it were brought to our own shores, we would probably discover to our cost that a French general of the Republic would not be more scrupulous where money is concerned than a Napoleonic marshal. An enemy within the nation would soon make short work of its finances.

There is not a great statesman in Europe, an able general, nor a distinguished admiral who is not ready and willing to accord honour and praise to Count von Moltke, and to the intelligent officers of the Prussian staff, and who do not recognise the amount of time and brainwork which must have been bestowed upon the elaborate calculations and plans prepared for such a campaign against a neighbour so powerful as France. But the concentration of an army upon the frontiers of France dwarfs into insignificance beside the labours devolving upon the Admiralty of England at the first outbreak of a naval war.

We have seen what Germany did, at the beginning of the war of 1870, in the despatch by rail of cavalry, artillery, infantry, and all the impedimenta required for so large an army, all of which were timed so as to arrive at a given date at the various points indicated, so as to concentrate in the manner contemplated by the chief of the staff and Commander-in-chief, and that so successfully was all effected from the beginning to the end of the campaign as to carry into practical effect all that had been previously planned and arranged Twenty years and more have elapsed since this grand scheme, which took so many years to mature, was attended with such brilliant success, and rewarded those who had expended time, labour, and deep thought upon it. Surely

what the Germans accomplished by land, this country, with
its boundless wealth, immense natural resources, and national
intelligence, ought to be able to effect by sea.   They have
set us the example—they have shown us how to do it.
Nothing but the will and firm determination is needed to
organise a fleet equal to the requirements of the empire, and
to adopt such military precautions as may be needed to
protect our shores   We possess admirals and generals equal
to the task, but our weak point is, unhappily, the want of
method, foresight, and harmony in our naval and military
administration, in which the civil and parliamentary element
has hitherto been permitted to exercise too predominant an
influence.

It was exceedingly fortunate for Lord Salisbury as Prime
Minister, and equally so for Lord George Hamilton as First
Lord of the Admiralty, that they should have had the valuable support of two such able and experienced statesmen
in the Cabinet as Mr. W H. Smith and Mr. Goschen, when
the naval requirements came under consideration.   As ex-
First Lords of the Admiralty, they had great departmental
experience, and were thus able to bring their personal knowledge to bear upon the subject, and consequently Mr. Smith
as First Lord of the Treasury, and Mr. Goschen as Chancellor
of the Exchequer, were more inclined to provide the funds
for the efficiency of a service so indispensably necessary
to protect the best interests of the empire, both at home
and abroad   Especial merit was due to Mr Goschen, who
run the chance of incurring unpopularity by increasing the
expenditure of the country rather than again behold it
liable to those risks to which it has been subjected in the
past, for the want of an adequate naval force.   It is not
less satisfactory to observe that Lord Salisbury is likewise
fully alive to the paramount necessity of a naval force for
whatever military operations the exigencies of the nation

may hereafter require.* Twenty-one millions may appear a very large sum, but everything depends upon the point of view from which it is regarded, the purposes for which it is to be expended, and the security it offers in return. Large as the sum undoubtedly is, it is after all only a sixth according to Mr. Gladstone, and but an eighth part according to the late Lord Overstone, of the annual increment of wealth of this country for a single year. Let us be careful that we do not make the same mistake as the miser who could not bring himself to incur the expense of locks, bolts, and bars to protect his treasures, for we know that the result of his sordid avarice was sad indeed.

History clearly indicates that England, during the last two centuries, has always exhibited an astonishing unreadiness for war, though constantly involved in hostilities. And even up to the present period it is an undeniable fact that our preparations for war, both naval and military, are the reverse of satisfactory. I have adduced elsewhere the representations of " One Who Knows the Facts," the practical testimony of Lord Charles Beresford, and those of the most distinguished flag-officers of the fleet who have expressed their views with unmistakable clearness, so as to impress upon the Government the necessity of adopting those judicious measures for the augmentation of the fleet which have received such general approbation throughout the country. The Royal Commission of 1890, presided over by the Marquis of Hartington,† goes far to show that this country is not in that defensive position which prudence and self-interest would alike suggest. Much has been done of late in the way of preparation and organisation, yet it is painfully evident that

---

* As the estimates for this year, 1897, bear ample testimony. *See* footnote on page 198.

† Now Duke of Devonshire, President of the Council of Imperial Defence.—Ed.

no combined plan of operations for the defence of the Empire in any given contingency has ever been worked out or decided upon by the naval and military departments; that some of the questions connected with the defence of military posts abroad, and even at home, are still after much correspondence in an unsettled condition; and the best mode of garrisoning some of our distant coaling-stations is also undecided.

It is perfectly clear, from the evidence given before the commission, that if a war were to break out suddenly, the state of affairs is not in a satisfactory condition, caused by the want of pre-arrangement and harmony between the naval and military authorities and the diversity of opinion which prevails upon the fundamental principles of action. Some unpleasant passages were apparent in the body of the report, and calculated to create an uneasiness in the public mind as to the confidential communications which were held back from grave prudential considerations   Nor is this feeling of uneasiness in the slightest degree diminished by the closing remarks made by Lord Randolph Churchill * in his separate memorandum, in which he begs the commissioners to "bear in mind that the evidence before us discloses in many particulars a state of things more seriously unsatisfactory, and possibly more pregnant with danger, than Parliament or the public imagine." For a long time past it has been notorious that serious differences of opinion are entertained by naval, military, and engineer officers in respect to the best mode of defending Malta, Bermuda, and several of our most important coaling-stations, to say nothing of Scilly, the Channel Islands, and the towns upon the south coast. How long this state of things will continue is a matter of interesting conjecture †

* Died in 1895.

† The Marquis of Lansdowne has, to a certain extent, settled the question by his Military Bill, asking for £5,458,000, brought forward for

Great stress was laid upon the confidential communications made by distinguished admirals and general officers before Lord Hartington's Commission, who would, no doubt, express themselves on such an occasion with far more caution and reserve than they are in the habit of doing in clubs and private society. I very much question whether there is any subject of grave importance concerning which foreign powers are not fully informed, and of which the people of this country alone are kept in ignorance for political and departmental convenience.

The naval and military attachés of foreign countries are officers of high scientific attainments, admitted intelligence, considerable tact, and keenly alive to everything that passes in this country, and study with unremitting attention all that appertains to naval and military affairs, which is duly communicated to their respective governments. In a country like this, with a free press and everybody at liberty to give expression to his opinions upon every subject, it is impossible to prevent the weak points of our system being discussed by naval and military officers and others in the leading and professional periodicals of the day. It is greatly to be desired that those in power should be as ready to receive information as our continental neighbours are to acquire and turn it to profitable account. But, alas! it is a melancholy fact that such information, instead of being sought out and welcomed by responsible heads of departments, is generally

---

second reading 5th April this year. His lordship said: "The defence works in which the navy is largely, indeed primarily, interested are estimated to cost £1,120,000. . . . We propose to complete the defences of four great strategic harbours at Falmouth, Lough Swilly, Berehaven, and the Scilly Islands. Work at these places was commenced six or seven years ago in consequence of strong representations from the Admiralty. . . . Amongst the fortresses I may mention Gibraltar and Malta; and amongst the coaling-stations such places as the Cape of Good Hope, Hong-Kong, and the Straits Settlements."—ED.

received with disfavour and regarded as inopportune and leading to expense.

Successive governments, irrespective of party, have been only too ready to avail themselves of every plausible excuse for postponing and tiding over the plainest obligation of national duty, with a view of throwing the responsibility and the odium for additional outlay upon their political opponents, instead of having the moral courage to place the whole subject before the country, which, if put in full possession of facts, would willingly vote any sum that may be required for the substantial defence of the Empire, providing only the money is wisely and judiciously expended.

The country cannot fail to have observed with great satisfaction that it is not the intention of the Marquis of Hartington,* as Chairman of the Royal Commission, to allow the many valuable recommendations submitted for the grave consideration of the Government to be ignored, for at the end of a year his lordship very properly inquired in the House of Commons what steps had been taken to carry them into effect, and expressed his disappointment at finding that several which were, comparatively speaking, of easy accomplishment had not been undertaken

To show how imperfectly prepared are we at the present time for war, and how little a Royal Commission composed of the most distinguished statesmen of the day of both parties, admirals and generals, is able to effect, may be inferred from the statement of Lord Hartington * on the 23rd of February, 1891, as to the want of a combined naval and military plan for the defence of the Empire, and to the fact that the best mode of garrisoning the coaling-stations was still undecided. "Thus some of the most vital questions were left in a dangerously uncertain condition." What is perfectly evident to Lord Hartington * and some of the leading members of his

* *See* footnote, page 299.

Commission appears to have been equally apparent to an able and intelligent officer of the United States navy, an attaché at our Court, who thus reports to his Government what in his opinion is the state of our coast defences —" The coast defences of Great Britain is notably the most inefficient of any of the great European powers, owing to the divided control, lack of co-operation, absence of digested schemes for mutual support, and the mixing of naval and military duties; the defence is unwieldy in its administration, unprepared for sudden work, and labours under the disadvantage of placing military men outside their legitimate sphere of action" Although the defenceless condition of our shores is notorious to all the world, it is melancholy to observe that, as yet, Mr Stanhope * has not realised this discreditable state of affairs; and what is the excuse he makes for virtually ignoring the judicious recommendations of the Royal Commission? First, that these recommendations excited no general interest; and, secondly, that he was " waiting to see the drift of public opinion." It it difficult for those who take the liveliest interest in naval and military affairs to arrive at a just and independent opinion upon a subject when the evidence is regarded as so confidential that it is not even printed, and therefore have no data to go upon. Such being the case it does seem somewhat unreasonable for Mr. Stanhope " to be waiting for the expression of opinion " on the part of those who are unequal, by mental habit, to grasp a subject so large and intricating, even if they had the evidence before them

It is earnestly to be desired that ere long Her Majesty's Government will reconsider the recommendations of Lord Hartington's Commission, so that the time and labour of its members may not be entirely lost to the country, and that

* The Right Hon Edward Stanhope, Secretary of State for War, died in 1893.

they will arrive at a sounder decision as to the real value of the well-considered proposals submitted to them.

The defence of our coaling-stations is far too pressing and important a question to be thus shelved or even postponed. It often happens when a sound and practical proposal is made, and its consideration is deemed inconvenient, that exaggerations on the ground of expense and supposititious difficulties are ingeniously devised, as on the present occasion.

A proposal to place under the Admiralty such fortresses as Gibraltar, Malta, Bermuda, and such naval arsenals at home as Portsmouth, Plymouth, Dover, and others is one thing, and would indeed require mature consideration and take time; but the question assumes a totally different character when it is simply proposed to place under naval control such dependencies and coaling-stations as the Falkland Islands, Ascension, St. Helena, Table Bay, Mauritius, and Ceylon, to which might be added, at no distant date, Singapore and Hong-Kong. It is equally desirable that Falmouth and the Scilly Islands should be placed under the supreme command of the Port-Admiral at Devonport, more especially Scilly, the importance of which, from a naval point of view, has been so frequently and ably set forth by that experienced and distinguished admiral, Sir George Elliot.

The defence of the Channel Islands is a question to which the Duke of Wellington directed his special attention, because, as he justly observed, from their peculiar position they control the command of the commerce in the Channel.

It would surely be worth while to consider, without loss of time, whether these islands would not be far more efficiently defended if entrusted to the care of the naval Commander-in-chief at Portsmouth, by gun-boats, torpedo-boats, marine artillery, and submarine mines, than by the two infantry battalions now stationed there, who can know little or nothing about great guns. Submarine mining has of late been very extensively resorted to, but the sensible remarks recently made by Sir John Pope Hennessy, late Governor of Hong-Kong, upon the subject, clearly demonstrates that submarine mining would be far better managed by seamen or seamen-gunners, who know something about boats, currents, and tides, "than by soldiers who cannot even handle an oar." This, combined with the strongly expressed opinion of Admiral Sir Arthur Hood,* that the defences of the Empire should be "assisted by torpedo-boats," appear to me to render it still more conclusive that the Channel Islands and coaling-stations should be placed under the Admiralty, and not under the War Office, as the management of torpedoes cannot be entrusted to the military, which transfer would prevent a dual control

It is very gratifying to observe the sound, practical and unprejudiced views taken by Lord George Hamilton as to the expediency of placing under the Admiralty authorities and naval control some of our smaller dependencies and coaling-stations, and he will no doubt pay every deference to the opinions of such distinguished general officers as Sir Andrew Clarke and Sir William Jervois, and such able and competent flag-officers as Admirals Sir Houston Stewart, Field, and Mayne. I do hope this question will be taken up seriously, free from all departmental and professional jealousies; for those who have considered the question under its various aspects cannot fail to perceive that the adoption of the measures proposed would confer very substantial benefits upon the navy, and afford relief in various ways to the sister service. Looking at it from a financial point of view, it is difficult to believe that such a transfer could lead to an expenditure which would not be more than amply repaid by increased efficiency. The employment of marines and marine

* Made a peer of the United Kingdom in 1892.

artillery upon this service would put into responsible and important positions detachments of one of the most gallant and efficient corps in Her Majesty's service, and at the same time place at the disposal of H.R.H. the Duke of Cambridge, the Commander-in-chief,* several infantry battalions which could be far better employed at Aldershot in perfecting themselves in those military duties which, sooner or later, they will be called upon to perform in active service upon the north-western frontier of India.

The late Lord Carnarvon upon several occasions expressed his surprise at what he designated the "strange procrastination" of the Government in carrying into effect the recommendations proposed by the Royal Commission appointed to inquire into the defence of our colonies and coaling-stations in the year 1881, of which he was chairman ; and now, at the expiration of some ten or twelve years, points of vital importance are still undecided.

Coaling-stations, as the name implies, are established for naval and not military purposes ; therefore there can be no doubt that they ought to be under the control of the Admiralty, and not under the War Office. To quote the words of Lord Carnarvon :· "Coal has become the most potent factor in the arithmetic of naval war. Without it our foreign commerce and our vast carrying trade would cease to exist; without it, our ships-of-war could neither fight nor move ; and even with it, there is no security unless it is adequately protected, for it becomes a prey to the first hostile cruiser" It is to the interest of the Admiralty that these coaling-stations should be adequately protected, garrisoned, and provided with all that renders them truly efficient   If they were placed under naval authority entirely, the First Lord and Board of Admiralty would take care that

* Since the above was written the Duke of Cambridge has retired, and in his stead Viscount Wolseley has been appointed

none but able and competent officers were appointed to such responsible commands, and the naval commanders-in-chief upon the stations would receive instructions to personally inspect and report upon the general efficiency of their respective commands; and should there be at any time an insufficiency of coal, ammunition, provisions, or other requisites in an emergency, the country would be able to fix the responsibility upon the delinquent; whereas, under the present arrangement, divided authority must lead to disappointment and confusion, delays and misunderstandings, as the various requirements have to filter through a department which has no direct interest in the real efficiency of the coaling-stations.

It is a great step in advance to find that the military authorities concur with the naval in opinion that the navy must form the first line of defence, and the navy are equally right in their claim to freedom of action and in their objection to be bound by military requirements; but the naval officers, on the other hand, seem to ignore the fact that there may be occasions where it would be impossible for ships to afford adequate protection to all our commercial ports and towns upon the south coast, which latter are left without any defence whatsoever.

Under these circumstances, it is unreasonable for naval officers to complain of money spent upon land defences, though large sums expended upon elaborate fortifications are to be deprecated; but there is a great difference between that costly expenditure and the providing necessary protection for our commercial ports, and some moderate defence for the exposed towns upon the south coast, so as to secure them from desultory attacks from hostile cruisers—a danger the inhabitants of Brighton and other towns upon the coast may discover to their cost to be far more real than it suits their immediate interest to take measures to avert.

x 2

The difficulty which prevailed in days gone by in obtaining funds for ships, guns, coaling-stations, and barracks will in probability reappear when similar demands are made upon the public purse for coast defences and the construction of important works at Dover and Filey, which are indispensable for the protection of our commerce and shores, and which should be taken in hand without loss of time, as it takes years to improve or construct a harbour. The progress made with the great works at Dunkirk, Calais, and more especially at Boulogne, demand watchful attention on the part of our Government and the Board of Admiralty.

The torpedo flotilla from Alderney, at the commencement of the naval manœuvres of 1890, in attacking so promptly and successfully the men-of-war at anchor in Plymouth Sound, was an exploit deserving of far more serious consideration than has been accorded to it. The dash and spirit displayed on this occasion by our young officers was highly commendable, and clearly indicates the more than probable success that would attend such efforts in time of war.

A great diversity of opinion still exists in the service as to the value of torpedoes and torpedo attacks, but as yet no papers have been written which can be regarded as satisfactory or conclusive. This is, no doubt, mainly attributable to the impossibility of deciding the amount of damage inflicted upon either the attacking or defending force during peace manœuvres, as the attack is invariably made in the darkness of night; and as no one likes to admit that he is worsted, a difference of opinion is the inevitable result. Both parties advancing claims, it is difficult to substantiate in mimic warfare the ships claiming to have sunk the torpedo-boats and the boats to have hit the ships. The real value of torpedoes cannot be truly estimated until tested by actual war. But, to all unprejudiced minds, it is certain that torpedo attacks are a very real and formidable danger, and especially so to our commerce in the Narrow Seas.

When we consider the protection afforded to the torpedo flotillas of France by the fortresses of Dunkirk, Calais, and Boulogne, and the close proximity of these naval arsenals to our own shores, it is high time the Government of the day should take measures to avert a contingency so certain to arise, and be prepared by counter-attacks to meet it   In my opinion there is no doubt that torpedoes will prove far more efficacious in defending our shores and commercial ports than submarine mining

It is much to be regretted that a general officer of such acknowledged ability and high professional reputation as Sir Andrew Clarke should have had nothing better, or more substantial, to advocate for the protection of our shores and commercial ports than the laying down of submarine mines, which, unless adequately protected by heavy ordnance and quick-firing guns, can be, as Sir Edward Hamley * justly observed, as rapidly pulled up as they are easily and cheaply laid down , and then what becomes of the economy ? Lastly, Sir Andrew consoles the public with an elaborate calculation of the immense amount of shot and shell required to reduce Brighton to ashes—an expenditure no country would incur for the accomplishment of such an object, in utter forgetfulness that a few shots from a cruiser or gun-boat sent into the Métropole or Grand Hotels, or a few shells setting fire to some of the houses at Kemp Town or in Brunswick Square, would occasion such an exodus from Brighton, and bring an amount of ruin upon this fine town, from which it might never again recover.

The naval profession is ultra-Conservative and its pre-judices die hard; but a general impression exists, among the young and scientific officers of the service, that the value

* Has since died.

of rams and torpedoes is only beginning to be appreciated, and in any future naval war they will exercise a powerful and decisive influence

That our naval and military forces may be duly prepared for the exigencies of war we have annually naval and military manœuvres, but I am not aware that any similar steps have been taken for the organisation and training of the garrisons appropriated to the defence of our naval arsenals, commercial ports and towns upon the coast. Upon this subject I feel it would be utterly impossible for me to express in more brief and forcible language what is required, and the urgent necessity for precautionary measures, than that used by the late and deeply lamented Lord Carnarvon. These are his words:—

"On board our great warships all individuals are trained to work together and to concentrate their separate duties or functions on a common purpose; we have no corresponding combination for the defence of our commercial ports. We have outgrown the old system, and are making no determined attempt to cope with the new order; we spend on things obsolete, we economise on things vital, and we seem to imagine that our past fortune is a guarantee for our future safety."

When considering the naval force required for the protection of this Empire and its dependencies, the public at large and the naval profession dwell almost exclusively upon the naval power of France and Russia, regarding them as the only great naval powers likely to prove antagonistic to Great Britain; but, unhappily, there is a third power, namely, the United States, now developing its naval resources with an amount of energy, prudence, and forethought which bids fair, at no distant date, to entail upon this country an anxiety against which the Admiralty at Whitehall would do well to anticipate.

It is earnestly to be desired that the two countries, bound by the ties of blood and mutual self-interest, may long remain in the bonds of peace ; but the history of the past goes far to prove that the ties of consanguinity offer but slender assurance for the permanence of friendship; and many of my readers will agree with me that no quarrels are more bitter and protracted than those in families where pride or personal interest happen to be in conflict

The United States are yearly increasing in wealth, power, and influence, and is a nation in which the *vox populi* is supreme. The Irish Nationalists constitute a powerful political party within it, always hostile and vindictive towards this country. In time of trouble they would fan the flame of national animosity against us. As a matter of course questions will arise, from time to time, in which the interests of the two nations are in opposite directions, questions in which arbitration could do little good, and violent and unreasonable passion might work immeasurable ill. In any controversy that might take place England would no doubt carry concession to the extreme; but there is a point, however, where our honour and interest are concerned beyond which it would be dangerous even for a great country to yield.

The United States is a young, ambitious, and aggressive power, keenly alive to its national interests, and at the present time possesses boundless wealth, and has, unfortunately, on many occasions proved so stubborn and unyielding that no alternative was left between concession or war.

There is a general received opinion that with whatever naval power we may be at war, that power will not risk the result of a general action, but endeavour to strike a blow at our widely extended commerce by attacking it in all quarters, and by carrying on harassing and desultory raids upon our beautiful and populous towns upon the south

coast, or upon the coast of Ireland, although I do not mean
to say that would ever decide the question at issue or wrest
from us our naval supremacy

The very interesting paper read by Mr. Biles at the
Institute of Naval Architects in 1891 indicates, with unmistakable clearness, the policy that would be adopted by
the United States in the event of war with this country—
a policy which, to a moral certainty, would be followed by
France, or any other great naval power, with whom we may
be involved in hostilities.   Mr. Tracey,* the Secretary for
the United States Navy, a statesman of no ordinary ability,
proposes to despatch, at once, four powerful cruisers of a
class something between the *Blake* and *Edgar* in four different
directions, which, as he justly calculates, would "scuttle or
settle" those vessels employed by us for the protection of
our commerce.   Mr. Tracey further proposes to despatch a
vessel of great speed and coal endurance, designated the
Pirate, with a roving commission as a "commerce destroyer,"
with rigid instructions not to encounter a vessel-of-war, her
sole duty being limited to the destruction of commerce.
This policy is admirably conceived and sound in theory,
and, if successfully carried into practical effect, would not
only be fraught with danger to our commerce, but equally
so to our numerous small men-of-war employed on foreign
stations.   But we have yet to see whether this "commerce
destroyer" comes up to the somewhat over-sanguine expectations of Mr. Tracey.   It is, however, most fortunate
that we already possess two such vessels as the *Blake* and
Blenheim, and that the list of the navy has been reinforced by such powerful ships as those of the *Royal Arthur*
and *Edgar,* etc., and further by the *Terrible* and *Powerful,*
an improvement upon the former vessels recently proposed
by Lord Spencer.

* Was Secretary of State when the above was written.

It is perfectly evident that the naval policy enunciated long ago by so many of our distinguished and gallant admirals, notably Sir Thomas Symonds and Lord Alcester, confirmed by the strongly expressed opinion of so able and experienced an expert as Lord Brassey, is the right policy to pursue, though entailing a heavy expenditure—an expense, however, the country must encounter if its commerce and dependencies are to be adequately protected and its wonted naval superiority to be maintained in the future.

I hope I may be pardoned if I request my readers to turn to the administration of Lord Melville, for they will there find that the very policy which the United States so successfully adopted in 1813–15 is identical with that which Mr. Tracey now proposes to carry into effect in reference to the construction of ships-of-war for the new American navy, which, from their size, speed, and coal endurance, will sweep from the seas all our *Medeas* and *Medusas*, and vessels of a still smaller type, upon which, in the name of economy, so much public money has been absolutely wasted.

The sound views expressed by Sir Thomas Hardy in regard to line-of-battleships and powerful frigates is even more applicable to the present time, with our immense commerce, than at the period at which he advocated their construction, when First Sea Lord in the administration of Sir James Graham, 1830. *Magnum est vectigal parsimonia.*

Procrastination has for years past been a chronic vice with our Admiralty; what ought to be done at once is invariably postponed to an indefinite period, which unfortunate habit has obtained for it the unenviable sobriquet of the "unready."

Too much importance cannot be attached to the actual state and condition of the vessels which constitute our first-class reserve. They may be required on the shortest notice and ought, therefore, to be at all times in the highest state of efficiency ; and as soon as any defects are discovered, no matter how trifling, in the carpenters', shipwrights', or engineers' departments, or those connected with guns, gun-fitting or torpedoes, they should be made good without delay. So essential is this that a certain number of efficient hands should be told off for this especial purpose No First Lord of the Admiralty ever displayed more energy cr practical sound sense, or more perfectly appreciated what would be necessary to meet the sudden exigencies of the service, than Lord George Hamilton ; and I have no doubt that he felt deeply indebted to the *Times* for directing his attention to a grave omission on the part of his Board in allowing the ships attached to the first-class reserve to remain up to the 14th February, 1891, without any steps being taken to make good the defects which had occurred during the summer manœuvres.

I remember, upon one occasion, Sir James Graham in-quiring of me whether a certain ship in the first-class reserve was, as reported, ready *in all respects* to proceed to sea   I replied, " Yes, sir, with the exception of a few trifling defects which could be made good in a short time." He replied, with a smile and a shake of the head, " Trifling defects and a short time, Mr. Briggs, are two very indefinite terms, and ought not to be applicable to ships in the first-class reserve "

It is a singular fact, and I state it from a long personal experience, that ships fitted out at Chatham or Sheerness scarcely ever arrived at Portsmouth without sending up long lists of defects of some sort or other to be made good. Constant complaints were made by various First Sea Lords upon this very subject, but, strange to say, they never applied that effectual remedy which was quite within their power, namely, issuing stringent orders that such remissness must not occur in future.

That there are not, at the present time, as many ships in the first-class reserve as could be desired, has been most satisfactorily accounted for. Lord George Hamilton judiciously reinforced the Mediterranean Fleet and Channel Squadron with new and powerful battleships of the most approved type, and gradually replaced the obsolete and inferior guard and district ships with vessels in all instances superior to those they superseded—a policy Lord Spencer has likewise adopted, the consequence of which is that the squadrons present a very different aspect from what they did when Lord George took his seat at the Board of Admiralty. I again repeat, the nation cannot feel too grateful to Lord Salisbury, as Prime Minister, and to Mr. Goschen, as Chancellor of the Exchequer, for the grand and patriotic vote of £21,500,000 for the augmentation of the navy—a programme which was carried to completion with energy and ability.

Nevertheless it must be borne in mind that this great addition to the navy, considerable as it may appear, is, to a certain extent, rather nominal than real, as the vessels now completed are in many instances merely replacing those which, from age and inferior qualities, are deemed unequal to take their place in the line of battle. The position of this country is very different from what it has ever been before. New and powerful navies are springing up which, in some future war, may effect combinations far more dangerous to British naval supremacy than those of France and Spain in days gone by. Our commerce has of late attained to such gigantic proportions that, in all probability, the enemy will be more bent upon the destruction of our trade and unprotected towns upon the coast than in attacking our fleets and naval arsenals

Lord George Hamilton has undoubtedly proved a very able and energetic First Lord, and too much praise cannot be awarded to him for the large and comprehensive view he has

taken of naval requirements, and the duties and responsibilities devolving upon the high office of First Lord of the
Admiralty; but it is by the Cabinet of the day, and not only
by the First Lord, that this great question of national defence
must be taken up.*   Great exertions have been made during
Lord Salisbury's tenure of office to this end, but the neglects
of former administrations have been so great and protracted
that the more the question of defending the Empire is gone
into, the more appears to be needed, and much of a pressing
character.

It is for merchants, shipowners and underwriters, who are
much too apathetic on the subject of commercial protection,
who ought to take up the matter seriously; they ought, as
men of business, to look ahead and turn their attention to
the necessity of providing for the safety of their own interests,
by using every effort and rendering every support in their
power to any government which evinces a real desire to
guard the great commercial interests of the country upon
which our very existence, as a nation, virtually depends
Grave political events are being silently, but darkly, foreshadowed which, ere long, will compel the legislature to devote its precious hours to commerce, protection, and national
defences, and no longer waste them in the fruitless discussion
on teetotal processions, Irish rowdyism, and parish councils.

The little interest taken in naval affairs was attributable
to various causes between the years 1827 and 1854, when
the Crimean War broke out.   A man-of-war was rarely seen
east or north of the Thames, and seldom if ever visited any
of our great commercial ports, added to which, for fifty-five
years, from 1830 to 1885, when Lord George Hamilton came
into office, there was only one First Lord amongst the many

---

* Doubtless it will now that there is a Council of Imperial Defence
composed of the members of the Cabinet, presided over by the Duke of
Devonshire.—ED.

who possessed sufficient influence in the Cabinet to secure those funds absolutely necessary to place and maintain the navy in a state of real efficiency; and that one was Sir James Graham, who, during his first administration, was supported, in all his important naval reforms, by his fast friends and political colleagues, Lord Stanley, Lord John Russell and Lord Palmerston, as well as by Lord Grey himself, the Premier. In his second administration, in 1854, Sir James Graham was equally fortunate, for it was the period of the Crimean War; and he then possessed the unbounded confidence of Lord Aberdeen, the Prime Minister, and had at his disposal the whole resources of the country.

During many administrations several First Lords, who took the deepest interest in the welfare of the navy and the defences of the empire, were not so successful, though as anxious as he for its welfare, amongst whom I will mention Lord Halifax, the Duke of Somerset, Mr. Corry, Mr. Childers and Mr. Ward Hunt. The difficulties have hitherto been those of finance, but the Government of Lord Salisbury has set a good example, which has happily been followed; and the country may fairly assume that the interest in naval affairs will not in future be allowed to relapse.

The system of annual naval manœuvres, so successfully established by Lord George Hamilton, has led and is leading to so many valuable results, and which go far towards keeping alive public interest in the navy. The regular visiting of our fleets and squadrons to our commercial ports alike tends greatly to popularise the navy. The Naval Exhibition, which was weekly attended by tens of thousands, did much to educate the inland population, and caused them to take an interest which they previously had never done; it gave them an idea of ships and guns, and the life of those on board men-of-war, of which they had before visiting the Exhibition no conception. All those who witnessed the field drill, broadsword exercise, and clever mimic warfare upon the artificial lake, and beheld the gigantic monster, the 110-ton gun, quick-firing guns, and the other wonderful implements of war displayed in the Armstrong Gallery, were greatly impressed; the thinking ones in the multitude realised, as they never did before, the necessity that existed to provide funds to keep our navy in a proper state of efficiency, though the lack of funds in bygone days was in no way attributable to want of generosity or patriotism on the part of the people. So long as Lord Brassey's interesting 'Naval Annual' continues to appear, and such clever brochures as Mr. Arnold Foster's 'In a Conning Tower,' and Mr. Laird Clowes'* 'All about the Royal Navy' (which the *Times* and daily press have so favourably reviewed) come from time to time before the public, they cannot fail to do good and keep alive the interest in naval affairs, and induce the public to meet the ever-increasing requirements of Her Majesty's navy with generosity and goodwill. To these must be added works of a far higher standard, such as that learned and scientific treatise of Captain Mahan, of the United States navy, entitled 'The Influence of Sea Power upon History,' and Rear-Admiral Colomb's† able work upon 'Naval Warfare: Its ruling Principles and Practice historically Treated.' Books of the description last named call for not only careful reading, but deep study; and as they submit important problems for consideration it is high time Admiralty lords, and the officers of the Intelligence Department, should devote their attention to solving the difficult and intricate professional questions they contain

---

* Mr. Laird Clowes is at present engaged upon an important work in five volumes—'A History of the Royal Navy, from the Earliest Times to the Present Day'—the first volume of which has been already published (Sampson Low.)

† Since been promoted to vice-admiral —ED.

Too high an estimate cannot be formed as to the valuable information embodied in Captain Mahan's book.* To many it may seem dry reading, but to statesmen, and all at the Admiralty, in the navy, as well as those engaged in trade and commerce, each and all should possess a copy, and should study and master its contents, as it reads lessons of vital importance, not only to politicians, the officers of the Royal Navy, but to the mercantile marine, and to the commercial interests of the whole Empire. If it is appreciated as it deserves, it cannot fail to be a standard text-book for generations to come.

The most satisfactory and encouraging feature of the day is to behold the increased and ever-increasing interest which the chambers of commerce, "Lloyd's," and the great mercantile and commercial bodies are taking in the development of the navy and the defences of the Empire

It augurs well for the future that the most distinguished officers of the day, and leading members of the Institute of Naval Architects, Lord Faversham, Lord Brassey, and other scientific naval experts, have for a long time past been directing their attention to the composition of the special classes of vessels which the country will stand most in need of in the future.

It is most gratifying to me to observe that the great deficiency in the number of our first-class cruisers is being rapidly made good by vessels of such a magnificent type as the *Terrible*, which is quite the *chef-d'œuvre* of Mr. William White,† the Director of Naval Construction and Assistant-Controller of the Navy.

---

* Captain Mahan has since brought out other important works, viz., ' The Influence of Sea Power upon the French Revolution and Empire, ' The Life of Admiral Farragut,' and, quite recently, a Life of Nelson (also Sampson Low).

† Was created a K.C B., Civil, 1895

The next question of importance, after an addition to our first-class cruisers, is that which relates to our coaling-stations and the coaling of our fleets during a period of war It has been satisfactorily tested during the manœuvres of 1890 that the fleet can be coaled in the open sea; it therefore becomes a question for prompt and serious consideration whether it is not most desirable that plans should be prepared for the construction of steamers, of great speed and coal-carrying capacity, to be specially employed for that specific duty, so as to render it unnecessary for the ships to be so frequently obliged to leave their stations to replenish their supply of coal. It is at all events an experiment worth a trial. It is also important that the properties of the *Vulcan* should be tested at an early date, so that a similar vessel may be constructed, should her services after trial prove equal to those anticipated.

There are other questions that might be discussed, such as vessels to be employed solely as rams, and whether such might not with advantage be added to the fleet; and also whether cruisers of an immense speed ought to be constructed, not to fight, but to be specially employed as scouts or vedettes, to obtain information as to what may be passing in the ports of the enemy, or to seek intelligence as to the whereabouts of any hostile cruiser. These are all matters which, sooner or later, must be dealt with by the Government and the Admiralty. Although it is most unfortunate that year after year should be permitted to roll by without any practical step being taken to defend our unprotected towns upon the south coast, to improve our harbours, or decide upon the several ports best suited for the protection of torpedo flotillas (destined to play a far more important part in the narrow parts of the Channel than the Admiralty has hitherto deemed fit to assign them), nevertheless I feel most grateful to have been spared to see the service, with

which I have been professionally associated for the last
sixty years, at length appreciated by the Government and the
country as it always ought to have been; and it is most
satisfactory to observe that the defence of the Empire and
the protection of our commerce are, temporarily at least,
regarded by both political parties in the State as outside the
contentions of party strife, and that whatever controversy
takes place, it is happily confined to those differences of
professional opinion which must inevitably arise in reference
to the class of ships to be constructed, their designs, armour-
plating, armament, and torpedoes. It is highly improbable
that the navy of this country will ever again be permitted
to fall into that " perilous condition " (to quote the words of
Lord George Hamilton) into which it had gradually sunk
when Lord Salisbury assumed the reins of power The
wealth and prosperity accruing from ships, colonies, and
commerce have excited the rivalry of other nations,
especially of Germany,* which has, in this case, been greatly
stimulated, no doubt, by the valuable work of Captain
Mahan, and if any further evidence is required to bear out
the desire of the United States to acquire ships, colonies,
and commerce, it will be found in the following extract from
the speech delivered by President Harrison on the 2nd May,
1891, at San Francisco.—

" I believe that we have now come to a new epoch as a nation. There
are opening portals before us inviting us to enter, opening portals to trade,
influence and prestige such as we have never seen before. We pursue
the paths of peace. We are not a warlike nation. All our instincts, all
our history are on the lines of peace. Only intolerable aggression, only
peril to our institutions or flag can thoroughly rouse us. With capabilities
for war on land and sea unexcelled in any nation, we are smitten with a
love of peace. We should have some good vessels. We do not need a

---

* To quote the strong language of Admiral Hollmann (Minister of
Marine), Germany's " influence and power would go to the devil " unless
she can exeit pressure with her navy.—ED

Y

great navy as some other people do, but we do need sufficient first-class ships to make sure that the peace of this hemisphere be preserved, simply that we may not leave great distant marts and harbours of commerce, and our few citizens who may be domiciled there, to feel lonesome for the sight of our flag.

" *We are making fine progress with the construction of the navy. The best English constructors have testified to the completeness of some of our latest ships. In San Francisco the energy, enterprise, and courage of some of your citizens have constructed a plant capable of building the best modern ships. We want merchant ships, and I believe we have come to a time when we should choose whether we will continue to be non-participants in the commerce of the world, or now vigorously, with the push and energy which our people have shown in other lines of enterprise, claim our share in the world's commerce* [The *italics* are mine.]

" The Postal Bill marks the beginning of methods to regain that commerce. My belief is, that under the operation of that law we shall be able to stimulate shipbuilding, to secure some new lines of American steamships, and increase the ports of call for those now established "

"Peace" is the last word on the lips of every diplomatist, but let such assurance be taken for what it is known to be worth.

The new policy about to be inaugurated by President Harrison is one which reads plausibly enough, but when carried into effect cannot fail to have an appreciable detrimental influence upon British interests. It is reasonable enough to dilate upon their claim to participate in the advantages of the world's commerce, and to assume that there is ample for all, but experience has shown that such is not the case when put to the practical test, as is clearly demonstrated by what has taken place, and is actually taking place, in Asia, Africa, and indeed upon the whole continent of Europe, in settling the different " spheres of influence."

The question which will have to be considered ere long will be, what is a fair participation in the world's commerce, concerning which difference of opinion is sure to arise; for national, like family interests, are no sooner affected than strife is engendered, and this ought to be provided for by

the Admiralty in the calculation of future requirements
Happen what may, one thing is certain, that the navy will
play a most important part in the future destinies of the
Empire. A powerful navy is much more likely to settle vexed
questions than the skill of the diplomatist, and to accomplish for England what the late Count von Moltke was
sanguine enough to believe the army of his Emperor will
achieve for Germany. The naval policy of England at this
moment calls for grave and serious consideration. So great
and continuous are the augmentations of foreign navies, and
so various are the views entertained by our own naval
officers and officials as to the classes of vessels that ought to
be built, that it is difficult, nay impossible, to lay down any
programme which may not, from year to year, call for
considerable revision. A very mistaken idea has got abroad
and prevails in certain naval circles, that the duties of
a naval Lord of the Admiralty are limited to those of
the particular department which he has been specially
selected to superintend. Now this is totally at variance
with the very object of the scheme propounded by Sir James
Graham, and with the spirit of everything he contemplated.
The great aim he had in view was that each member of the
Board should know exactly what the others were doing, and
offer any observation he might think fit upon the work of
any department. This course prevented any member from
complaining that he was kept in ignorance of what was
being done, as well as being charged with interfering with
the department to which his remark referred. It further
enabled the First Lord to ascertain the opinion of the
various members of the Board upon the questions submitted
for consideration and decision, and assured, to a certain
extent, unity of action and the harmonious working together
of the members of the Board. The system inaugurated by
Sir James Graham, during his first administration, proved,

ın the Crimean War and Indian Mutiny, pre-eminently successful, and was as sound when put to the test of practical experience as it was in theory

One of the greatest misfortunes of the naval profession is the diversity of opinion which prevails upon almost every subject amongst the leading members of the service, and it requires great tact and temper, combined with decision of character, to hold an even balance at the Board on the part of the First Lord. At an open discussion, at the United Service Institution or elsewhere, what one admiral of distinction proposes another gets up and flatly contradicts without any adequate argument being adduced. It matters very little whether ıt is the number of ships required, their classification, their speed, armour, armament, rams, torpedoes, or the extent and mode of garrisoning our coaling-stations; political, professional, and personal interests all come into play. Under these circumstances ıt is almost ımpossıble for the House of Commons or the general public to form a sound estimate of what the navy requires to render it efficient. Often when there is a definite proposal propounded upon which there ıs a consensus of professional opinıon, it is soon lost sıght of in a discussion upon some side issues which have little or no reference to the main subject, but are mere matters of departmental and executıve detaıl.

It ıs frequently said ın naval circles, that if a Lord of the Admıralty maintaıns an opinion at variance with the rest of the Board, and sees no chance of carrying hıs point, he should resign hıs seat, and great praıse was justly awarded to the late Sir Maurıce Berkeley* and Lord Charles Beresford for taking this patriotic and disinterested step; but, at the same time, it would be unreasonable to expect that officers of moderate means are going to throw up a lucrative appoint-ment and mar theır future career because they cannot succeed

* Created a peer in 1861 and took the title of Lord Fıtz-Hardınge.--ED.

in carrying their views. By resigning their seats they would not effect the accomplishment of their wishes, and someone else would instantly fill their places. All that can be expected from members of the Board is that they will use their influence to the utmost of their ability for the good of the service. If they fail in the accomplishment of their object, as many have done during my official experience, it has not been through the want of personal exertion and representations on their part; yet they may be fairly held to have done their duty. It is only in extreme cases that a Lord of the Admiralty is justified in resigning his seat. Sir Maurice Berkeley resigned his seat because the Government would not make that addition to the number of seamen for the fleet which he considered indispensably necessary for the safety of the country, and which he had, for so many years, been urging unsuccessfully upon the ministry Lord Charles Beresford resigned his seat at the Board because the Treasury refused to place the Intelligence Department of the Admiralty, to which he rightly attached so much importance, upon a more liberal, substantial, and permanent footing* As officers of rank and fortune the reasons they assigned amply justified them in adopting this extreme measure; but, under ordinary circumstances, it disturbs discipline, and is detrimental to the interest of the country. It is, however, certain that Lord Charles Beresford, as an independent member of the House of Commons, was able to accomplish much more good for the navy, supported as he was by the most distinguished officers of his profession and the Press, than if he had retained his seat at the Board; and it is to be hoped that, when he resumes his par-

* It was generally supposed that he resigned on the question of the Intelligence Department. He really resigned on the question of the strength of the fleet and the determined opposition he encountered to his proposal for proper war organisation.—ED

liamentary duties and takes his part in the administration of
the country, the powerful influence he possesses will always
be used to promote its best interests. It is not surprising
that naval officers, of the type of Lord Charles Beresford,
Captain Fitzgerald * and others, should look forward with
apprehension to the future, when they consider the active
part they may be called upon to take in any naval war,
conscious, as they must be, of the gigantic scale upon which
it must be entered upon. This country is anxious for peace,
and our rulers will, no doubt, act upon the sage advice of the
late Count von Moltke, and ward off war as long as possible;
but the time, if not in the near present, is not far distant
when events will, in various quarters of the globe, force
upon us a policy of concession or war. If the former, one
concession will lead to the demand for another, which will
at last compel us to have recourse to that resistance which
firmness, in the first instance, would have proved the safer and
more economical line of conduct. I have, at great length, set
forth the views and opinions entertained by Captain Lord
Charles Beresford. The full text of his valuable and ably
thought-out memorandum I have embodied in the administration of Lord George Hamilton, which Lord Charles, as a junior
member of his Board, submitted for consideration. The opinions
entertained by Lord Charles Beresford are identical with
those I have held for the last sixty years, with this difference
—that Lord Charles took the tide at the flood, whilst I
throughout the whole of my official career had to fight against
it, and I heartily congratulate him upon the signal success
which has rewarded his efforts, as well as upon the high
reputation he has so justly attained as a naval reformer. It
affords me the greatest satisfaction, before I sing my *Nunc
Dimittis*, to behold the navy in its present condition, and the
certain prospect of what it will be in the future; also the

* Now rear-admiral.

Charles Bereynd

security which now exists that, in days to come, it will never again fall so far below the standard of safety as that in which Lord Salisbury's Government found it when they came into office in 1886. Never again will eight millions be locked up in the dockyards on ships in various stages of construction; never again will the navy be found devoid of all organisation and without a single plan devised for protecting our commerce, defending our shores, or attacking the enemy, as was the case until a very recent date.

The defence of the Empire, considered in all its bearings, is one of those great questions which no government in this country is at all likely to boldly face, except under the apprehension of war or consequent upon a very strong expression of public opinion, unless there should happen to be at the head of the legislature of the two combatant forces men of sound knowledge, proved ability, and experienced in the difficulties to be met; and who, not being politicians only, but really acquainted with the work to be done, can, from practical knowledge, devise a plan of campaign which will result in the whole possibilities of a great war being thought out and provided for—vast and numerous as the problems to be solved undoubtedly are, combined with the difficulties resulting from the diversity of opinion which prevails, not only between the navy and army, but between the officers of both services respectively.

The word "impossible" ought not to be found in the statesman's vocabulary. The expenditure such a scheme requires could be met, to a large extent, by necessary economies where waste and extravagance still prevail But the question must be faced unless this overgrown population is to endure all the horrors of starvation, riot, anarchy, and disloyalty, which want of organisation will inevitably cause when food supplies are cut off or diverted, the channels of trade thrown into confusion, and the wage bill no longer paid. A strong navy without defence, properly surveyed, is useless   To make arrangements for these things is most necessary to our existence as a nation, *not* for *war*, but for peace   The British Empire has nothing to gain and all to lose by war. The efforts of its statesmen should therefore be directed to making its defences *so strong* that war may be deferred as long as possible, and that each succeeding year may add to the numbers, the wealth, the strength, and the power of the Anglo-Saxon race, so that in the future the statesmen of this mighty Empire may become the arbiters of universal LIBERTY and PEACE.

INDEX.

LONDON
PRINTED BY WILLIAM CLOWES AND SONS, Limited,
STAMFORD STREET AND CHARING CROSS